CHINA ON STAGE

CHINA ON STAGE

AN AMERICAN ACTRESS IN
THE PEOPLE'S REPUBLIC

LOIS WHEELER SNOW

Random House, New York

Copyright © 1972 by Lois Wheeler Snow

All rights reserved under International and Pan-American Copyright Conventions. Published in the United States by Random House, Inc., New York, and simultaneously in Canada by Random House of Canada Limited, Toronto.

Library of Congress Cataloging in Publication Data

Snow, Lois Wheeler.
   China on stage.

   CONTENTS: Introduction: reversing history.—Taking Tiger Mountain by strategy.—"For whom?" [etc.]
   1. Performing arts—China (People's Republic of China, 1949-   ). 2. Chinese drama—Translations into English. 3. English drama—Translations from Chinese. I. Title.
PN1582.C5S6   895.1′2′508   72-2724
ISBN: 0-394-46874-0

All plays published by the Foreign Language Press, Peking, China, printed in the People's Republic of China.

Manufactured in the United States of America

First Edition

To my teacher, DeMarcus Brown,
who opened up
the world of theatre to me,

A N D

To my husband, Edgar Snow,
who opened up
the world of China to me

The first problem is: literature and art for whom?

All our literature and art are for the masses of the people, and in the first place for the workers, peasants and soldiers; they are created for the workers, peasants and soldiers and are for their use.

MAO TSE-TUNG
*Talks at the Yenan Forum on
Literature and Art, 1942*

PREFACE

≋ In 1936, a young American journalist sat on a grassy plain beside a river in the tiny village of Pao-an, in China's war-blocked northwestern province of Shensi, watching an open-air "theatrical" performed by a Red Army troupe in an old Buddhist temple.

"Across the stage was a big pink curtain of silk, with the words, 'People's Anti-Japanese Dramatic Society', in Chinese characters, as well as Latinized Chinese, which the Reds were promoting to hasten mass education. The program proved to be a combination of playlets, dancing, singing and pantomime—a kind of variety show, or vaudeville, given unity chiefly by two central themes: anti-Nipponism and the revolution. It was full of overt propaganda, wholly unsophisticated, and the 'props' were primitive. But it had the advantage of being emancipated from cymbal-crashing and falsetto-singing, and of dealing with living material rather than with meaningless historical intrigues that are the concern of the decadent Chinese opera.

"What it lacked in subtlety and refinement it partly made up by its robust vitality, its sparkling humor, and a sort of participation between actors and audience. Guests at the Red Theatre seemed actually to *listen* to what was said: a really astonishing thing in contrast with the bored opera audience, who often spent their time eating fruit and melon seeds, gossiping, tossing hot towels back and forth, visiting from one box to another, and only occasionally looking at the stage."*

Edgar Snow (and, as he casually wrote at the time, Mao Tse-tung, among others, practically unnoticed amidst the crowd of factory workers, mule drivers, clerks, soldiers, villagers and children) was there in this forbidden area at the end of the Long March, having slipped through enemy lines to bring out a firsthand report of the revolutionary movement that was to sweep China and result in the establishment of the People's Republic.

In 1970, I stood beside this now-not-so-young-any-more American journalist in a large, recently constructed theatre in the center of a bustling, much bigger Pao-an, where a local troupe was in the process of staging a Peking opera for presentation on October first, the twenty-first anniversary of the founding of the People's Republic.

I had waited a long time to go to China. I had been married to Edgar Snow during the twenty-one years that mark the People's Republic's Liberation birthdays. I had been, and was still for some of those years, an actress on Broadway and television; our son and daughter had mostly grown up; we four had made homes in New York, New Jersey and in Switzerland. It had been an active, full period, enveloped by a profound interest in the Far East.

For two decades (1951–71), while the United States

---

* *Red Star Over China*, revised by Edgar Snow, Grove Press, New York, 1968, p. 120.

government attempted to isolate the People's Republic, the State Department forbade American citizens to visit China. Among the few exceptions was my husband (an old blockade-buster), who first returned there in 1960 and again in 1964–65. On both occasions I also was offered a visa but was unable to receive "permission" from the State Department (unlike my husband) for the first trip; the second time it was granted "too late." In July 1970, I didn't ask again--I went along.

We arrived in Peking in summer, via Hong Kong and Canton. My first glimpse of China was from behind windows of a modern, air-conditioned train operated entirely by women. After serving us mugs of hot tea they were as eager to sit and ask questions as we were to have them; they were alert, attentive people.

The southern summer landscape was a Chinese scroll. I watched leathery water-buffalo, elongated white heron, lichee trees, and shimmering green rice fields dotted with peasant farmers—as familiar to me as Hollywood actors—birdlike in wide-winged, woven palm-hair coats and peaked straw hats. My husband was impressed by the evidence of farmland mechanization new since his last visit five years before.

Peking's airport (we flew from Canton), when we arrived, was lighted by a full moon. As the plane touched ground I felt the strangeness of entering the Land of Oz. For years I had heard about, read about, received letters from, many foreign residents in China who had participated first or second hand in the events that formed the country from the 1920s to the present. I knew these people existed —but like Ozma and Dorothy and the Tin Woodsman; could they be *real*?

They were and are. Some of them were there to greet us at the airport; others I met during my five months in China. I am indebted to all of them for introducing me to a spectrum of Chinese life which gave me a deeper view of the country they live in and a better understanding of that country's revolution. Also, because of their appreciation of my special interest, they did everything possible to include some aspect of theatre wherever we went. It didn't seem frivolous to anyone; theatre plays an important role in China's revolutionary growth.

I stood with my husband beside Mao Tse-tung at Tien An Men (Heavenly Peace Gate) in Peking on China's National Day. I dined with Chiang Ching (Mme. Mao Tse-tung) and Premier Chou En-lai (whom I had first encountered at a Ping-Pong game several weeks before in the enormous gymnasium where some months later the China-U.S.A. Ping-Pong matches created international excitement and hope); was warmly greeted by Premier Chou's attractive wife, Teng Ying-chao; fell in love with Soong Ching-ling (Mme. Sun Yat-sen); was guided through many of the complexities of the Cultural Revolution(and a good deal of delicious food) by Huang Hua (now the Permanent Representative to the United Nations from the People's Republic of China) and lovely Ho Li-liang (Mme. Huang Hua); had the services of two efficient and attractive interpreters, Yao Wei and Hsu Er-wei, both of whom were pure gold in helping me find my way around the theatre; and walked and talked almost daily when in Peking with my husband's and now my good friends, Rewi Alley (a New Zealander who knows China better than most Chinese), Ma Hai-teh (the American, Dr. George Hatem) and his wife Su Fei, until then legendary figures to me—as were the many other friends I finally found in the flesh.

I also met Long March veterans, People's Liberation Army men who had been Little Red Devils as kids in the Red Army, actresses from pre-Liberation days, women who had been virtual slaves at that time, men and women who had been beggars, old ladies who had been child brides, and scores of others—peasants, factory workers, students, housewives, teachers, doctors, musicians, ballerinas, writers, actors, kindergarten babies, middle-school Red Guards, coal miners in universities and university students in coal mines, and foot-crippled, formerly illiterate grandmothers who can now at last read a newspaper.

It wasn't Oz. It was China. It's there, a combination of ancient culture and new revolutionary living, based on an ideology very different from ours and geared to the needs of nearly eight hundred million human beings who have pulled themselves out of the debris of war, poverty, ignorance, disease and untold misery heaped upon them for generations by the now-gone war lords and landlords, and the now-departed foreign exploiters of the past.

We spent a good deal of time in Peking. We traveled kilometers around its periphery within Hopei province, went up to the northwest, into the northeast (known as Manchuria under the Japanese occupation), and down to Shanghai, Nanking, Hangchow, Canton and environs. Everywhere I saw the theatre—professional troupes often supplemented by factory, school, or common groups entertaining us with local talent after a day's work. It was invaluable to have as companion my husband, who had known the country intimately in the infancy of its revolution, later during the postwar struggle, during the days of the Great Leap Forward, and just prior to the Cultural Revolution. China was emerging from its turbulence when I was there—August through December 1970.

A long-held hope was realized for me when we flew up to the northwest province of Shensi. There are special roots in its soil for me. Our daughter bears the name of its ancient capital, Sian (Western Peace). And it was here—under the noses of Japanese spies, Kuomintang troops, enemy agents and real-life bandits—that Edgar Snow had begun his hazardous trip to encounter the Communist "bandits" protected in the crumbling mountain caves to its north. It was in Sian, December 1936, that the course of the Sino-Japanese battle changed. From the splendid spa of a fabled courtesan (we had a soothing bath in her mineral-water pool) Chiang Kai-shek had taken flight in nightdress in a vain attempt to escape capture by the troops of his own marshal, Chang Hsueh-liang. Chiang's life, bargained for on word that he would cease his extermination campaigns against the Communists and cooperate in defeating the Japanese invaders, was spared—his promise was more or less kept till the end of World War II.

Sian was special to me; Yenan was even more so. It is Mecca to the Chinese, and almost every foreign guest has an ambition to visit this training town of China's Eighth Route Army. Headquarters of Mao Tse-tung and his followers for ten years (1937–47), the dusty little city saw the completion of four revolutionary training institutes, a library, a fine arts academy, and an army school that educated thousands of rebels in battle strategy, tactics, guerrilla warfare, and a political ideology that changed the life of China. Yenan became a symbol of hope for liberation against unsurmountable odds. Yenan was also nursery for today's Chinese theatre, a cultural child of the revolution.

Even so, it was Pao-an I wanted most to see. In one of its earthen caves Mao Tse-tung had told his life history to Edgar Snow, who included it, along with the story of the Long March, in *Red Star Over China*.

One September morning we drove out onto the paved highway now darting from Yenan to the mountains topped by loess soil blown in over centuries from Central Asia. Pao-an lies a hundred kilometers to the west. Few people, even in China, remember this first refuge of the survivors of the Long March. Its name has been changed to Chih-tan, in memory of the hometown hero-martyr who set up its first Communist base. Years had passed since any foreign visitor had set foot in this village. It had survived bombing, strafing, pillage and enemy mutilation. One wouldn't have suspected this from the number of local inhabitants who came out to see us. We stared at them; they stared at us. There was a world of separation. Infants cried; little children ran away or hid behind a familial pantleg to peek out with wide, round eyes. Slowly our smiles produced shy smiles in response; our proffered hands met eager ones stretched out.

Most of these people were dressed in worn, patched clothes—shabby by some standards; but many could recall when a pair of pants and a coat comprised an entire wardrobe (the coat doubling as blanket at night). There were men who had been striplings when the Red Army had arrived on their cave steps. We shared a pre-lunch feast of apples, pears, grapes and enormous tomatoes with a veteran Long Marcher in charge of a carefully tended orchard. He retraced years of battle with the Red Army, down to the defeat of the Kuomintang and his eventual "retirement" to Pao-an's peaceful fruit trees. Far from inactive, he has experimented with a new system of irrigation that has added acres of arable land, and with grafting methods that have produced many varieties of apples. For centuries this area was one of the very poorest, and it is still poor. Limited natural resources, lack of coal, a constant fight against the contour of land and the violence of weather keep villagers at work from dawn until past dusk every day. But the result is heretofore-unknown plenty. It was apparent from the firm, healthy bodies of children, from the well-stocked general store, from the smiles of pride on people's faces as they pointed out their fields and forests, their reclaimed homes and hillsides.

Passing Main Street's markets, bookstore, dentist's office, drugstore and clinic, we entered the open square where the newly built theatre—earth-floored, equipped with a movie projector and seats for more than five hundred people— was in the midst of a sprucing-up for the presentation of a model revolutionary Peking opera, *The Red Lantern*. The opening was a week away, so we missed being among the first-nighters. I left content at least to have seen the home ground of the revolution that has transformed China, and with it, China's theatre. My first look at this new theatre was not in almost forgotten Pao-an, but in the country's capital, Peking. —L.W.S.

CONTENTS

CHINA ON STAGE

*Lois and Edgar Snow with Chinese leaders on the Heavenly
Peace Gate, National Day celebration, October 1, 1970*

"Now you have reversed this reversal of history and restored historical truth, and thus a new life is opening up for the old opera."

—Mao Tse-tung, 1944, Yenan

INTRODUCTION: REVERSING HISTORY

CHINA CELEBRATES ITS LIBERATION ON THE first of October. National Day, 1970, began with spectacular parades (minus military armaments or boasts) of floats and marchers—to the tune of a million participants at Tien An Men Gate in Peking alone—and finished with music, dancing, and scenes from the new Peking operas played under night skies made kaleidoscopic by a display of fireworks hard to equal. The Chinese invented them, after all.

Over twenty years had passed since civil war ceased and a united country became the People's Republic of China. These years were permeated by battles of a different nature: to overcome floods and droughts, disease and superstition, illiteracy, material lacks, poor distribution and communication, ideological conflict. Immense construction and social achievements were made possible by the combined labor of hundreds of millions of peasants and workers, often using primitive tools or their own bare hands and callused shoulders. Reforestation, building of highways, heavy industry, land restoration, soil reclamation, scientific breakthroughs, technological progress, medical advances and rural health care, family planning and birth control, mass education and literacy campaigns, political rights, all have brought about a stunning improvement in this former obsolete giant that contains nearly a quarter of the world's people.

Theatre flourished. As the war ended thousands of towns and villages saw dramas of the everyday life of the people enacted before their eyes by the dramatic troupes of the People's Liberation Army. Through them the bitterness of the past was exposed and the promise of the future revealed. Catharsis, education, and entertainment came in one package.

Peking opera, artistically the most sophisticated form of Chinese theatre, with a heritage of close to two hundred years, resurged—renewed and resplendored after wartime wear and tear. Peking opera (*ching hsi*) is a dramatic form. It is not confined to Peking and is seen all over China, as it is the most popular, and it is considered the finest of the more than 250 local variations that have grown up in the different provinces: *shao-hsing* (from Lu Hsun's natal village in Chekiang); *kun chu* (Soochow); *pang tse* (Hopei, Shensi, Honan); *chuan chu* (Szechwan); *yueh chu* and *chao chu* (Cantonese); *y'ueh chu* (this is written with a different character than that used for the Cantonese and it comes from Chekiang), etc. Peking opera is sung in Mandarin, the others in regional dialects.

Origins twist back through centuries. The golden age of classical opera was the Yuan period (the Mongol dynasty begun by Kubilai Khan) of the thirteenth and fourteenth centuries. During this time a desire for social change began to be expressed through drama. Such "feelings of the

people" were discreetly stated in safely historical or legendary settings, as in the popular novels like *Three Kingdoms*
and *Water Margin* (or *All Men Are Brothers* as it is known
to us in the West) used as themes for operas. *Water
Margin* tells of a peasant revolt against the bureaucracy and
decadence of the Northern Sung dynasty (960–1279).

Kun chu opera grew up during the middle of the Ming
dynasty (1368–1644) in Soochow, Kiangsu province in the
south. Abstruseness made it a monopoly of feudal lords, and
following the destruction of Soochow during the nineteenth-century Taiping Rebellion it practically disappeared.
Through the absorption of *kun chu* and a combination of
local operas, principally from Anwhei (*hui chu*) and Northern Hupei (*pang tse*) provinces, popular Peking opera came
into being and flourished. The capital city became its center,
hence the name *ching* (city) *hsi* (play). It gained, and
retained, enormous mass popularity. With the arrival of
the Communists, old favorites like *Iron Faced and Un-
selfish, The Story of the White Snake, The Fisherman's
Revenge, The Four Scholars, Fifteen Strings of Cash* (*kun
chu*), *The Women Generals of the Yang Family* and *The
Butterfly Lovers* played once more to capacity houses, but
now many in the audience were workers clad in blue cotton,
enjoying the theatrical richness of the fallen dynasties for
a few pennies a seat.

Mei Lan-fang, the celebrated Peking opera actor, revived
and starred in splendid productions, even though he did
only female impersonations. (Until 1924, women had been
barred from the stage since the eighteenth-century rule of
Emperor Chien Lung.) Communist policy strove to popu-
larly establish male and female roles played by the respective
sexes and sung in natural rather than falsetto (false)
voices. Mei Lan-fang and a few other aging exceptions were
recognized by the young government. When the Chinese
Opera Research Institute was founded in Peking in 1954,
and the Peking Opera School in 1955, Mei Lan-fang was

named director of both. Several of his best-known roles were recorded on film. At the age of seventy-four he was acclaimed in *The Sword of the Universe*, a thousand-year-old Chin dynasty drama. Mei Lan-fang became a Party member in 1957, along with many personages in artistic and intellectual circles.

Recognition was accorded to theatre greats of the past as well. Hung Sheng, the anti-Confucian dramatist of the Manchu dynasty, received honor in Peking in 1954, on the anniversary of his death two hundred years before. The actor-hero Li Wen-mou, who died while leading a group of actors to fight in the Taiping Rebellion, was commemorated in Canton in November 1955. In 1958, the seventh centenary of the thirteenth-century dramatist Kuan Han-ching ("the Shakespeare of China") was greeted by productions of his works throughout the country.

A play bearing his name, a dramatization of how Kuan wrote his famous Yuan dynasty drama, *Snow in Midsummer*, was written for the occasion by the playwright Tien Han. During the Cultural Revolution, when artistic dimensions were remeasured to fit the model of revolutionary theatre outlined in Yenan years before, Tien Han was denounced as a "representative of the bourgeois, revisionist line for art and literature."*

Many of the people and dramas mentioned here were no longer accepted during the Cultural Revolution. Theatre (and cinema) from the time of Liberation up to the Cultural Revolution was mainly under the direction of those within the Communist Party who were "weeded out" during 1966–70 as "revisionists." A great many people had been honestly mistaken or simply fooled or confused by such leadership, which preached one line (Marxism-Leninism-Maoism) and practiced another (liberalistic, middle-class, revisionist). The Cultural Revolution sought to dig out the bourgeois elements and cement the cracks that had

* From an article in *Kuang-ming Jih-pao*, May 5, 1966.

appeared during the building of Chinese socialism. A vast process of education and reeducation had not eliminated deeply ingrained feelings of self-promotion, monetary incentive, and a tendency even on the part of persons who truly believed in the new society to rebuild a class with privileges above and beyond the ordinary people, the proletariat. "For whom" had been distorted; more and more the theatre, in content and form, was serving an elite. Many of those held accountable for this trend were not considered traitors by any means, but their responsible positions were filled by others with more reliable revolutionary goals. "Weeding out" in most cases meant temporary retirement for criticism and reeducation. The Chairman himself said the majority of the people were good.

There were a few who knowingly opposed proletarian socialist principles and promoted "the black line," a term used for anti-Party and antisocialist ideas reflected in literature and art. Furthermore, *Red Flag* (*Hung-chi,* the chief theoretical central organ of the Chinese Communist Party) points out: "Modern revisionists in the field of literature and art use a whole battery of arguments to support what they describe as the 'central principle' in aesthetics—'writing honestly.' Brandishing this 'principle' they denounce as 'dishonest' works of art and literature which describe the people's revolutionary struggles, faith in the revolution, and communist ideals. They use this 'principle,' too, to justify their approval of works which indiscriminately wax eloquent about bourgeois humanism, bourgeois pacifism and the bourgeois 'ideal' of a life of creature comforts and indulgence in the trivialities of home life. Only such works, they say, are 'honestly' written, and any work that is 'honestly' written must be a good work.

"It should be noted that the 'honesty' they advocate is in essence the 'honesty' of the bourgeoisie. If we discard examination of the class content of this 'honesty' and accept the thesis that as long as it is honest it is good, then there would of course be grounds for what they advocate."*

In following years Mao Tse-tung sounded further warnings; his instruction of December 12, 1963, "The social and economic base has changed, but the arts as part of the superstructure, which serve this base, still remain a serious problem," was followed in 1964 by an alert to national mass organizations in the field of literature and art: *"By and large,"* he said, "the people in them [that is, not everybody] have acted as high and mighty bureaucrats, have not gone to the workers, peasants and soldiers and have not reflected the socialist revolution and socialist construction. *In recent years*, they have slid right down to the brink of revisionism."

The ground was to be cut out from beneath their feet, and eminent personages were to fall, among them two "successors" to Mao Tse-tung.

Before Liberation a kind of "reformed" opera had been experimented with, the ancient plots modified and social significance instilled. With the Communists, versions of old classics incorporating modern ideas became more usual, but it wasn't until 1964 that revolution struck again, fundamentally affecting the seemingly sacrosanct Peking opera and the burgeoning foreign drama known before 1949 in only a few big cities.

Early in this century, urban Chinese students, returned from Japan, experimented with Western plays. By 1907, *Uncle Tom's Cabin* had been staged in Chinese, and a Chinese *Camille* (with an all-male cast) had played in Shanghai. It was in 1919 that among intellectuals interest in imported drama increased, and from this time on, left-wing writers and dramatists seriously engaged in modern works of social protest. The May Fourth Movement, begun in that year by Peking students as a protest against China's treatment under the Versailles Treaty set off a massive reaction resulting in changes that demonstrably shook China's feudal heritage. Literature and art became an important part of the cultural front from that event on.

* *Hung-chi (Red Flag)*, No. 21, 1962.

"After the May Fourth Movement the political leader of China's bourgeois-democratic revolution was no longer the bourgeoisie but the proletariat."*

Peking had a modern theatre school in the early twenties; a National School of Theatre was established in 1935 at Nanking. Among their productions were Gogol's *The Inspector General,* Ibsen's *An Enemy of the People,* and Shakespeare's *The Merchant of Venice.* Works of O'Neill, Strindberg and Chekhov were also shown.

This development, from the early stages of the revolution, included both violation of and support for the doctrine of service to workers, peasants and soldiers. Theatre reflected the various wartime mentalities: that of the undimmed stage lights of Japanese-occupied cities, that of Chiang Kai-shek's mountain bastion capital in Chungking, and that of the revolutionary Red Army touring troupes which helped swing the countryside over to support of the Communist guerrillas. The form of foreign drama was in some ways used by all three, but in the Communist areas the essential content was political education expressed through resistance to Japanese aggression and the various aspects of the proletarian revolution.

Mao Tse-tung stated the goal in 1940: "Not only do we want to change a China that is politically oppressed and economically exploited into a China that is politically free and economically prosperous, we also want to change the China which is being kept ignorant and backward under the sway of the old culture into an enlightened and progressive China under the sway of a new China. Our aim in the cultural sphere is to build a new Chinese national culture."**

Theatre made strides after Liberation. Ideas spread, nourished by the People's Liberation Army theatrical troupes that had sprung from the people's theatre during the years of battle. Shunned by much of the outside world—led

* *On New Democracy,* by Mao Tse-tung, January 1940.
** *Ibid.*

by the United States—and ostracized by the community of the United Nations, China at first relied on her socialist neighbors of East Europe and the Soviet Union as models and helpmates for industry, agriculture, medicine, science, education—and the arts.

Soon after the war a special category of drama arose, serving a short-term educational function for players and audience alike, perhaps akin to the off-Broadway *Daytop*, the ex-drug addict presentation. Australian journalist Wilfred Burchett saw some of these plays during his visit to China in 1951. *Gate No. 6*, about the Tientsin dockers and the smashing of the gang system, had more educational than artistic value because, he wrote, "it was necessary to show the public exactly how the system worked and how dockers lived" and "it went into too much detail. It took two nights to perform and was played by the dockers themselves. Eventually, because it had good dramatic content, it was radically overhauled, shortened and made suitable for the permanent repertoire." He describes similar plays, including one about prostitution after brothels were made illegal in China: "It was written by the girls themselves and graphically portrayed the terrible life they led from the time they were sold or tricked into prostitution. It was performed by the former prostitutes in the Peking People's Art Theatre, and was a powerful weapon in exposing the sordid and criminal behind-the-scenes story of the racket in brothels." Another educational drama dealt with and was played by a former band of Tientsin pickpockets—"a roaring success," wrote Mr. Burchett.*

Shakespeare, Molière, Chekhov, Shaw, Ibsen and other alien giants now were performed by hundreds of groups in dozens of cities. Chinese playwrights, employing "socialist realism," produced a flood of plays modeled on foreign drama. Ballet began in earnest, executed by novice Chinese dancers who learned, perhaps too quickly, the extrinsic

* *China's Feet Unbound*, by W. G. Burchett, World Unity Publications, Melbourne, Australia, 1952.

technique of Russian and visiting experts. Dance and ballet groups arrived from Albania, Burma, Poland, Vietnam and Yugoslavia. A Peking opera company played Paris in 1955 and later toured many European capitals and South America, revisiting Paris in 1957. Thus contact with the outside world broadened, influencing China's literature and art with concepts welcomed by many—but not necessarily the peasant masses.

During this time a parallel upsurge in music was created, pouring from symphony orchestras, virtuosos on concert stages, and the fingertips of youngsters practicing Tchaikovsky, Prokofiev, Beethoven, Mozart, Chopin and Liszt on alien pianos, harps and violins. Experiments with new Chinese instruments were made, and improvements were made in ancient ones. Researchers compiled archives containing thousands of heretofore-unrecorded classic opera arias, folk tunes, and popular songs. Composers used these, and their own inspirations, to produce new melodies and symphonies, and music for films and stage. National minorities' songs and dances spread beyond their boundaries. Old-style, new-style, Eastern and Western melodies surged up in every corner of the land. The Ninth Symphony could be heard as easily as the fully orchestrated *Yellow River Cantata*, which had had its debut before soldiers of the Eighth Route Army in Yenan in 1939.

The cultural creativity was astonishing, especially from a country recovering from the onslaught of war. A sampling of post-Liberation, non-opera Chinese drama (*hua chu* or "dialogue drama"), based on revolutionary-struggle themes, includes such titles as *Dragon's Beard Ditch* (residents' concern over a centuries-old malarious drain in the suburbs of Peking), written by Lao She,* known in the United States for his *Rickshaw Boy*; *Bright Skies* (ideological education of doctors in a Peking medical college from 1948 to 1952) by Tsao Yu, a leading dramatist remembered for his dramatic trilogy *Thunderstorm*, *Sunrise*, and *Wilderness*;

---

* In the West: Lao Shaw.

Steeled in Battles (liberation and reuniting of a peasant family by the Eighth Route Army) and *Locust Tree Village* (pre-Liberation class struggle during the agricultural cooperative movement), both by Hu Ko; *To Fight the Waves* (solidarity of seamen); *To Try the Chair* (commune struggle against the landlords); *The Crossing of the River Tatu* (the Long March); *A Bucket of Dung* (a dialogue between a man and a woman over the use of a pail of night soil); *Red Storm* (Peking-Hankow railway workers fight against imperialists and war lords); *Young People in a Far-off Place* (college graduates working in Sinkiang); and *Golden Eagle* (Mongolian feudal serfdom), written by Tsogtnarin, a young Mongolian dramatist.

Other themes were dealt with. The Lumumba struggle in the Belgian Congo: *War Drums Below the Equator*; Vietnam: *Fires of Wrath Under the Coconut Trees* and *Letters from the South*; women: *Girl in the Air Force* and *Sister Chiang*; children: *Little Sisters on the Grassland* and *Magic Aster*; and the behavior of peasant People's Liberation Army soldiers patroling the fashionable Nanking Road in Shanghai just after Liberation: *On Guard Beneath the Neon Lights*. In 1964, an enormous extravaganza, *The East Is Red*, with a chorus and cast of three thousand, was a magnificently staged pageant of the revolution and a paean to Chairman Mao. It was made into a color film, and the sound track, available in the United States, is a good example of the blend of Western-style symphony, chorus and indigenous songs.

Film studios recorded classic theatre and produced modern cinema on a wide variety of subjects, many of them concerned with historical peasant uprisings or current problems of the day. Though lacking experience and equipment, the People's Republic produced 170 full-length films between 1949 and 1957; less than two years after Liberation a "Month of Films" took place in twenty Chinese cities. In the period of the Great Leap Forward, 1958, 103 film productions appeared, the majority the work of the Seagull Studios in Shanghai, then still using mainly imported equipment. Seagull's output included, among other titles, *A Permanent Spring in the Time of Flowers, The Patriotic Mandarin, The Tai Doctor, Song of Victory on the Shores of the River, The Basketball Player,* and *The Railway Workers' Guerrilla Group.**

Imported films were largely from the U.S.S.R.; in 1950 alone there were forty-eight Soviet products. Along with a dusting of Albanian, Cuban and Korean films, *Bicycle Thief, The Red Balloon, Hamlet,* and *Pickwick Papers* represented the West wind. Some Chinese films went abroad. London, in 1952, saw *Daughters of China* and *The White Haired Girl.*

Chinese cartoons of excellent quality used a variety of media, such as the ancient art of marionettes, paper cutouts and folded paper, and a wash-tint technique reminiscent of Chinese painting.

In 1959, Edgar Snow's capsule assessment of the theatrical situation was "Many younger artists have reason to be grateful to the new state, which has welcomed talent and opened wide opportunities for it to develop. More than 80,000 professional artists and musicians were guaranteed full-time employment . . . Hundreds of new theatres have been built in China. . . . Nearly every province maintains at least one company to carry on its own opera in the several regional styles, dialects and traditions . . ."**

Soon Peking had more theatres than New York City, and in Shanghai alone seventy professional companies were working in a dozen different theatrical forms, comprising regional operas, and modern and vernacular drama. A rough estimate cited 3000 theatrical companies in the country in

* *China Triumphs,* by Julio Alvarez Del Vayo, Monthly Review Press, New York, 1964.
** *Red China Today,* revised and updated edition of *The Other Side of the River,* by Edgar Snow, Random House, New York, 1970.

1964 (not including amateur troupes). Of these, around ninety were professional modern drama companies, eighty-odd were cultural troupes, and the rest, over 2800, were companies staging various kinds of operas and balladry.*

Behind all this activity the problem of "two lines"— one reflecting bourgeois tendencies, the other the proletarian revolution—was growing and affecting the world of theatre in a particular way: a resurgence of bourgeois thinking conflicted with the criteria for literature and art counseled by Mao Tse-tung at the Yenan Forum in 1942. In the fervor of post-Liberation theatrical events this advice had been largely, if in many cases unintentionally, shunted aside. Copying of "the foreign" dominated indigenous creativity; refurbishing "the old" took priority over constructing the new. The roots were deep. By the outbreak of the Sino-Japanese War in 1937, socially conscious intellectuals were already splitting; choosing of sides went on, both in and out of the Party** down to the present day. Lu Hsun, who was the first to throw out old literary forms of expression to write in the vernacular, is revered today as a consistent promulgator and supporter of proletarian revolutionary goals; though he never became a Party member. "His thinking, action and writing were all marxianized."† Chou Yang, who joined the Communists in the early days and became Vice Minister of Propaganda for the Central Committee, was denounced during the Cultural Revolution as symbolizing anti-Lu Hsun and the "black line." He was accused of having begun his conspiratorial activities as a political opportunist as early as the thirties.

The question of "for whom" became more theoretical than applied. "For whom," demanded the Cultural Revolution leaders, were Communist ballerinas dressed in tutus

---

* *On the Revolution of Peking Opera*, by Chiang Ching, Foreign Languages Press, Peking, 1964.

** The Chinese Communist Party was formed in 1921.

† Mao Tse-tung, in a speech commemorating the first anniversary of Lu Hsun's death, 1937.

dancing "court" ballet and "for whom" were revolutionary actors clothed in velvet and silk presenting Shakespeare and Molière? Not for peasants, workers or soldiers with no background to understand the anomaly. Form without social meaning, art for art's sake, began to cut the war-born bonds between the masses and the artists. Privilege arose in position and class as actors and writers began to be paid more, have better living quarters than "workers," and receive special advantages.

The main problem stemmed from content, and this was especially true of classical theatre. Matured in feudal times, it reflects feudal society. Emperors, empresses, concubines, despots, court beauties, seducers, monsters, spirits, and imperial heroes people its stories; deceit, trickery, violence, exploitation, submission and servility mark its plots; questionable themes and superstition abound. Now after two decades, the Cultural Revolution mentors began to sweep away what the founding fathers considered undesirable and to assimilate the usable old with the necessary new in order to approach Mao Tse-tung's Yenan-given ideals of revolutionary truth.

In a twenty-day discussion held in Shanghai in February 1966, certain points were made concerning work in literature and art in the armed forces. If it seems odd that the armed forces were concerned, it is well to recall a quotation from Mao Tse-tung: "An army without culture is a dull-witted army and a dull-witted army cannot defeat the enemy."* Noteworthy was the citing of five writings by the Chairman as filling the needs of proletarian literature and art for a long time to come: *On New Democracy* (1940), *Talks at the Yenan Forum on Literature and Art* (1942), *Letter to the Yenan Peking Opera Theatre after Seeing "Driven to Join the Liangshan Mountain Rebels"* (1944), *On the Correct Handling of Contradictions Among*

* *The United Front in Cultural Work*, by Mao Tse-tung, October 30, 1944.

the People (1957) and *Speech at the Chinese Communist Party's National Conference on Propaganda Work*
(1957).

"However," stated the report on the discussion,* "since
the founding of our People's Republic, the ideas of these
works have basically not been carried out by literary and
art circles. Instead, we have been under the dictatorship
of a black anti-Party and anti-socialist line which is dia-
metrically opposed to Chairman Mao's thought. This black
line is a combination of bourgeois [and] modern revisionist
ideas on literature and art and what is known as the literature and art of the 1930s (in the Kuomintang areas of
China). Typical expressions of this line are such theories
as those of truthful writing, the broad path of realism, the
deepening of realism, opposition to subject matter as the
decisive factor, middle characters, opposition to the smell
of gunpowder, and the merging of various trends as the
spirit of the age . . . As a result . . . there have been few
good or basically good works in the last decade or so (although there have been some) which truly praise worker,
peasant and soldier heroes and which serve the workers,
peasants and soldiers . . . After this black line is destroyed,
still others will appear. The struggle will have to go on.
[It may demand] decades or even centuries of effort. This
is a cardinal issue which has a vital bearing on the future
of the Chinese revolution and the world revolution."

An example of revisionist drama, incorporating the de-
ceptions of "truthful writing" and other theories listed
above, is a film called *The Life of Wu Hsun*, produced by
Sun Yu in Shanghai in late 1950. After its debut in January
1951, it became the first dramatic wave to rock the revolutionary theatre.

Wu Hsun was an actual person who lived in Shantung
province in the last century. So poor that he could not go

* *Summary of the Forum on the Work in Literature and Art in the
Armed Forces with Which Comrade Lin Piao Entrusted Comrade Chiang
Ching;* Foreign Languages Press, Peking, 1968.

to school, he educated himself by listening outside the schoolhouse walls. He saved up coppers, bit by bit over a long time, earned by allowing the rich children to use him as an animal—so many pennies to kick him, so many to beat him, or to ride him as a horse. Once all his money was stolen by a landlord's son and Wu could not accuse him. He saved up again, starving and in rags, until he had enough to buy some land during a famine. Always begging and saving, he accumulated more land and money and eventually opened a school for poor peasant children. Many of them grew up to pass the Imperial examination and become high officials. Wu Hsun continued his life of penury. When he was an old man the Emperor gave him the "golden vest" which, when worn, made the wearer higher than a magistrate. Not used to luxury Wu Hsun threw it away. He died a beggar.

In China I heard that the picture was very moving. One solidly placed and intelligent Party member told me, "I found it hard to keep tears." He was not the only enthusiast; the film received highly favorable reviews in the press.

A few months later, criticisms began to create controversy; on May 20, *The People's Daily* in Peking carried an editorial written by Mao Tse-tung called "Pay Serious Attention to the Discussion of the Film *The Life of Wu Hsun*." In it Mao wrote, "The praise lavished on Wu Hsun and the film show the degree of ideological confusion reached in our country's cultural circles! Where on earth is the Marxism which certain Communists claim to have grasped? There should be discussion on the film . . . so as thoroughly to straighten out the confused thinking on this picture."

Discussions followed. The Party member who had found it "hard to keep tears" said that after lengthy and heated debate he was convinced that the film was motivated by bourgeois reformism and filled with reactionary thinking: Wu Hsun was tied up with speculators when buying land, and the education he gave the peasants resulted only in producing officials who exploited the people and propagated scholar-gentry rule.

It was banned soon afterward. Some high Party officials had lauded the picture, among them Chou Yang, the influential, soon-to-be-ousted Vice Minister of Propaganda for the Central Committee. In spite of his "error" (he made a public self-criticism) he was reelected Vice Chairman of the All-China Federation of Literary and Art Circles in 1953. Liu Shao-chi, Chairman of the National Congress and Mao Tse-tung's apparent successor, Lu Ting-i, Minister of Culture, and Peng Chen, then mayor of Peking, in addition to Chou Yang, had great influence in China's artistic circles. Though ostensibly they were all ardent Maoists, it was in a conflict of power and methods with them and their followers that Mao launched the Cultural Revolution in 1966. Liu Shao-chi himself was personified as the chief villain "taking the capitalist road."

It wasn't till 1960, when the Soviet Union abruptly recalled her technical personnel from China and canceled all commercial contracts—seriously crippling industry and suspending China's economic progress—that the tip of the ideologically distorted iceberg came into view. The Russian blow came during a period of weakness when natural disaster—floods and droughts—gravely affected agriculture and economy. The precipitous withdrawal of Soviet aid compounded the emergency. Meanwhile the United States threat intensified in Southeast Asia. As antagonism with China's socialist neighbor grew, it grew too within the ranks of the Party.

It was Chiang Ching, the Chairman's wife, who brought her talents and experience into the looming battle in the world of literature and art. As a young actress Chiang Ching had, in 1933, secretly joined the Party and gone to the revolutionary base in Yenan. There she worked at the Lu Hsun Academy of Fine Arts, directing rehearsals for the institute's theatre troupe, and there she met and married Mao Tse-tung, divorced the year before (1937) from Ho Tzu-ch'en.

My husband met Chiang Ching in Yenan a few months after her marriage and recalls her as a slender, attractive young woman. In this guerrilla capital of caves she bore Mao a daughter, Li Na.

For years after Liberation Chiang Ching was seen but rarely in public, and then as Madame Mao. Her official activities were limited, though she was a member of the Film Enterprise Guiding Committee, an advisory board of censorship capacity under the Ministry of Culture. During this time, in 1950, she had criticized a movie entitled *Inside Story of the Ching Court* as reactionary, but her denunciation of the film caused hardly a ripple. Then, in July 1962, Chiang Ching sent a statement of reproval to Hsia Yen, an influential member of the All-China Federation of Literary and Art Circles and of the All-China Motion Picture Workers' Federation, calling attention to the seriously reactionary political tendencies of a historical play, *Hai Jui Dismissed from Office.* To all appearances Hsia paid no attention. *Hai Jui*, written by Wu Han, a deputy mayor of Peking, was said to be an allegorical screen used to censure Mao Tse-tung for dismissing his minister of defense, P'eng Teh'huai in 1959, and replacing him with Lin Piao. Mao later publicly called it "a film of national betrayal."

Chiang Ching continued what soon would prove to be a veritable crusade to uphold the proletarian revolutionary line of Mao Tse-tung Thought: Peking opera was the means for its promotion; a change in content and in direction— "for whom"—was the crux of the attack.

"We must have unshakable confidence in the staging of Peking opera on revolutionary themes," she wrote in July 1964. "It is inconceivable that, in our socialist country led by the Communist Party, the dominant position on the stage is not occupied by the workers, peasants and soldiers, who are the real creators of history and the true masters of our country. We should create literature and art which protect our socialist economic base . . . the grain we eat is grown by the peasants, the clothes we wear and the houses we live in are all made by the workers, and the People's Liberation Army stands guard at the fronts of national defense for us and yet we do not portray them on stage. May I ask which class stand you artists take? And where is the artists' 'conscience' you always talk about?"*

Chiang Ching was supported by the respected mayor of Shanghai, Ke Ching-shih. It was mainly through him that the East China Drama Festival, held in the city from December 25, 1963, to January 22, 1964, broke the ground for reform of Peking opera. Mayor Ke spoke at the festival, publicly encouraging the creation of a new revolutionary theatre. In the same period Premier Chou En-lai called for the creation of literature and art on contemporary themes dealing with the socialist revolution.

Yet two and a half years after Chiang Ching had initiated her attack on *Hai Jui Dismissed from Office,* another criticism of the play, written by literary critic Yao Wen-yuan and published in Shanghai, was ignored by the powerful Peking press. Yao's article sharply stated that the nature of the struggle was a political one, not something for academic discussion. Chairman Mao was in Shanghai at the time and on hearing of Peking's refusal to publish the criticism he is said to have replied: "If they do not print this, we will print it in pamphlets to be distributed all over the country." It is said too that Peking's mayor, Peng Chen, blocked the pamphlets and prohibited the huge bookstore Hsinhua from ordering them.

Why all this over one play? *Hai Jui* had become the center of a publicly emerging "struggle between the lines" —the line of Maoist socialism that sprang from and depended on the workers and peasantry, and the line of Lui Shao-chi, who through the years leaned ever more toward the Moscow-oriented "revisionist" idea of socialism which the Maoists believe leads inevitably to capitalism. Behind Wu Han, author of *Hai Jui,* was Mayor Peng Chen and

* *On the Revolution of Peking Opera,* by Chiang Ching, Foreign Languages Press, Peking, 1968.

his followers. Behind them was Chairman of the National Congress Lui Shao-chi. Facing them all was Mao Tse-tung (then reported to be sick, feeble, and on the verge of giving up) and the Great Proletarian Cultural Revolution. It is now clear *Hai Jui* contained a deep and critical violation of revolutionary unity.

In 1964, Chiang Ching's campaign blossomed. The festival of Peking Opera on Contemporary Themes, involving thousands of actors and musicians from eighteen provinces, started what would soon become China's model theatre: *Sparks Amid the Reeds*, which became *Shachiapang*; *Taking the Bandit's Stronghold*, later retitled *Taking Tiger Mountain by Strategy*, and *The Red Lantern*. *The White Haired Girl* and *Red Detachment of Women*, the first full-length revolutionary ballet, made their debuts. "The reform of Peking opera is a major event," editorialized *Red Flag*, the Party's theoretical journal. "It is not only a cultural revolution but a social revolution."

Such was the beginning; a lot was to follow. When we entered the People's Republic in 1970, China had moved even further along on the proletarian path, and a handful of model operas and ballets heralded a theatre for those "for whom" it was intended from the start.

1

TAKING TIGER MOUNTAIN

PEKING OPERA NOW IS A MIXTURE OF DRAMA, music, dance, acrobatics, poetry, propaganda and revolutionary history, with indefatigable heroes (more adroit than James Bond, and with a purpose he never dreamed of) and fabulously wicked villains—the whole socking out a message of exemplary struggle and courage.

Five model operas* and two model ballets, representing a breakaway from hundreds of years of traditional Peking operas, form the basic theatrical fare in post-Cultural Revolutionary China. They are flanked by model orchestral works and a heaping hors d'oeuvre selection of skits, songs,

---

* Two of these are undergoing revision: *White Tiger Regiment* (setting: Anpingli, Korea, near the Chincheng front lines, 1953) and *On the Docks* (setting: Shanghai, 1963). The final versions were not yet ready for publication at this writing.

folk dances and music, national minority compositions, poems and patter, performed the length and breadth of the country in schools, factories, commune farms, army posts, steel mills, coal mines, People's Halls, threshing grounds, city parks and distant mountain regions. Excerpts and entire performances are televised to millions of viewers; full-length films have been made of all but one. Trains, courtyards, restaurants, stores, playgrounds, harvest fields, and workshops echo with their broadcast tunes.

The film and television prints reach remote areas still lacking adequate electricity. They are projected by a bicycle-powered generator manned by a dedicated comrade or two who "serve the people" with strong legs and the spirit of Yenan. (We saw a model in Shanghai's Trade Exhibit. In this instance the energy-producing limbs belonged to two attractive girls.) The generator not only provides power for documentary and Peking opera films, but fills in on all sorts of needed occasions where, for example, power fails and is needed for emergency operations.

Kids at play sing bits and pieces of favorite arias, and radios mix news and educational programs with the songs and music. Some days an energetic voice sang out across the courtyard of our hotel, awakening us with an early-morning rendition of a popular Peking opera tune. Bouncing into my shower, I enjoyed the song as much as the unseen singer.

With my love of the stage, I spent all the time I could in the theatre of China today. I had little direct knowledge of its traditional past: Mei Lan-fang—a glorious name to me, but never personally seen; beguiling Shanghai movie queens pictured on candy boxes purchased in my childhood in San Francisco's "Chinatown"; New York City's Oriental offerings; and an exciting evening at the Chinese "opera" (more like a musical circus in this version) when it played to packed audiences in Geneva's ice-skating arena some years ago. In China, accompanied by those who had seen the old and know the new (and what has created the new)

I watched and learned what I could about the present. I read each play in English before attending a performance; an excellent translator-companion explained subtleties I might otherwise have missed. Sometimes earphones with simultaneous English translation were available, but I preferred the less pervasive interpreter, or my own "self-reliance." I returned several times to some of the plays in order to better understand.

Theatre tickets cost very little. Seats in the first row are priced at the equivalent of about thirty cents in U.S. money,* those further back at around fifteen cents, though to a Chinese family this is more than it is to us. (Seventy cents buys a good meal for a family of four.) Theoretically, tickets can be bought ahead of time at the theatre, but they are mostly obtained through factories, communes, schools, and various organizations, either from the workers' accumulation fund, or for a fraction of the box-office price. Tickets are not easy to acquire; too many people want to see what is still too little theatrical fare. (Yet in small factories we visited as far away as Shenyang, most of the workers had seen three operas and two ballets.)

My initial experience was a performance of *Taking Tiger Mountain by Strategy*, one of the current model operas. It was presented in the Hall of the Political Consultative Council, a pleasant Peking "off-Broadway" auditorium functionally prepared for note taking, and with a seating capacity of about a thousand.

We arrived, in time for the seven-thirty curtain, and caused quick turning of heads and sharp surprise in black eyes till we settled into our seats. Western foreigners are conspicuous, even in a Peking theatre. The hall was already full of men and women—old, young, in-between—all dressed (as by this time I was) in cotton pants and light shirts. Khaki green of army sprinkled the spectators' near-uniform blue, and occasional flashes of bright color shot from the hair-bows and gay blouses of children out for a

* The official exchange rate is 2.44 yuan to one U.S. dollar.

treat. Tiny fans fluttered like hummingbirds throughout the audience on this unseasonably sultry evening. The golden-bronze curtain glowed with light; on either side of the stage were oblong screens that flash the libretto (printed in Chinese characters) simultaneously as an actor sings. (The notes of a song are drawn out in such a way as to make words often not understandable, hence the need for visual assistance.) They also identify acts and scenes. Distracted by them at first, I got used to these illuminated scroll-like aids—though, due to my lack of Chinese, they became and remained only familiar decorations.

Audience buzz-and-chatter stopped when a member of the cast, dressed in army uniform, sprang out onto the spot-lighted apron and recited, high and loud as a drill sergeant, an appropriate quotation from Mao Tse-tung. This is customary procedure now, and is not only a tribute to the Chairman but an ideological guide to the performance about to be seen.

As lights dimmed the curtains parted on a semi-ballet, semi-acrobatic, dance depicting a PLA (People's Liberation Army) pursuit detachment forcing its way forward in a blizzard. The illuminated signs at the sides of the proscenium identified the scene: "Winter, 1946, somewhere in Northeast China, a forest deep in a snow-covered mountain." Snow whirled, a huge crimson flag reeled in the music-howling gale; actor-dancers leaped and sprang through the storm; biting cold seemed to pour out across the footlights. I sat up straight at the breath-taking pace and energy.

Stage right, an orchestra of some twenty musicians, both men and women, using a combination of Chinese and Western instruments, remained scrim-screened but visible during the play, pinpointing a gesture, emphasizing a mood, underscoring the text—and in full accompaniment when arias or dances took over. (In old Peking opera the musicians—at that time, usually seven or eight players—used to sit on the stage in full view.) Unobtrusively the orchestra becomes part and parcel of the action. The conductor assumes particular importance as he punctuates striking moments with a sharp "tac" produced by clapping together two pieces of wood, a time-beater called a *pan*.*

The scenery was a blend of "revolutionary realistic-revolutionary romantic," the term the Chinese use to describe the new style. A house that Walt Disney might have designed if Snow White had been lost in a Chinese forest was indicated by outlines of exterior walls and a snow-topped roof framing a snug room with a window frankly painted on the back flat. Outdoor scenes used photographed scenery on the "cyc," while a cutout tree or two served the actors as a "forest" in the playing area. (Peking opera used to be setless and sceneless.) Stage properties were few, as they were in classical opera.** A table and chair sufficed as furniture in the army headquarters; a map on the wall made it look official. The interior of a hunter's house was achieved with a rough-hewn stool front stage and a *k'ang* (the peasant stone bed) against the back of the set. Realistic doors—that didn't always stay tightly shut—were used to enter from "outside" to "inside," but the actors sometimes employed a modified version of the old Peking opera high-step device for entering a room. Snowstorms were created by projected swirls of white spots and cloudbursts by streaks and slashes of simulated rain. (Bits of white paper thrown up in the air by the stage manager formerly produced a snowstorm in classic opera, as a flag with black lines drawn across it used to indicate a storm, or a flag with the character for water, a flood. Rain was equally easy to distinguish before—the actors simply carried umbrellas or dodged imagined pools of water.)

* See Chapter III.
** Present productions vary from province to province (sometimes within a province itself), especially when the model opera is presented in a local form with regional speech and singing replacing the traditional Peking opera style (Szechwan opera, Shensi opera, etc.) and thus a variation in physical setting occurs, some productions going in for more complete or elaborate backgrounds and stage properties.

Costumes today are realistic, though not carried to extremes—if a character is supposed to be poor and dirty, the idea is conveyed by neat patches and splashes; landlords are convincingly but not lavishly well-clothed. Gone is the sumptuousness of the past, when even beggars wore rags of silk and satin on stage. "Revolutionary romanticism" modifies straight realism and is apparent in carefully controlled color and design; it is an idealized or symbolized heightening of reality.

Actors use an extraordinary amount of unrealistic make-up, particularly the young men, who point up revolutionary goodness and health by startlingly rosy faces and upswung black-painted brows. The Chinese, however, are accustomed to exaggeratedly painted stage faces and don't seem in the least surprised by pink-cheeked heroes or yellow-green villains. Make-up ("face-painting"—*lien p'u*) was an ancient and complicated art in classical Peking opera, by means of which characters could be immediately categorized as they stepped on stage. Color played an important role: red, for example, was traditional for the honest. The more heroic the heroes looked, the better; the worse the wicked, the better. So it has been for centuries. Revolutionary Peking opera has considerably toned down what used to be a technique of enormous importance.

Similar emphasis—stressing good and bad—affects staging and lighting. Good people always take a prominent place on stage, singled out by light; villains and ne'er-do-wells—even when the scene is theirs, and even when occupying the stage alone—are kept off center and in dim light. This is skillfully done, though for me it tended to highlight the villains, somehow eye-catching in their obscurity.

Taking Tiger Mountain (I'm dropping the "by Strategy" from here on; most people do, and I've also heard some criticism about the grammatical use of the word) is adapted from a once-upon-a-time best-selling novel entitled *Tracks in the Snowy Forest,** written by Chu Po, a

---

* Foreign Languages Press edition, Peking, 1962.

PLA soldier-author who based his book on a combination of fact and fiction. Before making its way onto the Peking opera stage, the novel was first made into a film with the same title as the book. The dramatic content of the opera is basically one incident from a series of similar happenings in the novel—condensed, emphasized, and with some changes in names and characters.

Its title recalls Mao Tse-tung's well-known statement: "Imperialism and all reactionaries are paper tigers," by which he meant that in appearance enemies are terrifying, in actuality they have caused great destruction; but in the long run it is the people who are really powerful and who will prevail.

The opera describes a situation often encountered in the Civil War of 1946–47—a battle in which a detachment of the PLA overcomes a gang of Kuomintang bandits. *Taking Tiger Mountain* proves the power of the people "even when the enemy is strong and the people are weak, provided the masses are aroused, armed, and organized to struggle."* China had been devastated by war for many years. The Japanese had occupied large areas of the country, but Chiang Kai-shek had capitulated time and again to the invaders, expending his troops and his might on "extermination campaigns" against the Communists, who were becoming increasingly strong.

In contrast to the disciplined, dedicated peasant soldiers of Mao Tse-tung—who fought against modern-armed Japanese and puppet troops and the Nationalist armies of Chiang Kai-shek, equipped with weapons and supplies donated by the United States, with bamboo spikes, captured rifles, and Communist guerrilla technique—the Kuomintang's manpower consisted to a large degree of troops often "conscripted" by a rope around their necks. The fall of Japan in 1945, symbolized by mushroom clouds over Hiroshima and Nagasaki, released Chiang from his reluctant coalition with the Communists against the enemy. By 1946

* *Hsinhua News Bulletin*, August 5, 1970.

he threw all his resources into civil war. As battles raged and ravaged, many remnant bands of Kuomintang deserters or deserted, with no purpose except survival, established themselves in hideouts to lead predatory lives, making the most of their guns, cunning and brute strength.

With this historical background we move on stage: entrenched on Tiger Mountain, a stony fortress dominating the valley of Chiapi, a gang of such bandit renegades, headed by their chief, Vulture, and protected in their mountain stronghold by nine units of twenty-seven forts, have terrorized the surrounding countryside and the village of Chiapi. The residents have lived in destitution under this siege of violence, miserably oppressed by "the three mountains of imperialism, feudalism, and bureaucratic capitalism."*

Li Yung-chi, a railway worker, was kidnapped and taken to Tiger Mountain when Chiapi was pillaged; his wife and child were murdered. The mother and wife of Hunter Chang were killed, and he and his daughter, Chang Pao (disguised as a deaf-mute boy for her protection) have been forced to hide for years in the depths of a nearby forest. The PLA arrives to organize resistance and liberate the valley. When the people learn that this army is made up of worker and peasant soldiers who have come to help them, they eagerly take up the offered arms. Li Yung-chi, Chang and his daughter, along with many villagers, join the forces.

Yang Tzu-jung, a scout platoon leader of the PLA, supported and encouraged by his chief of staff, Shao Chien-po, disguises himself as a bandit and makes his way, alone, into the enemy's fort. His courage, firm revolutionary consciousness and ingenuity enable him to outwit Vulture and his gang of "Terribles," establish communication with the army and the people below, and join in the attack by the militia and the PLA. A fierce battle culminates in defeat of the bandits. Chiapi is freed; the villagers, won to the side

* Referred to in Mao Tse-tung's writings. See also, *Hsinhua News Bulletin*, August 5, 1970.

of their Communist liberators, celebrate, determined to continue the revolution.

Artificial, formalized conventions of old Peking opera combine with the contemporary theme and new techniques of *Taking Tiger Mountain* in a hand-in-glove rapport. The use of highly stylized gestures is fascinating. The scout-hero, Yang Tzu-jung, is clad in a bandit cover-up of tiger-pelt blouse and black pants under a long white chamois-lined coat, legs encased in high leather boots, with a hat of wolf fur on his head. The scene in which he speeds on horseback in a blinding snowstorm through the dense forest to the bandits' lair, encountering and killing a man-eating tiger en route, is a gem of pantomime, ritual movement, dance and acrobatics. With the aid only of a red-tasseled whip, music, his two nimble legs and eloquent voice, the actor creates a galloping steed, a cold ride fraught with dangers, a ferocious tiger, a panic-stricken horse, and a howling victim as he shoots the tiger to death. The tasseled riding whip is a conventional prop used to indicate riding a steed. Mounting and dismounting is done with traditional, stylized footwork and body movements. A rapid walk around the stage, using tiny steps, means a long distance covered. Sharpening the moments of high drama, the *liang hsiang*, or pause (from traditional Chinese theatre), brings the actor to a poised standstill, and then the action resumes.

The character of the villainous bandit Luan Ping was played by a master craftsman who made the wretched traitor-spy an unforgettable dreg of humanity. Under the unrelenting pressure of Yang-disguised-as-bandit (but known for who he really is by the Kuomintang scamp) Luan disintegrates from a gleeful, boasting spy to a trembling, powerless, crumpled rag—the actor's body was swept from the stage as if it were a disemboweled scarecrow. It was worthy of Marcel Marceau.

Peking opera steps associated with warrior roles and hair-raising somersaults combined with gravity-defying leaps enrich the modern-dance pantomime movements of soldiers skiing over snow-covered hills. The final scaling of Tiger Mountain is a thrilling display of gymnastic grace and muscular skill. When the battle between the bandits and the PLA takes place in the grimy, dark fortress cave, kaleidoscopic action envelops the stage. One after the other, in circus-like tumbling, the soldier-acrobats knock off the drunken villains—who, using a Peking opera device, either roll themselves off the stage, or after falling dead, get up and run off. It happens so fast, in such excitement of music and pace, that this self-removal of the dead is perfectly acceptable. Acrobatics are concise and clear-cut, conveying the impression of fury with discipline and precision. Chinese Douglas Fairbanks and Errol Flynns swarm over the stage defying and defeating the ferocious, agile, cooperative enemy: actors in both categories duck, dodge, leap, kick, and swing, in mutually assisted gymnastic feats.

As minutely planned as dueling episodes in a topflight Shakespearean company, these scenes in modern Peking opera have the added value of humor, and the cool comfort of rapport with the audience. The villains are destroyed without a trace of spectator sympathy: the triumph of sheer good over stark evil is mandatory and inevitable. No tears are shed for the vanquished. On reading the still-recent history of China it is easy to understand the Chinese acceptance of a totality of evil. The wildest imagination would be hard-pressed to come up with horror stories equal to those related by eyewitnesses in book after book about pre-Liberation China.*

Through the eyes of Jack Belden** we can get a conception of the Chinese peasants' passionate hatred of their

---

* See Jack Belden's *China Shakes the World*; Graham Peck's *Two Kinds of Time*; Edgar Snow's *Red Star Over China* and *Battle for Asia*; Agnes Smedley's *The Great Road*; Han Suyin's trilogy: *The Crippled Tree, A Mortal Flower* and *Birdless Summer*.

** *China Shakes the World*, by Jack Belden, Monthly Review Press, New York, 1970, p. 4.

Copyright © 1949 by Jack Belden; reprinted by permission of Monthly Review Press.

oppressors—"The extent and depths of which," he wrote, "could be felt and seen and heard in the trampling rush of peasant feet toward the landlord's manor; in the dying gasp of a village noble whose body, as well as whose land, was divided by club-swinging peasants; in the flash of a pig knife plunged into the heart of a clan leader whose ancestral tablets the farmers might normally have worshipped; in the shriek of a girl whose mother led Chiang Kai-shek's secret service to chop off her daughter's head and pull out her intestines; in the religious groans of village witches who called down gods to their incense tables and chanted in sepulchral tones: 'Chiang Kai-shek comes!'; in the snick of scissors wielded by women cutting off the flesh of a village oppressor; in the lamentations of village brides beaten by their husbands and in their murderous cries of vengeance as they organized themselves into Women's Associations and beat, scratched and tore the flesh of their hated lords and masters; everywhere on the good Chinese earth, across the plains, the mountains and the fields, these passions rose up as a new and unconquerable force."

To my Western, bourgeois stage eyes, the evil ones are often more successful dramatically than the heroes. They are so bad they are interesting. If I had seen Tiger Mountain's Vulture when I was a child, I would have gone to bed with the shivers; watching with more sophistication I found him fascinating. The actor we saw was superb in the role. His physical dexterity and grace added a supernatural quality as he literally rose in the air or bounced on his rocky throne in the throes of wily wickedness, like an Oriental Nome king. It is difficult to achieve the portrayal of complete bad or complete good on stage. Somewhere in conveying badness an interesting contrast is bound to appear, even if it is only unintentional humor. All good is sometimes all bore. But here it is important to remember the "for whom" the new Chinese theatre was created to reach. Audiences whose heritage is deep suffering from Kuomintang bandits, invaders, imperialists, landlords, war lords, traitors, spies, and the like, are apt to accept—and relish—absolutely drawn heroes and villains than bourgeois theatre audiences in the U.S.A. or Europe, thousands of miles and ideological light years away from such immediate suffering.

Heroes in socialist China have little in common with capitalist-grown varieties. Model revolutionaries are people revered by the masses for having led—and often lost—lives dedicated to service beyond the call of socialist duty, and who are meant to be emulated in daily life. They are not *apart* from ordinary citizens. They may have flashed to recognition in one heroic, if prosaic, moment, perhaps dying in an attempt to save state property—as in the case of a national hero whose young life was swept away in a raging flood as he endeavored to rescue some vitally important telephone poles. Communist youths are taught to go *beyond*—to be the first to do the dirtiest jobs, to brave the utmost danger, to volunteer ahead of others, to be living examples of courage, hard work and truth. Adoration of movie stars, prize fighters, pop singers, baseball players, cosmonauts, is inconceivable in today's China. Heroism is hitched to political and ideological performance. The PLA member who "serves the people" by enduring painful self-experiments with an acupuncture needle in an effort to find a cure for others' deafness has more public approbation in China than the stage and screen actors who portray heroic characters.

Actors (who have spanned times of both social ostracism and public adulation) are now workers, with all the dignity and honor attached to the name in socialist China. Glamour and wealth are no more for them than for others —though they do pick up reflected limelight, as I found out from a young Chinese friend. She was elated that my husband and I shared the high podium at Heavenly Peace Gate (Peking's Times Square) with distinguished persons, foreign and Chinese, at the October first celebration. The event was photographed and televised and we, accordingly, gained honor in the eyes of those who saw us—especially our hotel "comrade waiters"—up there "chatting" with Mao Tse-tung—a privilege we very much recognized. From the exuberant Chinese youngster I gathered that the following were causes of delight: it was wonderful to see us with Chairman Mao! it was wonderful to see Chou En-lai (a person with a special place in the hearts of the young)! it was wonderful to see Chen Yung-keui, the national peasant hero of Tachia commune! And it was wonderful to see Tung Hsiang-lin, who created the part of Yang Tzu-jung on stage, and who is seen in that role in the new film version of *Taking Tiger Mountain*. The actor, due to this role, was among the heroes.

China's children use their formative years to develop into politically and socially responsible human beings. Education is political instruction, study and theory combined with work and practice, productive labor and militia training. No cinema, literature, or advertising touches on the indulgent, romantic or licentious. Discothèques, bars, and night clubs are replaced by sports, folk dancing, country hikes, bike rides, and theatre and movies on revolutionary themes, or documentaries—all enjoyed by throngs of boys and girls relaxing after hard work and study. The past has given these heirs of the revolution a different present from their contemporaries elsewhere; they accept ideals and heroes as to be emulated that we in the West only profess to accept.

What Faubion Bowers calls the "archaic morality" of classic Peking opera has changed to the proletarian, revolutionary morality of new China. He points out that old theatre was "either a model of ideals or the nadir of infamy . . . aesthetically a purer theatre than our own; humanly it is a lesser one."* What we see now is both pure and human in content; it is the externals, the form that seems "unnat-

* *Theatre in the East*, by Faubion Bowers, Grove Press, New York, 1956.

ural" to us. Mr. Bowers uses the phrase "a distillation of humanity"; that holds true today, but the characters and plots are no longer the same.

For peasant audiences—ninety percent of the "for whom"—there is no such problem of the form seeming unnatural. They have emerged so recently from war, poverty, exploitation and the starkness of life and death, that primary-colored drama without subtleties of ideological shading is as readily accepted as the vividly painted, highly stylized characters of yesterday's Peking opera were by the Chinese theatregoers in the past. Total projection of evil and virtue is a custom. Enough of the traditional is retained in form and music to be familiar; politically oriented content has added substance, and is a means of teaching "past bitterness and present happiness" to the masses.

Collectively written and produced by members of the Peking Opera Troupe of Shanghai, *Taking Tiger Mountain* was begun in 1958 (during the Great Leap Forward) under the title *Taking the Bandits' Stronghold*. It has gone through much reshaping to reach its present "model" form, that is, one geared to "awaken the masses, fire them with enthusiasm, and impel them to unite and struggle to transform their environment." Revolutionary theatre is meant to educate and politicize as well as entertain, to present models and heroes that "propel history forward," in the words of Mao Tse-tung. "Revolutionary realism" combined with "revolutionary romanticism" equals "revolutionary truth"—"life as reflected in works of literature and art on a higher plane, more intense, more concentrated, more typical, nearer the ideal, and therefore more universal than actual everyday life."*

The effort to achieve this took place in conflict between those in the opera company who clung to the old ideas and conventions (including some, we were told repeatedly, who were downright counterrevolutionary) and those who rec-

---

* *Talks at the Yenan Forum on Literature and Art*, by Mao Tse-tung, 1942.

ognized the need for a new, original theatre: "new, in the sense that it is socialist; and original, in the sense that it is proletarian."*

The play received a new name (which stresses the success of the heroes, rather than putting the villains into prominence); scenes were added or deleted; the name of the bandit chief was changed from Eagle, as it was in Chu Po's book, to Vulture. Extensive changes were made in music, décor, and lighting.

An article written by the *Taking Tiger Mountain by Strategy* group of the Peking Opera Troupe of Shanghai describes the "remolding" of the hero Yang. In the text it is explained that the original script (until changed in 1963) "blatantly clamoured for prominence to give Yang Tzu-jung 'dare-devilry and dashing roughness,' that is, 'bandit-like airs.' " It called upon the hero "to hum obscene ditties on his way up the mountain to the bandits' stronghold . . . We criticized and repudiated this erroneous trend and made great efforts to achieve a typical portrayal of Yang as a hero in the image of the proletariat. The original script did not make the least mention of Yang's contact with the masses, to say nothing of describing the flesh-and-blood relationship and class feelings between him and the working people . . . We cut out the two scenes about superstition and murder which were specially written to play up the negative roles [the villains]. These were replaced by a new scene 'Asking About Bitterness,' purposely designed to demonstrate the fish-and-water relationship between our army and the people and the flesh-and-blood relationship between the working people and Yang Tzu-jung who relies on the masses and conducts propaganda among them . . . Thus the two essential sides to his character—class love and class hatred—are clearly defined. Without this it would be impossible to detect the class traits in the hero's inner world and Yang would remain a reckless adventurer divorced from the masses . . . Without accentuating Yang's political

* *China Reconstructs*, February 1970.

consciousness due to his being armed with Mao Tse-tung Thought, the audience would not know what ideological force propels him to go deep into the enemy's stronghold, and would even feel worried about him or even doubt if he could succeed in his mission."*

The guiding light in this battle between the "two lines"** was Chiang Ching (Mme. Mao Tse-tung). She watched rehearsals, discussed and criticized the play with the performers and writers, helped with rewriting. The model opera was presented at the National Festival of Peking Opera on Contemporary Themes in 1964. Chairman Mao attended a performance on July 17. He had encouraged and supported the work. Even after that, in April 1965, more editing of the script ensued to accentuate Yang's integration with and reliance on the people.

The result is *Taking Tiger Mountain*, which is playing to packed houses in the cities of China, and is seen in local theatrical versions or excerpts, or by means of cinema or television, in thousands of hamlets, villages and towns throughout the People's Republic.

The cast in the Peking production that we saw was filled with the kind of spirit associated with an opening night, yet this is the longest-playing opera in the city. Every actor performed as if Chairman Mao himself were in the auditorium, and with a feeling of ensemble that comes only from cooperative, extensive rehearsing. The bronze curtains closed at the end of the show to reopen on the assembled cast singing "Sailing the Seas with the Helmsman" and waving "little red books" in time to the music. The audience stood and joined in the singing. At the final note the cast applauded the audience and we applauded back.

* *Chinese Literature*, No. 1, Peking, 1970.

** Or "two roads"—the capitalist road and the road of proletarian revolution. Revisionism is another term used to express the tendency toward restoration of capitalism. It applies to the Soviet Union in particular (and its supporters), as the Chinese Communist Party considers the Russian Party a betrayer of Marxism-Leninism and the dictatorship of the proletariat.

I am not a worker, a peasant, or a soldier—but through the conviction, the excitement, the beauty of production and the skill of the players, I entered that evening into the "for whom" and enjoyed the opera immensely. I looked forward eagerly to the rest of the repertoire.

"HONGQI" EDITOR'S NOTE:

The modern revolutionary Peking opera *Taking Tiger Mountain by Strategy*, carefully revised, perfected and polished to the last detail with our great leader Chairman Mao's loving care, now glitters with surpassing splendour. Here we publish the script of the opera as was staged in Peking in October 1969 and recommend it to worker, peasant and soldier readers at all posts. All theatrical troupes should take this as the standard version when they present the opera.

Taking Tiger Mountain by Strategy

(OCTOBER 1969 SCRIPT)

REVISED COLLECTIVELY BY THE "TAKING TIGER MOUNTAIN BY STRATEGY" GROUP OF THE PEKING OPERA TROUPE OF SHANGHAI

＝

CAST OF CHARACTERS

Yang Tzu-jung: *scout platoon leader of the Chinese People's Liberation Army (PLA)*
Shao Chien-po: *PLA regimental chief of staff*
Li Yung-chi: *railway worker*
Chang Pao: *hunter's daughter*
Shen Teh-hua: *PLA scout platoon deputy leader*
Medical Orderly: *PLA girl medical orderly*

This translation is based on the text published in *Hongqi*, No. 11, 1969. The 1967 stage version of the opera appeared under the title of *Taking the Bandits' Stronghold* in *Chinese Literature*, No. 8, 1967.

Young Kuo: *PLA guard*
Chung Chih-cheng: *PLA soldier*
Lu Hung-yeh: *PLA soldier*
Lo Chang-chiang: *PLA soldier*
Other soldiers
Hunter Chang: *Chang Pao's father*
Mother Li: *Li Yung-chi's mother*
Chang Ta-shan: *railway worker*
Li Yung-chi's wife
Other villagers
Vulture: *bandit chieftain of Tiger Mountain, leader of Kuomintang's "Fifth Peace Preservation Brigade of the Eastern Heilungkiang Region"*
Luan Ping: *liaison adjutant under Horse Cudgel Hsu, bandit chieftain of Breast Mountain*
Bandit Chief of Staff
Bandit Chief Adjutant
Bandit Captain
"Terribles" and other bandits

⤫

SCENE ONE

ADVANCING IN VICTORY

Winter, 1946. A snowy forest in northeast China.

(*A PLA pursuit detachment in battle array, a red flag at its head, enters swiftly. The fighters execute a dance depicting their march against the wind along a snow-covered mountain trail.*)

Lo: Halt!

(*The men form ranks.*)

Lo: Report, Chief of Staff. We've come to a fork in the road.

Shao: We'll rest here.

Lo: Right, Lu Hung-yeh!

Lu: Here.

Lo: Stand guard!

Lu: Right. (*Exit.*)

Lo: We'll rest here.

Other soldiers: Right.

(*Young Kuo hands Shao a map. Shao examines it and then looks at the terrain.*)

Lo: Supply Chief! We'll rest here.

(*A voice responds: "We'll rest here!" Horses neigh. The men stamp their feet to warm up and knock off the snow from their capes.*)

Shao: You must be tired, comrades?

Soldiers: Not at all.

Shao: Good. Comrades Yang Tzu-jung and Shen Teh-hua are scouting up ahead. We've arranged to meet them here. The regiment Party Committee sent us as a pursuit detachment into this snowy forest in accordance with Chairman Mao's directive "Build stable base areas in the northeast." Our job is to arouse the masses in the Mutanchiang area, wipe out the bandits, consolidate the rear, coordinate with our field army and smash the U.S.-backed Kuomintang attacks. It's a task of great strategic importance. That Vulture and his die-hard gang have hidden themselves deep in the mountains. We've been trudging through the snow for days, but there's still no sign of them. We must display our style of continuous fighting. (*Decisively*) "Be resolute, fear no sacrifice and surmount every difficulty—

Shao and soldiers: To win victory."

(*Lu Hung-yeh enters.*)

Lu: Report! Platoon Leader Yang and Comrade Shen are back.

(The two enter and salute.)

Yang: Report!

Shao: Comrade Tzu-jung, you have had a tiring job.

Yang: We went out in disguise, according to orders, and on our way we rescued a boy—a mute, in an isolated ravine. Thanks to his father's directions, we reached a little hamlet called Black Dragon Valley. Our investigations there put us on the trail of the Vulture.

Shao: Excellent!

Yang (*sings "hsi pi yao pan"**): This section is infested with bandits. They call themselves "Third Regiment of the Fifth Peace Preservation Brigade."*
Last night they pillaged Black Dragon Valley.
(Changes to "kuai pan")
Vulture, vicious and cruel, has committed monstrous crimes.
After their pillage they fled to Chiapi Valley,
I think they have returned to Tiger Mountain.

Shao: We're on the Vulture's trail, comrades. We must press on. Lo Chang-chiang!

Lo: Here.

Shao: We'll camp at Black Dragon Valley tonight.

Lo: Right.

Shao: Comrade Tzu-jung!

Yang: Here.

Shao: We need more information on the enemy. Take Comrades Shen Teh-hua. . . .

Shen: Here.

Shao: Chung Chih-cheng!

Chung: Here.

---

* *Hsi pi yao pan* and other similar terms found in the text such as *kuai pan, hsi pi hsiao tao pan, erh huang man pan, erh huang erh liu, liu shui* and *hui lung*, are various styles of singing in Peking opera. Each has its own fixed tune, structure, mode, rhythm and tempo. Modern revolutionary Peking opera has critically assimilated various styles of singing from traditional Peking opera wth many creative improvements to suit the portrayal of proletarian heroes.

Shao: And Lu Hung-yeh!

Lu: Here!

Shao: And do some more scouting.

Yang: Right.

Shao: Be off now.

(*Dramatic pose.*)

(*Curtain*)

⋈

SCENE TWO

CHIAPI VALLEY PILLAGED

Dusk. The edge of the village Chiapi Valley. A withered tree stands slanting by the side and crags lie in the gully.

(*The routed bandit gang of the Kuomintang "Fifth Peace Preservation Brigade" is retreating to its lair. Passing by Chiapi Valley, Vulture, the bandit chieftain, peeps at the village.*)

Bandit Chief Adjutant: On our way back this time we've made off with quite a pile, Chief. This village is right on our doorstep. We ought to leave it alone.

Bandit Chief of Staff: That's right, as the saying goes, "A rabbit doesn't foul its own hole."

Vulture: Who cares? Chief of Staff, go and grab me some of those paupers. We'll put them to work building fortifications. Men and women—both of them.

Bandit Chief of Staff (*takes hint*): Yes, sir.

(*He leaves with the bandit gang for the village. The adjutant starts to go too, but Vulture stops him.*)

Vulture: I say, it must be nearly ten days since Howling Wolf went off to find Luan Ping, isn't it?

Bandit Chief Adjutant: That's it, I'm getting worried about this too.

Vulture: The first thing we'll do when we get back to Tiger Mountain is expand our forces.

Bandit Chief Adjutant: Yes. If Howling Wolf can find Luan Ping and get his hands on Horse Cudgel Hsu's Contacts Map, the whole Mutanchiang area will belong to us.

Vulture: I hear Commissioner Hou is also looking all over for that map. We mustn't let him get it.

Bandit Chief Adjutant: Don't worry, Chief. Howling Wolf and Luan Ping are sworn brothers. That map won't fly away.

Vulture: You know, openly the Americans are pretending to be working for peace talks between the Kuomintang and the Communists, but actually they help Chiang Kai-shek on the sly, transporting soldiers north for him. I hear Chiang Kai-shek has turned up in Shenyang, taking personal charge of the fighting. They want to wipe out all the Communist troops north and south of the Great Wall in three months. Our chance has come, it seems to me.

Bandit Chief Adjutant: Fine. When the Kuomintang army returns, you'll be made commander of all northern Manchuria. First it was Marshal Chang, then the Manchoukuo of the Japanese, and now the Kuomintang of Chiang Kai-shek. None of them could do without you. Ha! Ha! Ha!

Vulture: Ha! Ha! Ha!

(*Dogs bark in the village. Vulture swaggers off with Bandit Chief Adjutant in the direction of the village. Flames leap up and shouting is heard.*)
(*Li Yung-chi enters hurriedly, carrying a hunting rifle and some game.*)

Yung-chi (*sings "hsi pi hsiao tao pan"*):
Flames leap to the sky and people shout,
(*Changes to "kuai pan"*)
Mothers call to their sons, children cry for their mothers;

Again the bandits burn, kill and rob,
I'll have it out with them though I die.

(*Bandits enter dragging villagers, young men and women bound by ropes. Li Yung-chi fights with the bandits while the young people are beaten by the bandits and dragged off.*)
(*Yung-chi's wife is pulled on followed by her mother-in-law holding her baby. Bandit Captain snatches the infant and throws it over the cliff. Yung-chi, furious, attacks bandits desperately. His left arm is hurt.*) (*Vulture enters and shoots at Yung-chi.*)

Yung-chi's wife: Yung-chi! (*Flings herself to cover him and falls dead.*)

(*Vulture and the other bandits exit.*)

Yung-chi (*heartbroken and enraged, gazes at his wife*): Baby's ma . . . baby's ma. . . .
Mother Li (*rushing over, overwhelmed by grief*): Daughter-in-law. . . .
Yung-chi (*sings "hsi pi kuai pan"*):
Disaster comes like a bolt from the blue,
Fury burns in my breast;
I swear that I shall avenge
You Vulture!
I'll hack you to pieces for this blood debt.

(*He starts to go for Vulture. Bandits swarm on, and tie him up. He struggles with all his might.*)

Mother Li: Yung-chi!
Yung-chi: Mother!

(*Yung-chi is taken away.*)

Yung-chi: Mother! Mother!
Mother Li (*following in on her knees*): Yung-chi!

(*Curtain*)

⸺

SCENE THREE

ASKING ABOUT BITTERNESS

Afternoon. A remote mountain valley. In a small log cabin bowls and chopsticks lie in disarray on a table.

(*Chang Pao is clearing the table. Hunter Chang is looking outside.*)

Pao: That man and woman were rough types, dad. They finished off the bit of venison we'd just got.

Chang: Do you know who they were?

Pao: He said he was from the Chinese People's Liberation Army.

Chang: Huh! Eight years ago, when the bandits dragged me away, I saw him in their lair on Tiger Mountain. People call him Howling Wolf. He's a bandit.

Pao: Oh!

Chang: We can't stay here any longer, Pao. Let's get our things together at once and go to your uncle Ta-shan's in Chiapi Valley.

Pao: Right. (*Gets some belongings together.*)

Chang (*to himself*):   Those two fur traders who came through here a few days ago said the Communists were now in our old home village helping the poor to win emancipation. I wonder if it's true.

Pao: They're good men, those two. If they hadn't carried me home, I would have frozen to death in the ravine.

Chang: That's true. Hurry now.

Pao: Yes.

(*Chang ties a bundle. Pao gets the pelts down from the wall, and sees figures moving outside the window.*)

Pao: Somebody's coming again, dad.

(*Chang covers Pao's mouth with his hand.*)

Chang: Hush!

(*They listen attentively. Yang, Shen, Chung and Lu enter, muffled in capes and hoods which hide the red star on their caps. Alertly they walk across the snow.*)

Yang (*sings "hsi pi san pan"*):
We've been closely following a suspicious pair,
But here in the mountains we've lost the trail—
Shen: Say Old Yang, isn't this where Hunter Chang lives?
Yang: Right. (*Sings.*)
We'll call on the hunter again for help to solve our problem.
Comrades Shen and Lu!
Shen and Lu: Here.
Yang: You two scout on ahead. Report back here if you have any information.
Shen and Lu: Right. (*Exit.*)
Yang: Young Chung! Stand guard.
Chung: Right. (*Exit.*)
Yang (*walks up to the cabin and knocks*):   Hey there, neighbours!

(*The hunter comes out with apprehension.*)

Chang (*examines Yang*):   You are. . . .
Yang: Don't you recognize me? I'm the fur trader who was here a few days ago.
Chang: Fur trader?
Yang: Yes.

(*Pao runs out.*)

Yang (*to Pao*):   Your father doesn't remember me, little brother. Wasn't I the one who brought you home that day?

(*Pao examines him closely, wants to speak but stops, nods.*)

Yang (*has observed and guessed the truth but doesn't let on*):   What a clever child!

Chang (*observes Yang carefully, recognizing him*): Ah, you're Yang the trader.

Yang: Yes.

Chang: That's right. And we discovered we're from the same province. Come in, come in.

(*They all go in.*)

Yang (*to Pao*): Are you feeling better now?

Chang (*quickly*): He's a mute.

Yang: Ah, I see.

Chang: You're a trader, but today you're in uniform. What's your job, after all?

Yang: I'm not a trader. (*Throws back his hood to reveal the red star on his cap.*) I'm a soldier of the Chinese People's Liberation Army.

Chang (*sceptically*): You too from the People's Liberation Army?

Yang: Yes. Have you seen any PLA men before?

Chang (*guardedly*): No . . . no, never.

Yang (*sitting down on a wooden block*): We didn't have a chance to talk much, last time. We came over from Shantung Province. We are battalions led by Chairman Mao and the Communist Party.

Chang: But what are you fellows doing all the way up here?

Yang: Fighting bandits. (*Picks up an axe and slams it down on the wooden block.*)

Chang: Fight bandits? Can you do that?

Yang (*standing up*): We've got a big force not far behind. Our PLA has won several big victories in the northeast. The whole Mutanchiang area has been liberated. We've smashed most of the bandits. Only Vulture and his gang are left. They've buried themselves deep in this mountain forest, but we're going to wipe them out too, and soon.

Chang (*bitterly*): That Vulture! . . .

Yang: Old Chang, Vulture has devastated these parts.

You two have hidden yourselves here in this forest, you must have been deeply wronged.

Chang (*sits down and passionately seizes the axe*): . . . .

Yang: Go ahead, Old Chang, tell us about it.

Chang (*not wanting to mention the painful past*): It happened eight years ago, why talk about it? (*Puts down the axe.*)

Pao (*bursts out*): Dad! . . .

Chang (*startled and then bitterly*): Pao, how could you. . . .

Yang (*with deep feeling*): It's all right, child. The Communist Party and Chairman Mao will back us up. Speak.

Pao: I will, uncle, I will. (*Sings "fan erh huang tao pan"*)
Disaster struck one snowy night eight years ago,
(*Switches to "kuai san yen"*)
Vulture killed my grandma and carried off my mum and dad;
Uncle Ta-shan in Chiapi Valley took me in,
My dad escaped and came back,
But my mum threw herself off a cliff and died.
Oh, dear mum!
In the mountains we hide;
Afraid I'd fall into those devils' hands,
Dad dressed me as a boy and said I was mute.
(*Changes to "yuan pan"*)
We hunted in the mountains during the day,
At night we thought of grandma and mum;
(*Changes to "to pan"*)
We looked at the stars and the moon
And longed for the time
When the sun would shine over these mountains,
When I would be able to speak out freely,
When I could dress like a girl again,
When we could collect our debt of blood.
If I only had wings I'd take my gun

And fly to the summit and kill all those wolves!
Oh, dad! (Flings herself into Chang's arms.)
Yang *(furious, sings "hsi pi yuan pan")*:
Pao's tales of the bandits' crimes
Brimming with blood and tears,
Rouse me to the utmost rage.
Oppressed people everywhere have blood accounts
To settle with their oppressors.
They want vengeance,
An eye for an eye and blood for blood!
(Switches to "lui shui")
Destroy Vulture, and win liberation for the people,
Rise as masters and greet the sun in these deep moun-
tains.
Follow the saviour the Communist Party,
And bring the land a new life, .
Like our old home in Shantung,
Good days will be here forever.
Chang *(with emotion)*: Old Yang!

*(Chang sits down with Yang. Pao fondly hands Yang
a bowl of water which he drains.)*

Chang: You've said what's in my heart, Old Yang. But
beating Vulture won't be easy. His Tiger Mountain
stronghold is protected by nine groups of twenty-seven
forts. He can attack, he can defend, and he can slip
away. Nobody can touch him.

Yang: I see. They say it's very hard to get to the top of
the mountain.

Chang: Exactly. There's only one path up front, and it's
very steep. Besides it's very carefully watched. How
can anyone get up there?

Yang: Then how did you manage to make good your
getaway that time?

Chang: There's a dangerous trail down the back of the
mountain with steep cliffs and crags. No one dares to

use that trail, so it's unguarded. Eight years ago, that's where I came down. If I hadn't been lucky enough to fall on a tree branch, I'd have been dashed to pieces.

Yang: You've given us some very useful information. As long as we all pull together, there's no mountaintop we can't conquer.

Chang: Right. We're all looking forward to that day. Ha, ha, ha! You mustn't blame me for taking you as a stranger. A man and a woman were here a while ago. He obviously was a bandit, but he said he was from the PLA.

Pao: My dad saw him eight years ago on Tiger Mountain. He's called Howling Wolf.

Yang: Howling Wolf, eh? What else did he talk about?

Chang: He called the woman sister-in-law and said he was Luan Ping's sworn brother.

Yang (*bursts out*): Luan Ping? (*Leaves his seat.*)

Chang (*stands up*): The woman must be Luan Ping's wife. Howling Wolf had a big row with her over some map or other.

Pao: A Contacts Map.

Chang: That's right.

Yang: Contacts Map?

(*Chung enters and comes into the cabin.*)

Chung: Platoon leader, Old Shen and Lu are back.

(*Shen and Lu enter. They go into the cabin.*)

Shen: Old Yang, in the forest northeast of here we found the body of a woman with a blood-stained glove lying beside her. (*Gives glove to Yang.*)

Lu: There was a strong blizzard and the snow had already blotted out any footprints. We couldn't tell where the murderer had gone.

Yang: Have you seen this glove before, Old Chang?

Chang (*examines glove*): Yes. It belongs to Howling Wolf.

Yang (*coming to a conclusion*): He must have killed her
and snatched the Contacts Map. This is a complicated
business, comrades, and that Luan Ping we caught is
mixed up with the case. Lu Hung-yeh!

Lu: Here.

Yang: We are going after the murderer. You report back
to the chief of staff and tell him I suggest we interrogate
Luan Ping and dig out the story of the Contacts Map.

Lu: Right. (*Goes out at a run.*)

Yang: This is urgent, Old Chang, we've no time to chat
now. Here's a bit of food for you and Pao.

(*Yang unties his ration bag and hands it to Chang.
Shen unties his and gives it to Pao.*)

Chang: Old Yang!

Shen: Please accept it.

Pao (*moved*): Uncles. . . .

Yang: Goodbye for now. (*Turns to go.*)

Chang: Where are you going, Old Yang?

Yang: After Howling Wolf.

Chang: You can't get him. He's sure to be heading for
Tiger Mountain. That trail has always been hard to
follow, and a stranger could lose himself in this snowstorm. Come, Pao and I will show you the way.

Yang (*touched, goes to Chang*): Thank you, Old Chang.

Chang: Let's go.

(*Dramatic pose.*)

(*Curtain*)

<hr>

SCENE FOUR

DRAWING UP A PLAN

Early morning. Black Dragon Valley. The detachment has
spent the night. Inside the command post, a charcoal fire

burns bright. Outside the wind roars and heavy snow falls. In the background, majestic mountains and deep forests.

Shao (*with composure sings "erh huang tao pan"*):
Icy wind howls through the woods,
Rustling branches shake the deep gully.

(*A gust blows the door open. He goes to the door and looks out.*)

(*Sings, changing to "hui lung"*)
Snowflakes dance in a hazy mist,
The mountains are mantled in silver;
What a magnificent scene of the north!

(*He closes the door, changes to "erh huang man pan"*)

Beautiful our land, majestic and grand,
How can we let ravening beasts again lay it waste?
(*Changes to "yuan pan"*)
The Party Central Committee points the way,
Revolutionary flames cannot be quenched.
Bearing the hopes of the people, the PLA fight north and south
And plant the red flag all over our country.
Let the Yanks and Chiang gang up,
Prating about peace while making attacks,
Fighting openly and sniping in the dark.
Let them resort to a hundred tricks,
With justice in our hands, class hatred in our hearts,
One against ten, we'll still wipe them out.

(*Yang enters.*)

Yang: Report!
Shao (*recognizes his voice*): Old Yang!

(*Yang goes into the room. Shao rushes to greet him.*)

Shao: Did you catch the murderer?
Yang: We got him. We found this letter and this map concealed in his clothes. (*Hands them over.*)

Shao: Well done!

Yang: The trails in these parts are hard to find. Luckily, Hunter Chang acted as our guide. The murderer passed himself off as one of our PLA scouts, but the hunter exposed him. He admitted that he's a Tiger Mountain man named Li Chung-hao, better known as Howling Wolf.

Shao: Good. That hunter has been a great help. Long ago Chairman Mao told us: "The revolutionary war is a war of the masses; it can be waged only by mobilizing the masses and relying on them." Without the masses we can't move a step.

Yang: How true! Hunter Chang also told us of two trails up the mountain. I've sketched them, according to his description. (*Hands Shao a sketch map.*) Howling Wolf admits to the open trail going up the face of the mountain. He says there are no fortifications along it and that it's easy to climb.

Shao: Hm. Obviously a lie. Have you made arrangements for the hunter and his daughter?

Yang: We left them our grain rations. They're planning to move to Chiapi Valley.

Shao: Good. (*Looks at map and letter.*) I say, Old Yang, Luan Ping never said anything about this map.

Yang: No, he never. Howling Wolf says it shows the location of three hundred secret contact places of the Breast Mountain gang here in the northeast. It's something very important.

Shao: Luan Ping has been brought here. We ll question him right away and find out all about the Contacts Map.

Yang: I'll get Luan Ping. (*Turns to go.*)

Shao: He's your old adversary, Old Yang. You'd better do the questioning.

Yang: All right.

(*Shao goes into inner room.*)

Yang (*to the guard at the door*): Young Chang.

Young Chang: Here.

Yang: Bring Luan Ping.

Young Chang: Right.

(*Young Kuo brings Luan Ping into the room. Luan Ping sees Yang and wants to come over to greet him. Yang waves him to a chair. Luan sits down.*)

Yang: Luan Ping.

Luan: Yes, sir.

Yang: How are you getting on with your confession?

Luan: I want to come clean. I'm owning up to everything I know.

Yang: There's something you haven't mentioned yet.

Luan: Officer, I don't own a thing in the world except the clothes on my back.

Yang (*suddenly*):   What about that map?

Luan: Map?

Yang: The Contacts Map.

Luan (*startled*):   Oh! (*Pretending to be calm.*) Ah, let me think. . . .
(*Strikes a thoughtful pose.*) Ah, yes, yes, I remember now. They say Horse Cudgel Hsu had a map of secret contacts.

Yang: They say?

Luan: Don't misunderstand, officer. Horse Cudgel Hsu considered that map precious. I never had a chance of setting my eyes on it.

Yang: Luan Ping, you ought to understand our policy.

Luan: I do, I do. Leniency to those who confess; severity to those who resist.

Yang: I'm asking you—what was your job on Breast Mountain?

Luan: You know that. I was a liaison adjutant.

Yang: A liaison adjutant who says he knows nothing about liaison stations and has never seen anything of the Contacts Map. Huh! It's plain you don't want to tell the truth.

(*Luan pretends to be helpless.*)

Yang (*with sudden fury*):   Take him out!

Kuo: Get out!

Luan (*leaning against the chair, panic-stricken*):   No, no.
I . . . (*Slaps his own face.*) I deserve to die for trying to
fool you, officer. I'll tell you the truth now. There is a
map showing Horse Cudgel Hsu's secret contacts all
over the northeast, three hundred in all. That map is
now in my wife's hands. Let me out, and I'll find her
and get the map and give it to you. I want to make
amends and earn lenient treatment. (*Bows.*)

Yang: Besides those three hundred places, where else did
you have contacts?

Luan: Where else? Tiger Mountain. But for a long time
Vulture has been trying to get sole control of northern
Manchuria by himself. He and Horse Cudgel Hsu were
only friends on the surface, so I had very few dealings
with him. Last year, Vulture invited me to a Hundred
Chickens Feast to celebrate his birthday, but I didn't
go.

Yang (*listens with attention to his confessions*):   I want
a detailed report on all your contact points. You'd better
come clean.

Luan: Yes, yes.

Yang: Take him away.

Kuo: Now get out. (*Takes Luan out.*)

(*Shao comes out from other room.*)

Yang: He's a crafty one.

Shao (*humorously*):   The craftiest fox can't escape the
skilled hunter. Anyhow, his story about the Contacts
Map is the same as Howling Wolf's.

Yang: And he also let slip a mention of the Hundred
Chickens Feast.

Shao: Umm.

Yang: And in that letter, Vulture is again inviting him to the feast this year. There's something queer here.

Shao: I agree.

(*Shen Teh-hua enters.*)

Shen: Report!

Shao: Come in.

(*Shen goes into room.*)

Shen: Chief of Staff, the comrades are eager to attack Tiger Mountain. They have written requests for battle assignments.

Shao: You're behind this, I suppose?

Shen: I. . . .

Shao (*laughs and sits down by the fire*): I can understand how the comrades feel. Our fraternal units have sealed off all the roads and ferry points in the Mutanchiang area. Vulture can't get away. But he's a wily bird, hard to deal with. Haven't we discussed it several times? If we sent a large force after him, it would be like trying to hit a flea with your fist. No good. Since the task is urgent, we haven't the time to lure the bandits down the mountain and destroy them one by one. Ours is a special mission. We must remember what Chairman Mao tells us—strategically we should despise our enemy, but tactically we should take him seriously. Comrade Teh-hua, please call another democratic meeting of the comrades and talk it over again, in the light of the latest developments.

Shen: Right. (*Exit.*)

(*Yang starts to leave.*)

Shao: Old Yang, what's your suggestion?

Yang: I want to question Howling Wolf again and find out more about that Hundred Chickens Feast.

Shao: Go ahead. I'll be waiting to hear your proposal.

Yang: Right. (*Exit.*)

Shao (*sings "hsi pi kuai san yen"*):

> We've had the enemy sized up in the last few days,
> We've analysed carefully and pondered over our plan.
> Tiger Mountain has a system of bunkers and tunnels,
> So the better course is to take it by strategy.
> Select a capable comrade to disguise as one of their kind,
> Then penetrate into the enemy's lair,
> And strike from without and within.
> Who should we choose for this critical task?—(*Thinks.*)
> (*Changes to "yuan pan"*)
> Yang has all the qualificatins to shoulder this load.
> Born of a hired-hand peasant family,
> From childhood he struggled on the brink of death;
> Burning with hatred, he found his salvation
> In the Communist Party and took the revolutionary road.
> (*Switches to "erh liu"*)
> He joined the army, vowing to uproot exploitation,
> A veteran in battle, he's distinguished himself many times.
> By wits, he blew up many an enemy fort,
> He's entered enemy territory, killed traitors
> And rescued many comrades and villagers.
> He's fought many a battle with bandits here in the forest,
> Caught Luan Ping and Hu Piao and took Howling Wolf as well.
> If I send him on this dangerous mission alone,
> I'm sure, with his heart red as fire,
> A will strong as steel,
> He'll surely overcome Vulture.

(*Shen Teh-hua enters. Goes into the room.*)

Shen: Chief of Staff.

Shao: How did your meeting go, Comrade Teh-hua?

Shen: We analysed the situation and decided that taking

it by strategy is the only answer. We shouldn't try a direct attack. The best way would be to get a comrade into the enemy stronghold. . . .

Shao: You're right. Come, let's talk it over.

(*Yang enters and goes into the room. Shao srcutinizes him. Shen looks on in surprise.*)

Yang: Hu Piao is here to present the map. (*Waves his hand in bandit greeting.*)

Shao: You Hu Piao? Old Yang, ha, ha, ha!

Shen: Old Yang!

Yang: Ha, ha, ha! (*Sits down.*)

Shao: Tell us quick, what's your idea?

Yang: It seems to me, Chief of Staff, the best way to take Tiger Mountain is by strategy.

Shao: Precisely.

Yang: The enemy's Hundred Chickens Feast is a good opportunity.

Shao. Have we found out all about it?

Yang: Yes. Vulture celebrates his birthday on the last day of the last month of every lunar year. He gives himself a feast of chickens extorted from a hundred different families. They call it the Hundred Chickens Feast. (*Rises.*) I suggest we send a comrade up there in disguise to find out how the tunnels and bunkers are laid out. Then, when all the bandits are in the main hall during the Hundred Chickens Feast, get them drunk. . . .

Shao: And the detachment will spring an attack and take it before they know what's happening!

Yang: Right. Chief of Staff, put me on this job.

Shen: The comrades also propose Old Yang for the mission.

Shao: Good. Comrade Teh-hua, (*giving him the Contacts Map*) make a copy of this. Also notify the others there will be a Party branch committee meeting later on.

Shen: Right. (*Exit.*)

Shao: Old Yang, you're going to disguise as a bandit and make your way into the enemy stronghold. Are you sure you can do it?

Yang: There're three things in my favour.

Shao: The first?

Yang: Horse Cudgel Hsu and his Breast Mountain gang have just been defeated. I can go there as his adjutant Hu Piao who is in our hands and Vulture has never seen him. I've learned the bandit argot and won't be found out.

Shao: And the second?

Yang: If I present Vulture with the Contacts Map as a gift at our first meeting, I'll win his trust.

Shao: Fine.

Yang: The third condition is the most important. . . .

Shao: The loyal heart of a PLA soldier dedicated to the Party and Chairman Mao.

Yang (*from the heart*): You understand me completely, Chief of Staff.

Shao (*with deep feeling*): Old Yang, this is no ordinary task.

Yang: Chief of Staff! (*Sings "hsi pi yuan pan"*)
A Communist always heeds the Party's call,
He takes the heaviest burden on himself;
I'm set on smashing the chains of a thousand years
To open a freshet of endless happiness for the people.
(*Switches to "erh liu"*)
Well I know that there's danger ahead,
But I'm all the more set on driving forward;
No matter how thickly troubled clouds may gather,
Revolutionary wisdom is bound to win.
(*Changes to "kuai pan"*)
Like the Foolish Old Man who removed the mountains,
I shall break through every obstacle;
The flames that blaze in my red heart
Shall forge a sharp blade to kill the foe.

Shao: Good. You can take Horse Cudgel Hsu's black-

maned steed and ride northeast along the trail Hunter
Chang has pointed out. . . .

Yang: And wind my way up the mountain.

Shao: The detachment will go to Chiapi Valley, arouse
the masses and prepare for battle. We'll wait for word
from you.

Yang: I'll put a message for you in the pine grove south-
west of Tiger Mountain. The tree will be marked in the
agreed manner,

Shao: I'll send Shen on the twenty-sixth to pick it up.

Yang: I guarantee it will be there on time.

Shao: Good. The detachment will set out as soon as we've
heard from you. We'll strike from within and without
and destroy Vulture and his gang.

Yang: This is a well-thought-out plan, Chief of Staff. It's
decided then.

Shao (*grips Yang's arms, very stirred. After a pause*): Be
bold but cautious, Comrade Tzu-jung. (*Sings "hsi pi
kuai pan"*)
I'm confident you can fulfil this important mission,
Everything depends on this all-important task.
We'll call a Party committee meeting to approve the
plan,
With collective wisdom we'll defeat the enemy.

(*Yang and Shao clasp hands tightly in a dramatic pose.*)

(*Curtain*)

〰

SCENE FIVE

UP THE MOUNTAIN

A few days after the previous scene. In the foothills of
Tiger Mountain. A deep snowy forest. Tall, straight pines
reach to the sky. Sunshine filters down through the trees.

Yang (*sings offstage vigorously "erh huang tao pan"*):
I press through the snowy forest, spirit soaring!

(*Yang enters in disguise. He spurs his horse onwards. He executes dances depicting his journey through the dense forest, leaping across a stream, mounting a ridge, dashing down a steep slope, galloping across a distance and then looking all around.*)

(*Sings "hui lung"*)
To declaim my determination the mountains I staunchly face.
(*Switches to "man yuan pan"*)
Let the red flag fly all over the world,
Be there seas of fire and a forest of knives, I'll charge ahead.
How I wish I could order the snow to melt,
(*Changes to "san pan"*)
And welcome in spring to change the world of men.
(*Switches to "hsi pi kuai pan"*)
The Party gives me wisdom and courage,
Risks and hardships are as naught;
To wipe out the bandits I must dress as a bandit,
And pierce into their stronghold like a dagger.
I'll bury Vulture in these hills, I swear,
Shake the heights with my will.
With my courage the valleys fill,
At the Hundred Chickens Feast my comrades and I
Will make a shambles of the bandits' lair.

(*A tiger roars in the distance. The horse is startled, stumbles. Yang reins in, makes it rear, turns and halts it. Leaps from the horse. The tiger's roar draws nearer. Yang quickly leads his horse off. Re-enters, throws off his overcoat, pulls out pistol and fires at tiger. The beast screams and falls dead. Other shots are heard in the distance.*)

Yang (*immediately alerted*): Shooting! The bandits are

coming down the mountain. (*Calmly*) I've just killed one beast, and now a whole pack is here. I'll see that you go the same way.

(*Bandit Chief of Staff shouts offstage: "Halt!" He enters with a gang of bandits. Yang puts on his overcoat, walks forward boldly and gives a bandit salute.*)

Bandit Chief of Staff: What road do mushrooms travel? What's the price?*

(*Yang, head high, does not reply.*)

Bandit A (*seeing the tiger Yang has killed cries in fear*):   A tiger, tiger!

(*The other bandits hastily draw back.*)

Yang (*laughs*):   Brave, aren't you? That tiger is dead.

Bandit A (*looks at the beast cautiously*):   A beautiful shot. Right through the head.

Bandit Chief of Staff: Did you kill it?

Yang: It got in the way of my bullet.

Bandit Chief of Staff: Quite a man. Which mountain are you from? What are you doing here?

Yang (*taking the initiative*):   I suppose you fellows are from Tiger Mountain?

Bandit Chief of Staff: That's obvious. (*Realizes he has made a slip.*) Where are you from?

Yang: That's not for you to ask. I want to see Brigadier Tsui in person. I've important business with him.

Bandit Chief of Staff: How is it you don't know the rules of the mountains? You're not a *liutzu*. You're a *kungtzu*.*

Yang: If I were a *kungtzu*, would I dare come barging into Tiger Mountain?

Bandit Chief of Staff (*threateningly*):   Moha? Moha?*

* Bandit argot.

(*Yang, his mind made up, does not reply.*)

Bandits: Speak up.

Yang (*haughtily*):   I'm not saying anything till I see Brigadier Tsui.

Bandit Chief of Staff (*helplessly*):   All right, then, let's go.
Where's your gun?

Yang: Don't be scared. (*Tosses his pistol to Bandit A.
Points at the tiger and his horse.*)

Bandit Chief of Staff: Carry the tiger. Lead the horse.

The Bandits: Yes!

(*Yang in a dramatic pose. Then resolutely, calmly and
courageously he strides ahead.*)

(*Curtain*)

SCENE SIX

INTO THE BANDITS' LAIR

Immediately after the previous scene. The interior of Tiger
Hall. A gloomy cave lit by several lamps.

(*Vulture sits on a chair, his lieutenants—the "Eight
Terribles," stand on either side in a disorderly fashion.
Other bandits stand on the left rear side of the hall.
Vulture signals to Bandit Chief of Staff to summon the
newcomer.*)

Bandit Chief of Staff: Chief's order, bring *liutzu* in.

Bandits: Bring *liutzu* in!

(*Yang enters, head high.*)

Yang (*sings "hsi pi kuai pan"*):
Though I've come alone to the tiger's den,

Millions of class brothers are by my side;
Let Vulture spew flames ten thousand leagues high,
For the people I'll fearlessly take this monster on.
(Advances and gives a bandit salute.)

Vulture (*suddenly*): The god of the heavens shields the earthly tiger.*

Yang: Precious pagoda represses the river sprite.*

Terribles: *Moha? Moha?*

Yang: Speak exactly at the stroke of noon. No one has a home.*

Vulture: Why is your face so red?*

Yang: My spirits are flourishing.*

Vulture: Why so yellow again?*

(The bandits press closer, sword and gun in hand.)

Yang (*calmly*): I smeared it with wax to ward off the cold.*

(Vulture shoots out an oil lamp with his automatic. Yang takes a pistol from Bandit Chief of Staff. With one shot he knocks out two oil lamps. The bandits whisper among themselves and are stopped by the Terribles.)

Vulture: According to you, you're one of Brigadier Hsu's men?

Yang: I am his cavalry adjutant, Hu Piao.

Vulture: Hu Piao? Since you are Brigadier Hsu's man, let me ask you—when did you join his ranks?

Yang: When he was chief of police.

Vulture: I hear he has a few possessions he prizes the most.

Yang: There are two.

Vulture: What are they?

Yang: A fast horse and a sharp sword.

Vulture: What does his horse look like?

Yang: It has a curly coat and a black mane.

Vulture: What kind of sword has he?

* Bandit argot.

Yang: A Japanese officer's sabre.

Vulture: Who gave it to him?

Yang: The Japanese Imperial Army.

Vulture: Where was it presented?

Yang: At Wuholou in the city of Mutanchiang.

Vulture (*pauses*): If you really are Brigadier Hsu's cavalry adjutant, why did I see only Adjutant Luan Ping and not you at the last meeting called by Commissioner Hou?

Yang: I didn't rate very high with Brigadier Hsu. How could I compare with someone like Luan Ping? He was the one who went to all the important functions.

Vulture: Why have you come to Tiger Mountain?

Yang: I want to join you, Brigadier, and rise in the world. This is the first time I've crossed your threshold, but none of you big brothers seem to trust me. You aren't playing the game of our brotherhood, are you?

Vulture (*laughs*): We have to think of our stronghold's safety.

Terribles: Ha, ha, ha, ha!

Vulture:When did the Breast Mountain stronghold fall, Hu Piao?

Yang: The third day of the twelfth lunar month.

Vulture: What took you so long to get here?

Yang: It hasn't been easy for me to get here, Brigadier. After Breast Mountain was taken, I was hiding out in White Pines Dale for a while.

Vulture: White Pines Dale?

Yang: In the home of Luan Ping's uncle.

Vulture: Did you see Luan Ping?

Yang: Yes.

Vulture: And Howling Wolf?

Yang: Howling Wolf?

Vulture: Uh.

Yang: I don't know about him.

Vulture: Hu Piao, you are here but why isn't Luan Ping with you?

Yang: Luan Ping?

Vulture: That's right.

Yang: Ah, say no more about him.

Vulture: What do you mean?

Yang (*looks meaningly at other bandits*):   Well. . . .

(*Vulture signals and all the bandits except the Terribles leave.*)

Vulture: Hu Piao, what's the matter with Luan Ping?

Yang: It's a long story. (*Sings "hsi pi hsiao tao pan"*) *Just talking about him enrages me. . . .*

Vulture: What did he do?

Yang (*sings, changing to "hsi pi yuan pan"*):
He cares nothing for the code of our brotherhood.

Vulture: How did he go back on our code?

Yang (*sings*):   *We were lucky to get away when Breast Mountain fell,*
I urged him to come with me and join your brigade on Tiger Mountain.

(*The Terribles look at each other with satisfaction.*)

Vulture: Is he coming?

Yang (*sings*):   *Every man is free to make his own choice,*
But he shouldn't have—
He shouldn't have said such awful things about friends.

Vulture: What did he say?

Yang: He said. . . .

Vulture: What?

Yang: Well. . . .

Vulture (*impatiently*):   Out with it, Old Hu, be quick.

Yang: He said—(*sings*) *Vulture has to take Commissioner Hou's—*

Vulture: What?

Yang (*sings*):   *Orders.*

Vulture (*leaps to his feet in anger*):   Ah! What! I take orders from him!

Terribles: Rubbish, who does he think he is?

Yang: That wasn't all he said.

Terribles: What else?

Yang (*sings*):   *The Eight Terribles are a pack of worthless rats.*

Terribles (*enraged and shouting*):   What! That son of a bitch.

Yang (*sings, switching to "hsi pi liu shui"*):
He said he's a phoenix who wants a high branch to perch on,
That Commissioner Hou is a big tree and his roots are deep.

Terribles: To hell with him.

Yang (*sings*):   *As we were speaking he produced a map—*

Vulture: Map?

Yang (*sings*):   *A whole roll.*

(*Vulture dances around Yang coveting the map.*)

Yang (*switches to "hsi pi yao pan" as he continues singing*):
He was intending to take it to Commissioner Hou to earn a promotion.

Vulture: Was it the Contacts Map?

Yang: Yes, the secret Contacts Map.

Vulture (*worried*):   Then he's given it to Commissioner Hou?

Yang: Don't be impatient. (*Continues singing with a satirical smile on his face*)
Pleased with himself, he grinned all over.

Vulture: So!

Yang (*sings*):   *And brought out from the inside room,*
(*Switches to "hsi pi liu shui"*)
A jar of wine.
I filled him eight bowls, one after the other,
Luan Ping got so drunk he couldn't see.

Terribles: Haha . . . he got drunk.

Yang: So taking my chance while he was dead drunk, I. . . .

Vulture: Oh.

Yang: I. . . .

Vulture: Killed the dog?

Yang: I couldn't do that. We've been pals for years.

Vulture: Oh, oh. . . . (*Changing his tone.*) Of course, of course. Friendship is important! Friendship is important! Go on, Old Hu, go on.

Yang: He had his plans, but I had ideas of my own.

Vulture: What did you do?

Yang: I. . . .

Vulture: Yes?

Yang (*sings*): *I changed tunics with him while he was drunk,*
Then jumped on the black-maned horse, and through
The snowstorm galloped directly to Tiger Mountain.

Vulture: You mean you've got the map, Old Hu?

Yang (*laughs lightly. Changing to "hsi pi kuai pan," sings*):
Look, oh Brigadier Tsui,
This map here I present you. (*Holds up the map.*)

(*Standing high and looking down at the bandits, Yang holds out the map as Vulture respectfully flips the dust from his sleeves and takes it. He examines it avidly while the Terribles crowd around.*)

Vulture (*sings "hsi pi san pan"*):
The map I've thought of day and night,
Today is in my hands.
(*In wild joy*) Ha! Ha! Ha! Ha!

Terribles: You're a marvel, Old Hu, quite a man.

Yang (*meaningfully*): With the map in our possession, Brigadier, the Mutanchiang area is ours.

Vulture: Right. Well said. When the Kuomintang army returns, I'll be a commanding general. And I'll make the rest of you brigadiers and division commanders.

Terribles: We rely on your beneficence, Chief. (*Laugh wildly.*)

(*Yang laughs satirically.*)

Vulture: Because of what you've done for Tiger Mountain, Old Hu, I proclaim you Old Ninth.

Yang: Thank you, Chief.

Vulture: We belong to the Kuomintang army, you should
have a proper rank. I appoint you full colonel and deputy regimental commander in the Fifth Peace Preservation Brigade of the Eastern Heilungkiang Region.

Yang (*going up the steps*):   Thank you, Chief, for your
promotion. (*To Terribles*) I shall look to you brothers
for guidance.

Terribles: You shouldn't be so modest.

Bandit Chief of Staff: Bring wine!

Terribles: Hey, bring wine!

(Bandits enter with wine for all.)

Bandit Chief of Staff: Drink, everyone. Drink to congratulate Old Ninth.

Terribles: Congratulations, Old Ninth.

Vulture: For delivering the Contacts Map and winning
his spurs!

Yang (*sings with vigour "hsi pi kuai erh liu"*):
To their congratulatory toast I drink my fill,
I shall not rest until my mission is fulfilled.
The day is yet to come for me to show my skill,
To write history I'll willingly shed my blood.
(With a triumphant smile, he drains his bowl.)

Yang (*boldly*):   Ha . . . ha . . . ha . . . ha!

(Curtain)

⋈

SCENE SEVEN

AROUSING THE MASSES

Chiapi Valley. Home of Li Yung-chi, both inside and out.
Noon. A snowstorm is raging.

Mother Li (*sings "erh huang yao pan"*):
I'm ill and unwell, our grain is gone,
I call my son, but there is no reply.
Oh, the hatred of us poor, this debt of blood,
When will it ever be redeemed?

(*Chang Ta-shan enters.*)

Ta-shan: Aunt.
Mother Li: It's Ta-shan!

(*Ta-shan comes into the house.*)

Ta-shan: Are you feeling any better today, Aunt?
Mother Li: I was dizzier than ever when I got up this morning.
Ta-shan: Aunt, here are some tubers. . . . (*Hands over the tubers.*)
Mother Li (*stopping him*): Oh, Ta-shan you shouldn't. . . .
Ta-shan: Aunt, Yung-chi is away but you have us neighbours.

(*Ta-shan sets water to boil on the stove. Mother Li takes tubers into the inner room. Yung-chi, his chin stubbly, and clothes torn, pushes open the door and comes into house.*)

Ta-shan (*surprised*): Yung-chi!
Yung-chi: Ta-shan!

(*Mother Li emerges from inner room.*)

Yung-chi: Ma!
Mother Li: Yung-chi! (*Sings "erh huang san pan"*)
Can I be dreaming that you've returned?
It pains me to see you so battered and bruised;
How did you escape
(*Switches to "erh huang erh liu"*)
From the tiger's den?
Yung-chi (*sings*): *I jumped down a cliff at the back of the mountain and got away.*

Mother Li (*sings*):   *I'm overjoyed to see you home but I grieve*
For my daughter-in-law and grandson.
Yung-chi (*sings "erh huang tao pan"*):
The many crimes to be avenged are all
Engraved upon my heart.
The fury in my breast bursts into flame,
Someday I'll knife our foe to death.

(*Voices offstage cry: "Soldiers are entering the village!" PLA fighters shouting: "Don't go away, neighbours, we are your own people!"*)

Ta-shan: Another raid by Vulture?
Yung-chi: Are they after me?
Ta-shan: Hide, quick, I'll go out and take a look. (*Pulls out a dagger and exit.*)
Mother Li: You'd better hide yourself, son, do.
Yung-chi: Hide? Where can I hide, mother? It's better to fight it out. It's me or them now. I break even if I take one of them, and two better still.
Mother Li: Yung-chi, you. . . .

(*Chung and Lu enter.*)

Lu (*knocks at door*):   Anybody home?
Yung-chi: Yes. We're not all dead yet.
Lu: Neighbours!
Chung: Aunt!

(*Yung-chi wrenches the door open. Chung and Lu enter. Chung closes the door behind him. Mother Li is alarmed. She moves closer to Yung-chi protectingly.*)

Lu: Don't be afraid, Aunt. We're. . . .
Yung-chi: Come to the point.
Lu (*to Yung-chi*): Neighbours, we're the Chinese People's Liberation Army.
Yung-chi (*looks them over*): This "army" and that "army," I've seen plenty. Who knows what you really

are! Speak out, whatever you want. If it's money, we haven't got any. If it's grain, your gang has already robbed us clean. If it's our life. . . .

Mother Li: Yung-chi!

Chung: Neighbours, we are the worker and peasant soldiers. We protect the people.

Yung-chi: That's what you say.

(*Mother Li dizzy.*)

Yung-chi: Ma!

Lu (*to Chung*): Aunt's not feeling well. We'll get our medic to come.

Chung: Right.

Yung-chi: Who are you trying to fool! (*Supports his mother into inner room.*)

(*Chung signals to Lu. They go out together, closing the door.*)

(*Shao and Young Kuo enter.*)

Chung: Chief of Staff!

Shao: How are things going?

Lu: An old woman is sick inside.

Shao: Send for our medic. Tell her to bring some grain.

Lu: Right. (*Exit.*)

Chung: It's really tough to do mass work here.

Shao: The villagers here don't understand us. They've been fooled before. Don't you remember—Howling Wolf tried to pass himself off as one of our scouts?

Chung: I know that.

Shao: If we don't arouse the masses, Young Chung, we won't be able to get a firm foothold and wipe out Vulture. On the other hand, unless we destroy the bandits, the masses won't be really aroused.

Chung (*smiles*): I realize that.

Shao: Go and tell our men, we must be concerned about the welfare of the masses. We must explain our Party's policy patiently. We must carry out to the letter the

Three Main Rules of Disciplines and Eight Points for Attention. We've got to get things moving here by action.

Chung: Right. (*Turns to leave.*)

Shao: By the way, find out if Hunter Chang has arrived.

Chung: Right. (*Exit.*)

(*Medical Orderly enters.*)

Medical Orderly: Chief of Staff! (*Hands him a sack of grain.*) Where's the patient?

Shao (*points to house*): There.

Medical Orderly (*knocks at door*): Hello, neighbour.

Shao: Our medic is here, neighbour. Open the door.

(*Yung-chi rushes into outer room, a dagger in his hand. His mother follows, trying to stop him.*)

Mother Li: Yung-chi, you mustn't. . . .

Yung-chi: What do I fear? I can fight it out with them with this. (*Stabs dagger into table.*)

Mother Li (*very upset*): Yung-chi, I beg you. (*Faints.*)

Yung-chi (*supporting her hastily*): Ma! Ma!

(*Shao forces open the door. Goes in with Medical Orderly and Kuo. Protecting his mother, Yung-chi glares at Shao.*)

Shao: Give her first-aid, quick!

Medical Orderly: Yes.

(*Shao slips off his coat and wraps it around Mother Li. Medical Orderly helps her into inner room, followed by Kuo and Yung-chi. Shao pours some grain into pot and sets it to boil. Yung-chi comes out for some water. Shao goes into inner room.*)

Yung-chi (*discovering pot of gruel, deeply moved, pensively*): The People's Liberation Army? (*Sings "erh huang san yen"*)
These soldiers care for us folks and cure our ailments;
They're considerate, kind and helpful.

*But soldiers and bandits were always of the same brood,
always oppressing us.*
What's happened today is certainly very strange.
Can the saviours we've longed for have really arrived?
Mother Li (*offstage*): Water.

(*Yung-chi fills a bowl with gruel. Kuo emerges and
takes it in. Shao comes out.*)

Shao: Your mother has come to, neighbour. Don't worry.
Yung-chi: . . . .
Shao: What's your name, neighbour?
Yung-chi: Li Yung-chi.
Shao: Were you born in these parts?
Yung-chi: No. My family used to live in Shantung
Province. My father worked in Tsinan but after the
April 12 coup, he was killed by Chiang Kai-shek in a
strike. . . .
Shao (*angered and in sympathy*): Oh! . . . (*Warmly*) But
how did you people get here?
Yung-chi: After Father died, Mother brought me here to
try our luck.
Shao: What do you do?
Yung-chi: I'm a railway worker.
Shao (*extremely excited*): Fine! So we're all one big
family.
Yung-chi (*looks Shao over carefully*): Whose troops are
you anyhow? What are you doing here in these moun-
tain forests?
Shao (*fondly*): Neighbour! (*Sings "erh huang yuan pan"*)
We're the worker and peasant soldier, come
To destroy the reactionaries and change the world.
We've fought for years north and south for the revolu-
tion,
With the Party and Chairman Mao leading the way,
A red star on our army caps,
Two red flags of the revolution on our collars.
Where the red flag goes dark clouds disperse.

Liberated people overthrow the landlords,
The people's army shares the people's hardships,
We've come to sweep clean Tiger Mountain.

Yung-chi (*his feelings bursting out like spring thunder, sings*
"*erh huang peng pan*"):

Our eyes are nearly worn out, looking for you day and
night.
Who would have thought that here in the mountains
today
You've come, fighting the bandits and saving the poor—
Here before us our own army!
(*With feeling, switching to* "*yuan pan*")
Our own army,
I shouldn't have confounded right and wrong,
I shouldn't have taken friend for foe.
I am ashamed beyond words.
(*Pushes down the dagger stabbed into the table.*)
For thirty years I've been sweating like a slave.
Feeling these lashes and bruises I can hardly suppress my
rage,
I struggle in a bottomless pit.
We have untold misery and wrath to pour out,
Those bandits we all hate to the core.
Some said our days of suffering would go on and on.
Who would have believed an iron tree could blossom,
That we would at last live to see this day.
(*Changes to* "*to pan*")
I'll go with the Party to drive out those beasts,
Whatever the sacrifice and danger, be it fire or water,
When Tiger Mountain is being swept clean and free,
I, Yung-chi, in the front ranks will be.

(*Shao grasps Yung-chi's hand. Lu calls offstage:* "*Chief*
of Staff!" *Enters.*)

Lu: These villagers have come to see you, Chief of Staff.

(*Villagers swarm in, together with some soldiers.*
Mother Li comes out, supported by Medical Orderly.)

Villager A: Superior officer. . . .

A Soldier: Grandpa, we don't use such terms, call him commander.

Shao: Call me "comrade."

Chung: Chief of Staff, this is Old Chang.

Shao (*comes forward and shakes the hunter's hand*): So you're Old Chang, have you come from the forest?

Chang: We couldn't stay up there in the forest. We've moved in with Pao's uncle Ta-shan, here.

Shao (*pats Pao on the shoulder*): Good girl.

Yung-chi: Old Brother Chang.

Chang: Ah, Yung-chi, our saviours are here at last.

Ta-shan: Commander, we're all burning with one desire —to attack Tiger Mountain.

Shao: Our PLA is winning big victories at the front, neighbours. The Mutanchiang area has been liberated.

Villagers: Wonderful!

Shao: Vulture has no place to flee now.

Ta-shan: Let's destroy his nest.

Yung-chi: Give us guns, commander.

Villagers: Yes, give us guns, please.

Yung-chi: If we have guns, there isn't a man in Chiapi Valley who couldn't bring down two or three of those bandits.

Shao: You'll have your weapons. But none of you have any warm winter clothes and every family is short of grain. How can you go after bandits in the deep mountain forests?

Villagers: What can we do then?

Shao: There are plenty of medicinal herbs in Chiapi Valley and lots of timber. If we get the narrow-gauge train running again, we can ship them out and buy clothing and grain in return.

Villagers: That's right.

Shao: You can also organize a militia. We'll get the train running again and you'll have food and clothing. When we fight Vulture, you'll be all the stronger.

Yung-chi: When can we start repairing the railway?

Shao: We can start right now. Let's all work together.

Villager A: It's heavy labour, commander.

Chung: Grandpa, we fighters are all from poor families. When we've guns in our hands, we fight; when we've tools in our hands, we work.

Yung-chi (*steps forward and grasps Shao's hand*): We really are all one family, commander. (*Sings "erh huang to pan"*)
We mountain folk mean what we say,
Our words are straight, our hearts are true,
To seize a dragon we'll go with you—

Villagers (*join in chorus*): *Under the sea,*

Yung-chi (*sings*): *To catch a tiger—*

Villagers (*in chorus*): *We'll follow you up the heights.*

Yung-chi (*sings*): *With the thunder of spring the earth will shake!*
Then Vulture—

Villagers and Soldiers (*sing in chorus "erh huang san pan"*): *Your days are numbered.*

(*The army and civilians from a tableau of heroes, mighty and splendid.*)

(*Curtain*)

⤬

SCENE EIGHT

SENDING OUT INFORMATION

Dawn. A clearing on top of Tiger Mountain. Crags and forts are visible against undulating hills covered with snow in the distance. On right is a road leading to the foot of the mountain.

Vulture: Is this where Old Ninth usually does his exercises?

Bandit Chief of Staff: Yes.

Vulture: Where else has he been?

Bandit Chief of Staff: He's been around the forts on our
five peaks.

Vulture: What! You even let him inspect our nine groups
of twenty-seven forts?

Bandit Chief of Staff: He's one of us, isn't he? Why not
show him how strong we are?

Vulture: I don't like the look of things. There's a lot of
activity down below, and Howling Wolf still hasn't
returned. None of us ever set eyes on Hu Piao before.
Why did he show up at a time like this? We've got to
be careful.

(*Bandit Chief Adjutant enters from right.*)

Bandit Chief Adjutant: We've everything ready as you
ordered, Chief.

Vulture: Good. Put him to the test, the way I told you
last night.

Bandit Chief Adjutant: Yes, sir. (*Exit on right.*)

(*Vulture and Bandit Chief of Staff, seeing somebody
approaching, leave quickly on left front.*)

Yang (*offstage sings "erh huang tao pan"*):
Hacking through thorns and thistles,
I battle in the heart of the enemy. (*Enters.*)
(*Changes to "hui lung"*)
When I look into the distance and think of my
Comrades-in-arms, the army and the people, awaiting
the signal
To attack these wolves, my spirits soar.
(*Changes to "erh huang man pan"*)
The Party places great hopes on me,
Comrades at the Party committee meeting offer weighty
advice,
Their many exhortations give me strength,
Their flaming hearts warm my breast.
(*Changes to "kuai san yen"*)

I must never forget to be bold yet cautious,
And succeed through courage and wits.
The Party's every word is victory's guarantee,
Mao Tsetung Thought is eternally glorious.
(Changes to "yuan pan")
Tiger Mountain is indeed heavily fortified
With forts above and tunnels below.
The leadership's decision to use strategy is right,
A direct attack would mean heavy losses.
After seven days here I know the disposition well,
I have the secret report concealed on my person.
Now at daybreak, pretending to take a stroll, I'll send it out. . . .
(Notices something.)
Why have the guards suddenly been increased?
Something's up.
This message—
If I don't get this message out,
I'll miss the opportunity and ruin our attack plan,
And let the people and Party down.
(Changes to "to pan")
New Year's Eve is fast approaching.
I mustn't hesitate, I must push on,
Though the grass be knives and the trees swords,
Down to the foot of the slope.
What though the mountain be tall?
Standing in the cold and melting
Ice and snow, I've the morning sun in my heart.

(The sun rises filling the sky with red clouds which tinge the sharp crags.)
(Offstage voices: "Hurry up." "I'm coming.")

(Alert, Yang removes his coat and pretends to do traditional exercises.
Two bandit guards walk by pretending to be on patrol. They hail him.)

Bandit Guards: Good morning, Old Ninth!
Yang: Morning.

(*Bandit guards go off, Yang ends his exercises. Shots ring out.*)

Yang: Shooting!

(*Shouts in the distance: "Charge!" "Kill!" Nearer voices cry: "The Communists are coming!" The shooting increases.*)

Yang: What? Can the comrades be here? (*Thinks, comes to swift decision.*) No, not at this moment. The comrades wouldn't have come before Chief of Staff received my message.

(*The shooting becomes more intensive and shouts draw nearer.*)

Yang: That shooting sounds fishy, too. That's another test. I'll reply to their trick with one of my own and get this message off. (*Fires two shots in the air. Calls towards the left.*) Brothers!

(*Four bandits enter.*)

Yang: The Communists are here. Come with me and fight!

(*The bandits rush off. Vulture and Bandit Chief of Staff enter stealthily. Bandit Chief Adjutant comes forward.*)

Vulture: Just a minute, Old Ninth.
Yang (*shouts to bandits offstage*): Stay where you are.
Bandit Chief of Staff (*in same direction*): Stop shooting.

(*Bandits shout acknowledgment of order.*)

Yang (*to Vulture*): What's the matter?
Vulture: It's a manoeuvre I ordered.
Yang: I'd have fired this clip and got a few of them, if you hadn't stopped me.

(*Vulture laughs uproariously.*)

Yang: Why didn't you tell me you were arranging this
manoeuvre, Chief? You. . . .

Vulture: Don't let it bother you, Old Ninth. I didn't tell
anybody about it. If you don't believe me, ask him.
(*Points at Bandit Chief Adjutant.*)

Bandit Chief Adjutant (*pretentiously*): Why, I thought
the Communists were coming myself.

Yang (*chuckles with implied meaning*): I wish they would.
I'm just waiting for them.

Vulture: You're doing well, Old Ninth. (*Laughs.*)

(*Bandit Captain, offstage: "Get a move on!" Enters,
escorting another bandit who falls to the ground.*)

Bandit Captain: This fellow bumped into the wall outside, Chief.

Vulture: What!

Bandit A (*trembling*): We went down, under orders. Far
off, we saw the narrow-gauge train running again. But
before we got to Chiapi Valley, we ran into some Communist soldiers.

Vulture: Chiapi Valley, eh? (*Suspiciously*) And you're
the only one who got away?

Bandit A: Yes.

Bandit Chief Adjutant: Nine out of ten you were captured by the Communists and they let you go.

Bandit A: No, no.

Vulture (*draws his gun and points it at Bandit A*): You
bastard!

Yang (*intervenes*): Why get excited, Chief? If he really
had been a prisoner of the Communists he wouldn't
dare come back.

Bandit Chief of Staff: That's right. Everyone knows how
Chief hates any man who lets the Communists capture
him.

Vulture: Humph.

Yang (*to Bandit A*): Get out of here. Can't you see you're making Chief angry?

Bandit Chief of Staff (*kicks Bandit A*): Beat it.

Bandit A (*softly, as he goes out*): Old Ninth is a good man.

Bandit Chief of Staff (*to Bandit Captain*): Give the order —tighten all defences.

Bandit Captain: Yes, sir (*Exit.*)

Vulture (*dejectedly*): Eh!

Bandit Chief of Staff: I'll send some men down on a raid, Chief. That will be something to celebrate at the Hundred Chickens Feast.

Vulture: Not a bad idea, but you must be very careful this time.

Bandit Chief of Staff: Very well. (*Exit.*)

Yang: We've nothing to worry about, with the defences we've got on Tiger Mountain. But we shouldn't just sit here and wait for them to come after us.

Vulture: What do you think we should do?

Yang: We ought to practise charging—

Vulture: Oho!

Yang: And get our soldiers into top shape.

Vulture: Well.

Yang: Then, after the Hundred Chickens Feast, we'll roll down into Chiapi Valley.

Vulture (*grabs Yang's hand*): You're smart. Take command, Old Ninth. Put the men through some charging drill.

Yang: Right.

(*Vulture laughs and exit with Bandit Chief Adjutant.*)

Yang (*softly, contemptuously*): That dumb cluck. (*Sings "hsi pi huai erh liu"*)
A fool and cheat, who plays another trick,
It gives me my chance down the mountain.
Comrade Teh-hua,
To fetch the message, we count on you,

When the time comes to rout the bandits
At the feast, victory song we'll sing.
(Throws open his coat in a dramatic pose.)

(Curtain)

✕

SCENE NINE

OFF TO THE ATTACK

Morning. The day before lunar New Year's Eve. The scene is the clearing outside Yung-chi's house. A couplet written on red paper is pasted on the palisade gate. The joy of emancipation is everywhere.

(As the curtain rises the whistle of the narrow-gauge train is heard.)
(Smiling villagers, with sacks of grain on their backs, watch as the train sets out again, then they are off. A villager puts down the sack of grain he carries for Yung-chi's mother.)

Mother Li *(sings "hsi pi liu shui")*: *Soldiers and people are one family,*
Happiness fills our mountain village.
A good snow falls, everyone smiles,
Dividing food and clothing, we celebrate liberation.

(Shao enters.)

Shao: Aunt!

Mother Li: Commander!

Shao: Have you got enough food and things for the New Year?

Mother Li: Plenty. Who would have dreamed that Chiapi Valley could have such a good New Year? If you PLA boys hadn't come, I don't know what we'd have done.

Shao: The best is yet to come.

Mother Li: We owe it all to the Communist Party and Chairman Mao.

(Shao puts the sack of grain on his back, ready to carry it in for Yung-chi's mother. Offstage, Yung-chi is drilling the militia.)

Yung-chi *(offstage)*:   One, two, three, four!

Militiamen *(offstage)*:   One, two, three, four!

Mother Li: Those militiamen are full of pep. But the ones who will have to stay behind to guard the village are grumbling, especially Pao. She just won't hear of it.

Shao: Oh, that girl. . . .

(Offstage, the militiamen shout: "Charge, charge, charge!")

(Shao and Mother Li go off, talking.)

(Offstage, the drilling militiamen cry again: "Target straight ahead. Charge, charge, charge!")

(Pao backs in, with her eyes still on the drilling militia.)

Pao *(sings "erh huang hsiao tao pan")*:

Listen to the lusty shouts over the drill ground
(Changes to "hui lung")
Where they are busy training,
Full of fight to smash the enemy.
I'm so anxious to join them
That my heart's afire.
(Changes to "yuan pan")
How I long for the day
When the bandits are slain and a blood debt repaid.
With deep hatred, morning and evening
I sharpen my sword and oil my gun.
On the high cliff the blizzard may blow,
Storm the tiger's den—that I dare.
Why then pick on me to guard the village?
(Changes to "to pan")
I must see the Chief of Staff at once
And tell him again what's on my mind.

My resolve is to fight on the battlefield,
For I've pledged to kill them all.

(Medical Orderly enters.)

Medical Orderly: Pao!

Pao: Sister, put in a word for me. Let's go and see our Chief of Staff.

(Pao rushes Medical Orderly along. Shao comes out from Yung-chi's house.)

Shao: Hey, what are you two talking about?

(Yung-chi enters.)

Pao: Uncle, let me go.

Shao: Well, the militia have got to protect the village, too.

Pao: Humph, I hate that Vulture so much, I've got to kill him with my own hands. How could you keep me here? I must go.

Shao: But you're too young, Pao.

Pao: What, me too young?

Medical Orderly: Chief of Staff, Pao is class-conscious and skis well. She's a good shot, and she can help me look after the wounded. Do let her go.

Yung-chi: Commander, this girl has been through much bitterness and is thirsting for revenge. Let her come along with us.

Shao: Militia leader, you're feeling the same way, eh!

Yung-chi: Let it be so.

Shao: So you are all of one mind. All right, then. It's settled.

Pao: Hurray! *(Exit, leaping for joy, followed by Medical Orderly.)*

Yung-chi: Commander, the prisoners Luan Ping and Howling Wolf have been taken away. It looks like we're about to attack Tiger Mountain, eh?

Shao: Impatient, aren't you?

(Yung-chi grins.)

Shao: How long should it take us to reach the back path of the mountain at the rate we ski now?

Yung-chi: It's eighty *li* longer than the direct approach. I think we can do it in a day and a night at most.

Shao: Good. See that your militia is fully prepared.

Yung-chi: I'll see to that! (*Exit.*)

(*Chung and Lu enter.*)

Lu: Chief of Staff, why should we be marking time here? The comrades can all ski as fast as required. . . .

Chung: And the militia has been organized.

Lu: And we've been sent reinforcements. . . .

Chung: I think we ought to set out immediately. I'm sure we can win.

Shao: Comrades, we should guard against impetuosity at critical moments. (*Sings "hsi pi san pan"*)
Wait patiently for orders—

Chung: Right. (*Exit with Lu.*)

Shao (*sings and changes to "hsi pi yuan pan"*):
Although I've urged patience
I can't keep calm myself.
The day to close in on the enemy is nearing.
But there's no sign of Shen returning with the message.
If anything goes wrong. . . .
(*Changes to "kuai pan"*)
I've another idea. We mustn't miss
Our chance at the Hundred Chickens Feast.
Yung-chi says there's a dangerous
Trail up the back of the mountain,
Surprise and courage will carry us
Charging into Tiger Hall.

(*Lo shouts and enters.*)

Lo: Shen is back, Chief of Staff.

(*Shen enters.*)

Shao (*hurries forward*):   Comrade Teh-hua.

Shen (*hands the message over, panting*): I'm not late, am I?

Shao (*takes it*): No, go and get some rest.

(*Exit Shen supported by Lo.*)

Shao (*eagerly reads message*): ". . . A steep trail up the back of the mountain leads directly to Tiger Hall. . . . Burning pine torches will be the signal. . . ." (*Excitedly*) Good Old Yang! Hero! Hero!

(*Young Kuo shouts offstage: "Chief of Staff!" He enters running, followed by Ta-shan and Yung-chi.*)

Young Kuo: Report, Chief of Staff. When the train reached West Branch River, the bridge had been wrecked. We got out to repair it and were attacked by bandits. We drove them off. . . .

Shao: What about those two prisoners?

Young Kuo: Howling Wolf was killed by a stray bullet.

Shao: And Luan Ping?

Young Kuo: He escaped while we were chasing the bandits.

Shao: Escaped? (*Aside.*) If he heads for Tiger Mountain, that'll be dangerous for Comrade Yang, and it may ruin our plan. (*Turns to Young Kuo and Yung-chi.*) Assemble the detachment, quick.

Young Kuo and Yung-chi: Right. (*Exit.*)

(*A rail is struck, the call to fall in.*)

Shao: Comrade Ta-shan, you and Hunter Chang take over the defence of the village.

Ta-shan: Right.

(*Soldiers, militia and villagers enter.*)

Shao: Comrades! (*Sings "hsi pi san pan"*)
The situation has suddenly changed,
Our task is pressing,
Every second counts.

To arms, comrades,
Let's fly forward.
Forward march!

(Dark change.)
(A snowstorm. Soldiers and militia with Yung-chi as their guide set out quickly, braving wind and snow.)
(At the foot of a cliff, they remove their skis. One soldier starts climbing and slips; two others mount, carrying ropes. One of them slips and tries again. They lower the ropes when they reach the top. Shao and his men grasp the ropes and follow.)
(When the soldiers descend a slope, some roll down, others leap. They press onward quickly and boldly.)

(Curtain)

⟞⟝

SCENE TEN

CONVERGING ON HUNDRED CHICKENS FEAST

Lunar New Year's Eve. In Tiger Hall.

(The curtain rises amid shouting: "Bring 'liutzu' in!")
(Two bandits enter with Luan Ping.)

Luan: Chief.
Vulture: Luan Ping!
Luan: Yes, sir.
Vulture: Adjutant Luan!
Luan: Chief.
Vulture: What brings you here?
Luan: I've come—to wish you a happy birthday. Ho, ho. . . .
Vulture: Where did you come from?
Luan: I. . . .

Vulture: Humph!

Luan: I. . . .

Terribles: Speak!

Luan: I. . . .

Terribles: Out with it!

Luan: I . . . I've come from Commissioner Hou.

Vulture (*sneers*):   So you've been with Commissioner Hou.

Luan: Yes.

Vulture: Summon Old Ninth!

Bandit: Old Ninth, you are wanted.

(*Yang enters, an Officer of the Day sash across his chest.*)

Yang: Everything is ready for the feast, Chief.

Vulture: Look who's here, Old Ninth.

Yang (*startled at the sight of Luan Ping but controls himself instantly. Seizing the enemy's weaknesses, he decides on the course of action to take*):   Oh, Brother Luan. Why have you come here? How are you getting along? What post did Commissioner Hou give you? I, Hu Piao, congratulate you on your promotion.

Terribles (*mockingly*):   What are you now—a regimental commander? (*Laugh.*)

(*Luan is bewildered.*)

Vulture: What kind of post did Commissioner Hou give you?

Luan (*recognizes Yang and smiles wickedly*):   Hu Piao, my eye! No . . . you're mistaken. . . .

Yang (*sternly*):   Me mistaken or you the one who's mistaken? I, Hu Piao, was friend enough and was playing the game. Not at all like you, Luan Ping. I advised you to join Brigadier Tsui, but you tried to drag me off to Commissioner Hou. You can't say I wasn't playing fair. (*Presses on.*) Answer Chief. What business brings you here?

Luan (*turns away from Yang*): Chief, listen to me. . . .

Yang: Cut it out. Today is Chief's fiftieth birthday. There's no time for your nonsense.

Vulture: Right. Come to the point. I want to know why you've come.

Luan: To join Chief's forces.

Vulture: Oh!

Yang: Then why did you go seeking an appointment from Commissioner Hou?

(Luan gets confused, stumbles.)

Yang: Why has the commissioner sent you here? The truth, now!

Terribles: Out with it and quick! Why have you come?

Luan: I'm not from Commissioner Hou.

Bandit Chief of Staff: That's not what the bastard said a moment ago. He certainly changes his tune fast. Quite a bird.

(The bandits laugh uproariously.)

Luan: Stop laughing! You've been fooled. He is not Hu Piao. He's a Communist armyman!

(Terribles draw their guns and point them at Yang.)

Yang (*calmly*): Ha, ha, ha! Well, so I'm a Communist armyman, since you say so. Now tell Chief and big brothers here more about this Communist armyman.

Vulture: That's right. You say he is not Hu Piao but a Communist armyman. How did you come to know him?

Luan (*stammers*): He . . . he . . . he. . . .

Bandits: Heh.

Luan: He. . . .

Yang: All this fellow can do is stammer and contradict himself. He's up to some trick, Chief.

Bandit Chief of Staff: I bet he was caught by the Communists, and then released.

Luan: No . . . no. . . .

Yang: Did the Communists set you free? Or did they send
you here?

Terribles: Speak!

Luan: I. . . .

Bandit Chief Adjutant: The Communists sent you, didn't
they?

Terribles: Speak. Be quick!

(Luan stares, tongue-tied.)

Yang: Chief, our defences on Tiger Mountain are absolutely watertight, and the Communists can't get in. But
now this fellow has come. There's something fishy about
this.

Luan *(hastily)*:   There isn't. I swear!

Yang: Luan Ping! (*Sings "hsi pi kuai pan"*)
Capricious, sinister fellow,
Your evasiveness surely conceals tricks.
To our fortress you came, leaving your tracks
In the snow for the Communists to follow.
(Walks to the steps and calls.)
Captain—

(Bandit Captain comes forward.)

Bandit Captain: Here.

Yang *(sings)*:   *Double the guard and keep a close watch,*
Let no one off duty without my order.

Vulture: Right. Without Old Ninth's order, no one is to
leave his post.

Bandit Captain: Yes, sir. *(Exit.)*

(Terribles nod approvingly.)

Vulture *(comes down from his seat, grasps Luan and throws
him to the ground)*:   You treacherous dog. First you
tried to get Old Ninth to go with you to Commissioner
Hou. Now you come here to divide us and want to bring
the Communists in. This is too much.

Luan: He's not Hu Piao, Chief. He's really a Communist armyman.

Yang: What a snake you are, Luan Ping! (*Walks down the steps.*) You're trying to do me in by Chief's hands. Too bad I didn't bump you off when we had drinks at White Pines Dale.

Terribles: That's right.

Yang: Chief, I've never let myself be pushed around by little men. For your sake, I've offended this mad dog so he's attacking me viciously. If you believe that I'm a Communist armyman, then finish me off at once. If you believe that I'm Hu Piao, then permit me to leave this mountain. It's either him or me; keep him or keep me. You decide as you please, Chief. (*Removes his sash and tosses it onto the ground.*)

(*Vulture dumbfounded.*)

Bandits: You mustn't leave, Old Ninth, you mustn't leave.

Terribles: Old Ninth mustn't leave, Chief.

Bandit Chief of Staff (*picks up the sash and hands it to Vulture*):   Old Ninth mustn't leave, Chief.

Bandits: Old Ninth mustn't leave.

Vulture: Don't be childish, Old Ninth. Put it on, put it on. I will treat you right. (*Laughs.*)

(*Bandit Chief of Staff takes the sash from Vulture and puts it on Yang.*)

Bandit Chief of Staff: Put it on.

Luan (*realizes the situation is going against him, pleads*):   Chief. . . .

Vulture (*brushes him aside*):   Humph! (*Returns to his seat.*)

Luan: Chief! (*Prostrates himself before Yang.*) Brother Hu Piao!

(*Yang ignores him.*)

Luan (*slaps his own face*): I'm trash, I'm worthless, I ought to be hanged!

Yang (*shouts to the assembled bandits*): The hour has come. Let everyone congratulate Chief on his birthday.

Bandits: Get ready, everybody. Congratulate Chief on his birthday!

Bandit Chief of Staff: It's your fiftieth birthday today, Chief. You mustn't let this cur spoil everything.

Bandit Chief Adjutant: It will be bad luck for Tiger Mountain if you don't blot out this evil star.

Bandits: Yes. He must be killed, killed!

Luan: Big brothers, Brother Hu Piao, Chief. . . .

(*Luan kneels down before Vulture.*)

Vulture (*laughs ominously*): Ha! Ha! Ha! . . .

Luan: Chief, spare me! . . .

(*Vulture waves his hand.*)

Terribles: Kill him!

Luan: Chief, spare me! . . .

Bandit Chief Adjutant: Take him away.

Yang: I'll do it. (*Seizes Luan, who is paralysed with fright.*)

Luan: Old Ninth!

Yang (*sings "hsi pi kuai pan"*):
You've robbed and killed for dozens of years,
Your bloody hands have committed towering crimes.
To avenge the people, in the nation's name,
I sentence you to death.
(*Drags him out. Shots are heard. Yang re-enters.*)

Yang: Everything is ready for the celebration. Allow us to offer our respects, Chief.

Vulture: You're Officer of the Day, Old Ninth. You take over.

Yang: Brothers!

Terribles: Here.

Yang: Light the lamps in the hall, burn pine torches out-

side. Let's offer our best wishes for Chief's birthday.
(*Bandit Captain enters.*)

Bandit Captain: Yes, sir. It's time for the celebration.
(*Exit.*)

Terribles: Best wishes to you, Chief.

(*Terribles and other bandits bow to Vulture.*)

Yang (*jumps on a stump*):   Brothers, let's eat and drink
our fill. Get good and drunk.

Bandits: Right. We'll get good and drunk.

Yang: Please be seated at the table, Chief.

Vulture: After you, brothers.

Yang: It's your fiftieth birthday, Chief. You must be
seated first.

Terribles: Yes, yes. You must be seated first, Chief.

Vulture: All right. Let's go. (*Beside himself with elation.*)
Ha! Ha! Ha!

(*Vulture leaves for adjoining cave room. Bandits file in
after him and begin feasting. Bandit Captain enters.*)

Yang (*steps down the stump*):   Captain!

Bandit Captain: Here.

Yang: Call in the brothers on guard and let them drink
their fill.

Bandit Captain: Yes, sir. (*Exit.*)

(*Bandits can be heard playing rowdy drinking games in
adjoining cave room.*)
(*Yang returns to the stump and looks around.*)

Yang (*sings "hsi pi kuai erh liu"*):
The mountain is a blaze of lights on New Year's Eve,
(*Walks down the stump.*)
This is the signal to our troops.
The Hundred Chickens Feast has started as planned,
The bandits are drunk and befuddled.
I hope the comrades will come quickly
And smash this den of stubborn enemies.

How time drags, when I'm impatient,
Why haven't the comrades gone into action?
I long to go out and have a look.
(Controls himself. Changes to "yao pan")
But I must keep calm at this critical moment and block
this secret tunnel.
(Points at the spot below Vulture's armchair.)

(Vulture, Bandit Chief of Staff and others enter drunk,
staggering.)

Vulture: Why don't you join the feast, Old Ninth? Everyone wants to drink to your health.
Yang: Today's your fiftieth birthday. It's your health we
should be drinking to. Fill the Chief's bowl.

(Everyone drinks.)
(Shots are heard. Bandits throw down their bowls.
Terrible B, wounded, enters running.)

Terrible B: The Communists have sealed off the entrance
to Tiger Hall with machine guns.
Vulture: Let's get out, brothers. Hurry!
Bandits: Charge! Charge!

(PLA men, offstage, yell: "Lay down your guns or die!")

Vulture: Into the tunnel with me, Old Ninth, quick.
(Pushes over the armchair, but Yang shoves him aside.)
Yang: You're not getting away!

(PLA men charge in shouting: "Lay down your guns or
die!")

Vulture *(to Yang)*:   What! You're. . . .
Yang: A member of the Chinese People's Liberation
Army.
Vulture: Ah!

(Vulture draws his gun. Yang knocks it out of his hand.
Vulture runs off. Bandits follow.)

Shen: Old Yang!

Yang: There's a secret tunnel here, comrades. Rescue the villagers and catch Vulture alive. (*Runs to pursue Vulture.*)

Shen: Charge, comrades!

(*PLA men follow.*)

(*Shen fights with a Terrible. Bandit Chief of Staff enters and raises his pistol and fires at Shen, who dodges. Bullet hits the Terrible and kills him.*)

(*Lo rushes in after another Terrible. They fight. Pao pursues a bandit. They wrestle. She subdues him. She and Lo lead prisoners off.*)

(*Yung-chi, Medical Orderly, soldiers and militia, with villagers the bandits had been holding captive, walk across stage and are off.*)

(*Bandit Captain enters, running. Yung-chi shoots him dead. Another bandit runs in and is captured by Yung-chi.*)

(*Vulture enters, followed by two bandits, fleeing wildly. Yang pursues them and shoots the two bandits dead. He and Vulture lock in struggle.*) (*Chung and soldiers chase on Bandit Chief Adjutant and bandits. They fight.*)

(*Yang grabs a gun and kills several bandits.*)

(*Shao, Shen, Yung-chi, Medical Orderly, Young Kuo and militia enter. They capture Vulture and all the bandits.*)

(*Pao, raging, wants to stab Vulture. Medical Orderly holds her back.*)

Shao (*pumps Yang's hand, very moved*):   Old Yang!

Yang: Chief of Staff!

(*Shao introduces Yung-chi to Yang. The two warmly clasp hands. Dramatic pose.*)

(*Final curtain*)

為

誰

11

"FOR WHOM?"

THEATRE IN CHINA IS NOT TO BE COMPARED with theatre in the West any more than Chinese characters are to be compared with Western calligraphy. In China the theatre is for a precisely guided moral-political education, not for box-office profits. It is the largest theatre in the world, and its houses are packed.

The growth of revolutionary Chinese theatre closely parallels the growth of revolutionary China. From the early days of struggle, soldier-writer-actors and writer-actor-workers participated in the cultivation of the soil and fought against the Japanese while entertaining and giving meaning and motivation to the lives of bitter, incredulous peasants.

The Cultural Revolution brought about the new "model" theatre. Theatre also played a crucial part in bringing about the Cultural Revolution, just as it played a role in the Communist revolution itself. Communist guerrilla theatre, even further back than the early days on the grassy plains of Pao-an, was the fertile field from which the young drama grew, its extemporaneous skits and playlets bursting with educational material and revolutionary ideas to fill the needs of culture-starved, illiterate people.

"Every troupe had long waiting lists of requests from village soviets. The peasants, always grateful for any diversion in their culture-starved lives, voluntarily arranged all transport, food, and housing for these visits . . . Theatrical troupes were created in Soviet Shensi before the southern army reached the Northwest, but with the arrival of new talent from Kiangsi* the dramatic art apparently acquired new life. There were about thirty such traveling theatrical troupes there . . .

"There was no more powerful weapon of propaganda in the Communist movement than the Reds' dramatic troupes," Edgar Snow wrote in 1936, "and none more subtly manipulated." A flow of almost daily programs, "Living Newspapers," used military, political, economic and social problems as dramatic material "in a humorous, understandable way for the skeptical peasantry.

"When the Reds occupied new areas, it was the Red Theatre that calmed the fears of the people, gave them rudimentary ideas of the Red program, and dispensed great quantities of revolutionary thoughts, to win the people's confidence . . . in its broadest meaning it was art, for it conveyed for its spectators the illusions of life . . . For the masses of China there was no fine partition between art and propaganda. There is only a distinction between what was understandable in human experience and what was not."**

In May 1942, taking time out from critical battles,

* By 1931, the Gorky School in the Soviet area of Kiangsi had over fifty touring theatrical troupes; there were others in the Soviet bases in Honan and Hunan.

** *Red Star Over China*, revised, by Edgar Snow, Grove Press, New York, 1968, pp. 122–24.

Mao Tse-tung considered it important enough to personally address a forum on literature and art in battle-blocked Yenan, presenting his analysis of the work already done on the cultural front during the ten years of civil war, and the work still to be done to "insure that revolutionary literature and art follow the correct path of development and provide better help to other revolutionary work in facilitating the overthrow of the national enemy and the accomplishment of the task of national liberation."*

Talks at the Yenan Forum on Literature and Art remained a guide during the years that followed, applies to the present, and will stand as a valuable contribution in the years to come, not only in China, but wherever people seek a proletarian-revolutionary approach to literature, art, music and drama. Mao probed, counseled, scolded and taught the young artists gathered in Yenan, laying down a manifesto for creativity: the why and how for achieving truly new, truly revolutionary literature and art, based on conscious political (Marxist-Leninist) understanding, directed to the needs and wants of a (to be) proletarian-led society. He instructed a change of feeling, a remolding of thinking, a reversal of bourgeois forms and attitudes, in reaching out to the mass of people for whom the arts are intended.

"In the world today," Mao Tse-tung said in 1942, "all literature and art belong to definite classes and are geared to definite political lines. There is in fact no such thing as art for art's sake, art that stands above classes, art that is detached from or independent of politics. Proletarian literature and art are part of the whole proletarian revolutionary cause; they are, as Lenin said, cogs and wheels in the revolutionary machine."

We tend to ignore the fact that *all* theatre—all art, for that matter—is political, a reflection of the society that sponsors and controls it. The capitalist system produces "conformist" theatre and "protest" theatre, theatre that

* *Talks at the Yenan Forum on Literature and Art*, by Mao Tse-tung, 1942.

perpetuates bourgeois standards, and theatre that exposes its faults and weaknesses. We label the latter "political" theatre, denying or ignoring that even "entertainment" drama springs from a political and class foundation. That our theatre is different from China's is obvious, but it is not true that ours is nonpolitical, even if we often sugar-coat it to hide such manifestations. The Chinese are much more integrally politically conscious than we are; they have been taught and have learned to be so for compelling reasons. The process is as all-pervading as is the continuing revolution.

"There is a very clear realisation in China of the meaning of culture in the contemporary world, much higher than here, both among intellectuals and among the people. In fact, the importance attached there to the social meaning of a work of art over the individualist nature of its production process is such that it is quite normal for artists to remain anonymous, and the work of art itself to be discussed in terms of its purely cultural or aesthetic role. In China one sees culture and the masses so close together that it has become the culture of the masses. The word culture itself begins to become expendable insofar as its use traditionally defined what was cultured or higher class from what was uncultured or lower class . . . We may, if we wish, make comparisons between a country where the bourgeoisie dictates the culture and a country where the proletariat dictates it but we can do so only on the basis of class, of an analysis of class culture."*

The basic question asked during the Chinese Revolution, the principal one posed during the Cultural Revolution, and still a fundamental one today, is "for whom." It applies to every field, to all facets of government, to all areas of society and work. During the revolution it meant gaining liberation for China's vast population; its applica-

* "The Politics of Culture," an article by Roger Howard in *China Now*, published by the Society for Anglo-Chinese Understanding, London, January 1971, No. 18.

tion during the Cultural Revolution helped to eradicate a still-entrenched bureaucratic elite; and it remains of primary importance if China is to realize its goal—a Marxist-Leninist dictatorship of the proletariat.

For whom? For the masses: the workers, peasants, and peasant-worker-soldiers of China, the 90 percent of the population.

Mao Tse-tung states that literature and art for the landlord class is feudal; literature and art for the bourgeoisie is bourgeois; and literature and art which serve the imperialists is "traitor literature and art. Anything that is truly of the masses must necessarily be led by the proletariat." The form that it takes, the direction or meaning it contains, is determined by the needs of the people it serves: "We should take over the rich legacy and the good traditions in literature and art that have been handed down from past ages in China and foreign countries, but the aim must still be to serve the masses of the people. Nor do we refuse to utilize the literary and artistic forms of the past, but in our hands these old forms, remoulded and infused with new context, also become something revolutionary in the service of the people."

He was not barring the use of material from either the past or foreign. "We must on no account reject the legacies of the ancients and the foreigners or refuse to learn from them. It makes a difference . . . between crudeness and refinement, between roughness and polish, between a low and a high level, and between slower and faster work," Mao told the Yenan artists. "But taking over legacies and using them as examples must never replace our own creative work; nothing can do that.

"China's revolutionary writers and artists . . . must go among the masses; they must for a long period of time unreservedly and whole-heartedly go . . . into the heat of the struggle, go to the only source, the broadest and richest source, in order to observe, experience, study and analyse all the different kinds of people, all the classes, all the masses, all the vivid patterns of life and struggle, all the raw materials of literature and art. Only then can they proceed to creative work."*

Only by living with the people, in full participation that breaks down barriers between intellectuals, party cadres and the masses, can writers and artists know how and what to create to unite people in solid understanding of the aims of the revolution. Theatre, with its variety of techniques—skits, "Living Newspapers," storytelling, circuses, shadow plays, dramas and operas—and its inclusion of many different art forms—Peking opera, provincial opera, dance, ballet, music, acrobatics—was the most direct way of reaching the illiterate majority. Revolutionary theatre has to be understood and present the problems of those it is meant to serve; it has to use their materials, their language, their heritage. "A thing is good only when it brings real benefits to the masses of the people," said the young Mao.

With these words echoing in their ears, the revolutionaries infiltrated area after area, teaching, preaching, allaying the anxieties of the still-uncommitted, still-hungry, skeptical peasantry, who had viewed previous armies with loathing and contempt. They also helped to reeducate captured or defected Kuomintang and Japanese soldiers who, instead of being shot, put in chains or concentration camps as expected, were given food and placed in classrooms to study. Well-treated, they attended lectures and dramas and mingled with the troops, according to the American doctor Ma Hai-teh (George Hatem), who spent years in the battle area treating peasants and soldiers.

In contrast to such practices, Agnes Smedley describes a different situation in Chungking, the Kuomintang capital during the United Front period. She attended a play given there by Japanese captives organized in the "Japanese Anti-Imperialist League." "About twenty young Japanese soldier captives," she wrote, "under the leadership of the Japanese

* *Talks at the Yenan Forum on Literature and Art*, by Mao Tse-tung, 1942.

revolutionary writer Kadji* wrote their own plays, published their own magazine, and put on plays for the Chinese population and for war prisoners. The day after the play was given, the theatre was suppressed by Mr. Chen Li-fu, [Kuomintang] Minister of Education. The plays were considered revolutionary because they showed the effects of war upon the poor people of Japan."**

The People's Army was different. With the possible exception of the Taipings, China had not seen the like.

The years in Yenan (1937–47) drew vigorous, enthusiastic youngsters from all parts of China to participate in ridding their country of the Japanese, while the Kuomintang concentrated more and more on elimination of the Communists, rather than the enemy invaders. Girls and boys from middle schools, country lads and lasses, enlightened peasants from other liberated areas, university students, teachers, actors and actresses, writers of prominence, intellectuals—people from widely different backgrounds—responded to the call of Yenan. Smuggled in under siege conditions, they forsook families and braved death in their belief that this new manner of living, sharing and struggle would result finally in emancipation.

"Every enthusiastic young revolutionary who arrived in Yenan had to begin by helping to dig a cave. Afterwards they were given stools, with which they attended one of the open-air universities—there were at least six in Yenan—where political science, military science, medicine, and the fine arts were taught. . . .

"All the intellectual elite of the country was to be found at the Lu Hsun† Academy of Fine Arts. . . . They wrote and presented plays and organized entertainments of

* His wife, Yuki, was the main force in this revolutionary couple.

** *Battle Hymn of China*, by Agnes Smedley, Book Find Club edition, Alfred A. Knopf, New York, 1943, p. 500.

† Lu Hsun (1881–1936), the writer Mao Tse-tung called "the greatest and the most courageous standard-bearer of this new cultural force," is regarded as a national hero. Though never a Party member, he left behind a revolutionary example that is held high in China.

all kinds, as well as exhibitions. Touring shows went to the front to entertain the troops. Believe me, no one was bored in the evenings in Yenan. We worked very hard, but we relaxed too."*

So spoke Kao Fan-sian, a "super-veteran" of Yenan days, who in 1966, when he was reminiscing to K. S. Karol, was Vice Governor of Shensi province.

The Lu Hsun Academy, where hundreds of young people converged from all over the country to study under some of China's best writers, artists, musicians, and actors, was made up of several departments: literature, drama, art and music. In Yenan there was also the Lu Hsun Library and a fledgling motion-picture group (which eventually developed into the base for the major film studios in China, in Peking, Shanghai, Canton, Sian and Shenyang after 1949).

In 1944, after a performance of *Driven to Join the Liangshan Mountain Rebels* by the Peking Opera Theatre in Yenan, Mao Tse-tung wrote, "History is made by the people, yet the old opera (and all literature and art, which are divorced from the people) presents the people as though they were dirt, and the stage is dominated by lords and ladies and their pampered sons and daughters. Now you have reversed this reversal of history and restored historical truth, and thus a new life is opening for the old opera . . . I hope you will write more plays and give more perform-ances, and so help make this practice a common one which will prevail throughout the country."

Japan surrendered to the allies in August 1945. Im-mediately Chiang Kai-shek, with United States military assistance, moved to block the Communist-liberated zones. Full-scale civil war broke out in June. It was to take over three more years of combat before the People's Liberation Army marched into Peking.

Jack Belden gives us vivid highlights of the theatre during these last years before victory:

---

* *China: The Other Communism*, by K. S. Karol, Hill & Wang, New York, 1967, pp. 107–09.

"The night was bitterly cold, yet a crowd of at least two thousand people came to see the play. . . . There were a few benches on which some lucky early-comers sat, but most reclined on the ground, the children down front, directly in front of the stage, with others standing in the rear on small elevated humps of ground. Here and there in the audience one could see militiamen with rifles, some of them equipped with bayonets which glinted fitfully in the light.

"It would be hard to imagine a more democratic gathering. No tickets were sold, there was no dress circle and no preferred seats. . . . Sometimes the stage lamp went out. Then a stagehand would fetch a step ladder onto the stage and pump vociferously at the lamp for a few minutes until the illumination was restored. Afterward, the actors would pick up their lines as if nothing had happened. . . .

"The Communists' whole theatrical effort was extremely impressive. While at Yehtao [in the Taihang Mountains of Shansi province] during a three-day fair, I saw as many as five plays going at one and the same time. The stages were makeshift affairs and the properties the scantiest. Costumes, however, provided no problem as most all the plays concerned everyday people. The actors and actresses made up under a small awning in back of the stage, using flour and axle grease to produce the effects they wanted . . . Until very recently in China, as in Shakespeare's time, all women's parts were played by men, but in Communist areas, female leads were generally played by women. And it was quite a moving thing to see women with bound feet, who hitherto had not been allowed outside the home, toddling around the stage and acting out the part of an emancipated female."*

Another contribution to our knowledge of the theatre at this time is William Hinton's account of a small Chinese town swept up in the tide of the revolution in south

---

* *China Shakes the World*, by Jack Belden, Monthly Review Press, pp. 209–11.

Shansi. He describes the celebration following the December 1947 announcement of the Draft Agrarian Law which "With sentences as abrupt as the strokes of a fodder-chopping knife . . . proclaimed the death of landlordism.*

"Across the streets and alleys on all but invisible strings fluttered countless pennants of colored paper. Each bore a slogan supporting the new land law or denouncing Chiang Kai-shek and his bandit gang. . . . Along three of the four main streets . . . stages large enough for full-scale theatrical performances were set up on heavy timbers and hung with red silk.

"Peasants . . . jammed the roadways with their animals and vehicles. . . . Among the attractions which drew them to the town was the *yangko*** dancing. . . . In the lead came young men with red banners bearing the name of the . . . Association which they represented. Behind them came the musicians with their drums, cymbals, gongs, and pipes. Next came the acting group and then a long column of dancers."†

Hinton describes what he calls the "yangko rock," a peasant harvest dance. I remember Agnes Smedley, an avid folk dancer, showing it to me years ago, after her stay in Yenan. *Yangko* dancers often accompanied Red Army troops in an attempt to establish contact with village peasants.

"The girls all carried wide scarves of silk that were tied

* *Fanshen: A Documentary of Revolution in a Chinese Village*, by William Hinton, Monthly Review Press, New York, 1966, p. 7. Vintage Books, 1971.

Copyright © 1966 by William Hinton; reprinted by permission of Monthly Review Press.

** Ko (or keh) is the word for song. *Keh* and *ko* are different pronunciations; *keh* being the Peking sound. *Yang* here derives from the *yang* of *tsai yang*, the planting of rice. Old fertility songs and dances were performed at the time of planting of rice, coming north from the south of China where rice is grown. Rewi Alley told me that. In Sandan, in northwest China where he lived for some time, the *yangko* was always done prior to Liberation by dancers on stilts.

† Hinton, pp. 10–11.

to their waists with large red bows," writes William Hinton. "Like shimmering butterflies they wove figure eights and clover leaves and other intricate patterns and finally formed a circle inside of which the actors assembled to perform the plays and skits which they themselves had written.

"The most popular theme of these many plays was land reform. The two points . . . were the need to depend on the poor-and-hired peasants and the importance of uniting with the middle peasants. Many groups portrayed a villainous landlord who tried to sabotage all land division, a rich peasant who schemed with him, a middle peasant who worried lest the new land law be used against him, and a village political worker who sold out the poor for favors from the rich. But a hired laborer with the help of a Communist Party member always won the confidence of the people in the end. The landlord and his running dog cowed in disgrace, the poor peasants danced a merry jig with the middle peasant, while the boys and girls of the dancing brigade burst into joyous song and began their *yangko* all over again.

"Chiang Kai-shek came in for much buffeting about, as did the Soongs, the Kungs and the Chens—China's three other ruling families. These men were represented in typical fashion—Soong always with a Western-style hat, Chen in a black landlord's gown, Chiang in preposterous military regalia and Kung, the banker, always clutching a large briefcase stuffed with money.

"The streets overflowed with *yangko* and stick dancers, each orchestra trying to play louder than the last, each group of dancers striving to step out more vigorously than the one in front of it, each actor attempting to outdo in gesture and voice the others in the cast. Add to this the thousands upon thousands of country people milling about; the peddlars vending hot mutton soup, candy, peanuts and pears; the hundreds of carts going and coming; the red banners and the colored paper spinning and twirling in the air.

"And, as if all this were not enough, the three great stages on the three main streets presented a continuous succession of plays, each to an enormous changing crowd. Farther on . . . a traditional opera troupe sang to an audience of thousands.

"For two days and nights the festivities continued without letup."*

And so the civil war and the theatre—the military and the cultural, "the fronts of the pen and the gun"—pushed on toward Liberation. Mao pointed the way, expressing his faith in his followers:

"I believe . . . you will surely be able to bring about a transformation in yourselves and in your works, to create many fine works which will be warmly welcomed by the masses of the people, and to advance the literature and art movement in the revolutionary base areas and throughout China to a glorious new stage."

* Hinton, pp. 11–12.

III

SHACHIAPANG

THE FIRST OF THE ORIGINAL MODEL REVOLU-
tionary Peking operas received its title from a pleased Mao
Tse-tung.

Shachiapang is a market town in Changshu county,
Kiangsu province, south of the Yangtze River in East
China's Lake Taihu area, where

> The glory of the morning is mirrored in Lake Yangcheng
> The reeds in full bloom, the paddy so sweet
> Neat rows of willows line the shore
> By their own hands, the working people
> Have carved out a lovely landscape
> In this southern region teeming with fish and rice.
> Not one inch of our fair land will we surrender,
> Nor will we tolerate the brutality of the Japanese invaders.

In this setting the curtains open. The date is not pinned down to a specific year, but we know it is some time after the fall of Nanking, the former capital of the Nationalist government, to the Japanese in December 1937. From then to the end of 1941, in the densely populated eastern part of China and the lower Yangtze valley, the Japanese occupied most of the cities while the Chinese Red armies formed by Mao held most of the countryside areas.

The Chinese historian Immanuel C.Y. Hsu has written of this period: "The masses of civilians were gravely affected by the war, and their tribulations were exacerbated by the particularly atrocious conduct of the enemy. The Japanese bombed noncombatants, torpedoed fishing boats, strafed civilians, bayoneted ex-soldiers tied in batches of fifty, and burned, looted, and raped . . . Yet, in spite of everything, the Japanese could not quickly win the war. Tokyo finally resigned itself to a stalemate; it adopted the policy of living off the conquered land with the help of puppet governments."*

By 1937, following the Sian Incident, Chiang Kai-shek had been obliged to unite in a common front against the Japanese with the Communist forces left behind as a rear guard when the main Red troops made the Long March (1935–36) to the northwest. About ten thousand Communist troops still operating south of the Yangtze were organized into the New Fourth Army. Following the January 1941 attack by a Kuomintang force on a largely unarmed rear guard of this army ("it included many schoolteachers, students, nurses, hospital orderlies and hundreds of wounded, as well as many artisans"**) the united front disintegrated in the area. Plagued by both the Japanese and the Kuomintang, the New Fourth Army utilized the countryside, where the support of the people afforded

* *The Rise of Modern China*, by Immanuel C. Y. Hsu, Oxford University Press, 1970. p. 696.
** *Journey to the Beginning*, by Edgar Snow, Random House, 1958; Vintage Books, 1972.

protection and a mass base. Mao Tse-tung, analyzing problems of strategy in May 1938, pointed out: "As one aspect in the development of our nationwide guerrilla warfare, we should effectively organize guerrilla warfare in the Hungtze Lake region north of the Yangtze River, in the Taihu Lake region south of the Yangtze, and in all river-lake-estuary regions in the enemy-occupied areas along the rivers and on the seacoast, and we should create permanent base areas in and near such places."*

A digest of this history appeared on the illuminated screens flanking the proscenium of the Workers' Theatre in Peking as the red drapes opened on *Shachiapang*. Eighteen wounded New Fourth Army men are recuperating in this lakeside haven surrounded by the enemy. As soon as they are well they will rejoin their unit. The prologue has established that there is a midnight highway patrol by the Japanese. Villagers, led by Sister Ah-ching, an underground Communist Party worker who, as cover, runs a local tea shop, help the wounded soldiers cross the enemy lines to find sanctuary in the homes of the townspeople.

Early morning sun lights willow trees blending with sky and mountain. A peasant woman (and a for-real Women's Liberationist), Aunt Sha, is mending clothes in front of her modest house on the lake edge. Little Ling, an army nurse, tends a young soldier. It is a scene of peace. Suddenly the news of a Japanese raid is announced, and preparations commence to protect the invalid soldiers. Kuo Chien-kuang, the political instructor of the company, takes his wounded men to hide in the thick reeds of the lake marshes.

The savage Japanese raids last three days and are immediately followed by the arrival of the "Loyal and Just National Salvation Army"—Kuomintang puppet troops commanded by Hu Chuan-kuei and his chief of staff, Tiao Teh-yi. Sister Ah-ching had once saved Hu's live, before

* "Problems of Strategy in Guerrilla War Against Japan," in *Selected Works of Mao Tse-tung*, Vol. II. p. 96.

he became a collaborator, by hiding him from the Japanese. Totally unaware that she is a Communist, he remains grateful to her and praises her as a friend to Tiao as they refresh themselves outside her pleasant tea house. Ah-ching, cool as a sea-cucumber, replies:

Risking my life for another is a compliment I hardly deserve.
I keep a tea-house and hope for good business,
So I must observe the code of the brotherhood;
The commander was a frequent customer,
A big tree, and I wanted to enjoy its shade.

My stove is built for business,
My kettle doesn't ask where the water comes from,
My tables are used by travellers from everywhere;
Whoever comes here is a customer
And I have to be pleasant to him;
I greet all comers with a smile,
And once out of sight, out of mind.
When the customer leaves, the tea grows cold—

Here, with a deft flick of the wrist she picks up the chief of staff's cup and tosses the tea on the ground. He is startled, but she turns to him with a wide smile:

There is no question of giving anyone special care.

And the two men take it as a joke. (This is all done in song, with Peking opera gestures of hands and heads that give the incident a dimension not apparent in the script.)

Led by the Communist Party and supported by the local Party workers and villagers, Ah-ching lives her double life, playing Hu and Tiao against each other, skillfully overcoming danger and difficulties, and finally getting the wounded Communist soldiers out of the marshes and away safely. Hu and Tiao torture and kill the villagers in their efforts to find out who is behind the escape. Ah-ching, with Aunt Sha's help, gets information about the enemy's headquarters and the New Fourth Army returns to Shachiapang to free the people.

Shachiapang is a glowing achievement in revolutionary Chinese drama. The combination of a contemporary theme with sophisticated opera conventions, in a burst of music and action, creates a viable theatre. The script has scope; the characters are heroic and human at the same time.

Ah-ching (played by a charming actress) is a warm-hearted, convincing human being, motivated by deep loyalty to the Communist Party and the Mao Tse-tung Thought. Her goodness and boldness are revealed through action; her actions are impeccable, but as undercover Party branch secretary and liaison officer, she must play the game with the villains in order to outwit them. The viewer is never uncertain about *what* she is doing, but the complications of the situation, and the fact that she cannot be open, gives her a character of depth. This does not collide with the concept of the revolutionary hero—or heroine, in this case. Ah-ching is not a dubious, shaded, or "middle character"— a term used for persons in literature and in theatre who are not wholeheartedly dedicated to the principles of Chinese socialism, people "who are midway between good and bad, the positive and the negative, the advanced and the backward, people tainted by the 'old things'—'the mental burden which has weighed down on the individual peasant for thousands of years.' "* Pure Communist gold and goal, Ah-ching is entirely capable of manipulating the villains while keeping the audience aware. Carrying on a daring, devious struggle under the noses of her enemies, with the support of such stalwarts as Aunt Sha, Sha Szu-lung (Aunt Sha's son, who risks his life to take food and medicine to the wounded behind the enemy blockade), and other revolutionary comrades, she fulfills her demanding tasks with aplomb. As the Chinese put it, the minor characters serve as foils to Ah-ching "just as green leaves to a red flower."

Ah-ching is a key role; Kuo Chien-kuang is another. In

* From an article "Writing About Middle Characters—a Bourgeois Library Literary Notion," by Wen-i Pao, September 30, 1964.

spite of the woman's importance, Kuo, representing the New Fourth Army, dominates the scenes in which he appears. "A soldier born of the people . . . loyal to Chairman Mao, devoted to his people and motherland, and full of wisdom, courage and resourcefulness,"* he is the responsible, dedicated leader, a fierce fighter when he meets the enemy, an affectionate, pleasant young man when he relaxes and jokes with Aunt Sha. That he has reached the height of political maturity is stressed constantly. All the army men are heroes, but Kuo is the leader, set off prominently whenever he is on stage. He is the focal point of battle scenes, the center of group scenes, the major hero among all the others—and the actor makes him personal and personable. The part doesn't offer the flamboyancy of Yang-disguised-as-bandit in *Taking Tiger Mountain,* but just for this reason it's fun to see how Peking opera technique works in a more restrained and realistic role. One way is through long singing passages which were specially conceived to set off Kuo's role. Particular care has been taken to give him arias that realize the finest in Chinese music, I was told. These are so well-known and liked that audiences sometimes join in the singing.

Played by skilled actors, scenes attain a depth and brilliance not evident in the written script alone. There's a fine bit of acting when Ah-ching and Aunt Sha extricate themselves from a trap sprung by villainous Hu and Taio after the escape of guerrilla soldiers. A flip of the hand, a quick turn of the head, a registered facial reaction (punctuated by "tacs" from the orchestra) telegraph centuries-old "scoops" to initiated spectators. To those not in the know this physical language adds, at the very least, an unusual theatricality. It is far too intricate and refined to bear comparison to sentimental nineteenth-century melodrama. Rather it is a heightening of reality, a crystallization of truth, embroidered by suggestion and convention—gestures and footwork that recall the complexity of China's theatrical

* *China Reconstructs,* Peking, February, 1970.

culture, a high achievement in the art of symbolic representation.

To a Western viewer it is surprising to see an actor spring through a clump of realistic shrubs, look around, stumble in haste, and suddenly perform *hsiao mao*, a Peking opera movement which is described as a "light forward tumbling." So it is too in the scene "To the Attack," where the recovered soldiers prepare for battle. Kuo Chien-kuang issues orders to the men as he poses on one leg, strides forward, kicks high, and then, rising from a squatting position, circles around with leg extended, doing a completely airborne turn in a horizontal spin.

In battle scenes, dances based on the movement "running in a circle on the stage" are used to express quick marching. Advancing sideways mimes "taking cover to preserve oneself, and making full use of fire-power to destroy the enemy." Inaction is combined with movement, and serves to set it off. The rush of color and motion, disciplined as dance, is pointed up by the pause that here and there relieves or sharpens the pace.

I had the feeling of a first-night performance with members of the cast on tiptoe to do their best. The thoroughness of training and rehearsing is obvious; the enthusiasm of the participants is added spice. Such specialized technique is not required in Western acting; in fact, most Western drama would suffer from the ardor that emanates from China's revolutionary stage.

Shachiapang's villains are as wicked as they are supposed to be, but they are more within our ken than those in *Taking Tiger Mountain*, more complex than those in the fellow opera *The Red Lantern*. Kuomintang Hu poses as a jovial fellow when things are going his way. But he is always a "poisonous snake" and "vicious wolf," setting traps to lure the loyal guerrilla soldiers out of the reeds, or cold-bloodedly shooting the village hostages. One doesn't sympathize or identify with him or his natty chief of staff. Attention is *directed* to the poor and brave peasants and soldiers; the emphasis is removed from the villains also by staging and lighting that keeps them lurking in the background. It made me wonder how the actors who play the villains feel. Perhaps it is real selflessness that permits them to enact characters beyond the pale: the identification that an actor must establish between himself and the part of, say, Iago, cannot be possible as there is no element of empathy displayed. An actor playing a villain must subjugate himself to a purely evil role. With what emotional associations ("justification," a "method" actor would say) I cannot tell. Hao Lian, who plays Li Yu-ho in *The Red Lantern* said: "Villains *help* the heroes to stand out; they help to create the heroic image. Some actors don't like to play villains, but through political understanding they gain a clear understanding of a villain role." He also said that the company is received with warmth by the peasants—all except the villains. "Sometimes the peasants don't even want to feed them," Hao laughed. "That means they've played their parts well. They are good actors!"

Shachiapang is an adaptation of a Shanghai opera, *Sparks Amid the Reeds*. It was Chiang Ching who approached the Number-One Peking Opera Company of Peking with the script in play form and the request to make it into a new type of Peking opera embodying the principles of Mao Tse-tung's *Talk at the Yenan Forum on Literature and Art*. The first attempt was not successful. We were told that the company's bourgeois leadership clung tenaciously to old ideas, and that the young creators were under their control and influence. The resulting piece, *The Underground Liaison Agent*, even had a female impersonator—a custom that even before the revolution was becoming obsolete— in the role of Ah-ching. Rewriting and revising ensued. The entire company, librettists and directors included, paid as many as eight visits to army units and camped out for some time on a reed-grown marsh to benefit from theory put into practice. The standards of model revolutionary opera had been met by the time that

Sparks Amid the Reeds, title restored, was performed at the Festival of Peking Opera on Contemporary Themes in June 1964. When Mao Tse-tung attended the presentation he suggested a title change; *Shachiapang*, after the village whose reeds protected the wounded comrades, came into being.

In a nine-month run in Shanghai the opera achieved 436 performances to an audience of 655,000. Its rich music inspired a symphony that bears the same name. In September 1971, the Changchun Film Studio released a Technicolor film version.

Singing is an integral part of China's principle form of theatre, for it is still essentially opera. The script is in verse; the parts are almost entirely sung. When reading the plays it is important to remember this, (as well as the fact that translation—no matter how well done—tends to dull earthy, idiomatic values. Robert Frost might be aptly recalled here: "Poetry is the thing that is lost in translation"). In old opera spoken passages were needed to give the singers a rest, as performances went on for many hours; modern opera is tight in form and lasts, with intermissions, about two hours. The singing is almost continuous, though spoken dialogue mingles with the melodies.

Songs, and the manner of singing them, are vital to characterization. The orchestra plays a significant interpretive role as well. It was explained to me in Peking that many people talk about going to *t'ing* (listen to) an opera, rather than *k'an* (see) it. That is not really different from what we do in the West with our opera.

Much has been made over the difficulty of understanding or appreciating Chinese music. To many Westerners it seems discordant, bizarre, loud or shrill. But an attentive foreign ear can overcome the sound barrier and find a new musical world for the effort, especially since today's music has been moderated—"tempered," as they say. It is far from grotesque, if it ever was. Chinese is a lilting, singable language whose very tones give it the quality of song. Once

accustomed to the difference, the visitor is likely to feel
—not at *home*, but quite possibly delighted.

The music serves to knit the old and new together;
traditional melodies, well-known to opera goers, are retained, even though the words are changed. A rich de-
pository of folk music long since assimilated into Peking
opera bridges the years. Innovations have altered some
classic rhythms and melodies. An example is the inclusion
of modern military music and themes from revolutionary
army songs. Occasionally strains from "The East Is Red" or
"The International" rise up to encourage a troubled stage
comrade or to heighten a heroic moment.

One of Chiang Ching's major contributions to the
new Peking opera is the way she has added strength and
power to the music. Originally, aside from all the "noise,"
the characteristic of Chinese music was its thinness; to a
great extent this limited its capacity to express the full
range of human emotions. By adding many Western instruments, including the full range of winds, the kettle drums,
the piano and harp, Chiang Ching greatly augmented the
opera orchestras and made them capable of achieving far
more musically than in the past.

It would take long study to fully understand the
nuances and intricacies of Chinese music. I hope this brief
compilation will shed enough light on the subject to give
the texts more of the dynamism they have in the actual
theatre.

Terms like *hsi pi yao pan* and *erh huang san yen, yuan
pan*, and *kuai pan*, accompany the songs in the texts
printed here; they denote style, mode, rhythm and tempo.
Pan yen is timing: *pan* is the accented beat, *yen* is the un-
accented beat. The beat of *pan* is given by a wooden
instrument called *pan*, which is shaken by an orchestra
member to produce the main beat during singing. The
yen beat is produced by a small drum, the *tan pi ku*.
Man pan denotes slow time; *yuan pan*, medium time; *kuai
pan*, quick time; *san pan*, free time. *Yao pan* is a fast beat

particularly stressing emotion and anger. In this style the accompaniment is fast, while the singing is slow.

Hsi pi and *erh huang* are the two basic musical styles now employed in Peking opera. *Hsi pi* is quick and lively, used for expressing happiness or excitement. *Erh huang*, a deeper, more profound style, generally is used for reflection, conjecture, and for soliloquies. Thus a melodic style in a set tempo expresses a particular mood as the actor sings the accompanying words. At times, *pu teng ngo*, a recitative, breaks the singing, accompanied only by percussion instruments. For each model opera, a new set of melodies has been created; they are combined with many traditional musical devices. In *Shachiapang* a bamboo flute is used that is characteristic of the music south of the Yangtze. In *Taking Tiger Mountain*, notes from the centuries-old, militant *kun chu* melodies have been adapted to voice a woman fighter's "high-pitched indignation and hatred of the enemy"—a kind of Chinese keen.

The principle orchestral instruments in present Peking opera, beside the *pan* and *tan pi ku* mentioned above, are the *po*, cymbals similar to ours; *hu chin*, a high and shrill two-stringed fiddle of northern origin; *erh hu*, an important two-stringed fiddle through the south; *yueh ch'in*, or "moon guitar"; *pi pa*, a very old Chinese pear-shaped guitar with four strings and a mellow tone; *so na*, a brass horn like a trumpet with a piercing reedy sound; *ti-tzu*, a bamboo flute with eight holes; and the *shen*, a kind of mouth organ with ten, thirteen or nineteen bamboo tubes sprouting from its top. These are now augmented by Western instruments varying to some degree with each opera and ballet. The effect is different from that produced by the smaller orchestra (seven or eight players) that formerly accompanied Peking opera: softened, more melodic, but with the distinctive color and fervor of a revolutionary China built on the artistic richness of its past.

Shachiapang

(MAY 1970 SCRIPT)

REVISED COLLECTIVELY BY THE PEKING OPERA TROUPE OF
PEKING

≍

CAST OF CHARACTERS

Kuo Chien-kuang: company political instructor of the
    New Fourth Army
Sister Ah-ching: *member of the Chinese Communist
    Party, underground Party worker*
Aunt Sha: *peasant activist in Shachiapang*
Cheng Chien-ming: *secretary of the Changshu County
    Committee of the Chinese Communist Party*
Yeh Szu-chung: *platoon leader of the New Fourth Army*
Squad Leader: *squad leader of the New Fourth Army*
Little Ling: *woman nurse of the New Fourth Army*

Young Wang: *soldier of the New Fourth Army*
Hsiao-hu: *soldier of the New Fourth Army*
Lin Ta-ken, Chang Sung-tao and other New Fourth Army men
Sha Szu-lung: *son of Aunt Sha, Shachiapang militiaman and later soldier of the New Fourth Army*
Chao Ah-hsiang: *head of the market town of Shachiapang*
Wang Fu-ken: *Shachiapang militiaman*
Ah-fu: *revolutionary peasant of Shachiapang*
Other peasants, old and young, men and women, of Shachiapang
Hu Chuan-kuei: *commander of the puppet "Loyal and Just National Salvation Army"*
Tiao Teh-yi: *chief-of-staff of the puppet army*
Adjutant Liu: *adjutant of the puppet army*
Tiao Hsiao-san: *cousin of Tiao Teh-yi*
Other puppet soldiers
Kuroda: *colonel of the invading Japanese army*
Tsou Yin-sheng: *interpreter for the invading Japanese army*
Several Japanese soldiers

≂

SCENE ONE

MAKING CONTACT

During the War of Resistance Against Japan. Midnight. A highway held and patrolled by the Japanese in Changshu County, Kiangsu Province.

(As the curtain rises, Szu-lung, breaking through clumps of shrubs, enters from behind a tree. He looks round, stumbles, performs the Peking opera dance movement "hsiao mao"—light forward tumbling; then looks round vigilantly and beckons to people offstage.)

(Enter Sister Ah-ching, followed by Chao and Fu-ken.)

Sister Ah-ching (*sings "hsi pi yao pan"** *):
Party Secretary Cheng has sent word:
The wounded will be brought to our town tonight,
We are here to help them cross the blockade line. . . .

(Szu-lung blows on a reed blade according to an agreed signal. No response. He starts to go down the road to look for the wounded men, but Sister Ah-ching promptly stops him.)

Sister Ah-ching (*continues singing*):
Be on the alert against Japanese patrols.

(She pulls Szu-lung and signals to Chao to take cover. Fu-ken suddenly notices Cheng coming in his direction. He hurriedly turns to Sister Ah-ching.)

Fu-ken: Sister Ah-ching, here they are?

(Enter Cheng.)

Cheng: Sister Ah-ching! Comrade Chao!
Sister Ah-ching and Chao: Secretary Cheng!
Sister Ah-ching: Have all the wounded comrades come?
Cheng: They're all here. See, there's Instructor Kuo.

(Kuo enters, strikes a dramatic pose. Yeh and Hsiao-hu enter in his wake.)

Kuo (*to Yeh*):   Stand guard! (*Turns to Cheng.*) Secretary Cheng.
Cheng: Let me introduce you. This is Political Instructor Kuo. This is the town head of Shachiapang, Chao Ah-

---

* Hsi pi yao pan and similar terms in the text such as *erh huang san yen, yuan pan, erh huang yao pan, hsi pi yuan pan, lin shui* and *kuai pan* are various styles of singing in Peking opera. Each has its own fixed tune, structure, mode, rhythm and tempo. Modern revolutionary Peking opera has critically assimilated various styles of singing from traditional Peking opera, with many creative improvements to suit the portrayal of proletarian heroes.

hsiang. This is Sister Ah-ching, the Party branch secretary and liaison worker here. For cover, she runs the Spring Tea-house. Her husband is an underground messenger for the Party.

Sister Ah-ching and Chao: Instructor Kuo!

Kuo: Town Head Chao! Sister Ah-ching! (*Warmly shakes hands with them.*)

Cheng: Rest here in Shachiapang patiently and get well. If anything happens I'll get in touch with you. Let's cross the enemy line right now.

Kuo: Platoon Leader Yeh, go get the comrades.

Yeh: All right.

Hsiao-hu: Instructor! A Japanese patrol!

Kuo: Take cover!

(*The armymen and people take cover at once.*)
(*A small Japanese imperialist patrol crosses the stage, fierce and cunning.*)
(*Szu-lung emerges from behind the tree, and skilfully performs the Peking opera dance movement "tan man tze"—somersault sideways. His eyes searching the way the Japanese patrol took. Then he turns and beckons to Sister Ah-ching. The crowds enter. Szu-lung, Chao and others help the wounded soldiers cross the enemy line. Kuo and Sister Ah-ching shake hands with Cheng in farewell.*)

(*Curtain*)

≍

SCENE TWO

EVACUATION

Some two weeks later. In front of Aunt Sha's house on the bank of Lake Yang-cheng. Rows of willows. Rosy sky at sunrise.

(As the curtain rises, Aunt Sha is mending clothes. Ling is sorting out bandages and medicine. Wang is folding sacks.)

Ling: Young Wang! Come and let me change your dressing.

Wang: Change the dressing? No, I won't.

Ling: Why not?

Wang: Little Ling, it's so hard to get medicine. We should keep it for serious cases. My wound will heal soon enough.

Ling: It's true we don't have much left, but the mobile hospital will soon bring us more. Your wound may not be very serious, but it's not nothing, either.

Wang: I'm a light casualty.

Ling: Light casualty? Then why didn't the instructor allow you to go when he took the light casualties to help the peasants bring in the rice harvest?

(Wang can say nothing.)

Ling: Young Wang, come and have your dressing changed!

Wang: Nothing doing!

Ling: Orders from the instructor!

(Wang agrees reluctantly. He turns round and sees Aunt Sha.)

Wang and Ling: Aunt Sha!

Aunt Sha: Young Wang, you wounded comrades should do as the doctor and nurse say. Don't be pigheaded!

(Wang willingly lets Ling change his dressing.)

Ling: See, Aunt Sha doesn't like the way you carry on, either.

Wang: H'm! Aunt Sha's taken a fancy to you, so she always takes your part.

Aunt Sha: I take her part, you say. Well, yes, I do. The girl always talks sense and does what's right. That's why I like her.

Wang: All right. When we leave, we'll take Szu-lung along with us and leave Little Ling behind to keep you company. We'll give you a girl in exchange for a boy.

Aunt Sha: That'll be fine. I've had four sons, but never a daughter.

(Aunt Sha sits down. Ling takes a small stool and sits beside her.)

Ling: Aunt Sha, you often say you have four sons. But we have seen only Szu-lung, why?

Aunt Sha (*full of emotion, her heart overflowing with class hatred*):   That's all past and done with. Why bring it up again?

Ling: Aunt Sha, we all want to hear.

Wang: Yes, Aunt Sha, tell us about it, please.

Aunt Sha (*burning with hatred, unable to restrain herself from relating her bitter past, sings "erh huang san yen"*):
It's a long story. . . .
In the dark days we were too poor to raise our children,
Of my four boys, two died of hunger and cold.
I had to get a usurious loan from the Tiao's in a year of famine,
To pay the debt, my third son had to work for them as a farmhand.
(Changes to "yuan pan")
A poisonous snake, that bloodsucker Tiao (Rises to her feet with increasing anger.) had a murderous heart,
He made my son toil day and night.
Brutally beaten, the boy died of a mortal wound.
Szu-lung, my fourth, has such a fiery temper and is fearless,
He charged into Tiao's house to have it out with them;
The bloodsucker accused him of breaking in at night for robbery,

And had my poor sixteen-year-old thrown into prison.
Only when the New Fourth Army captured Shachia-
pang,
Was my son freed and could he see the light of day.
The Communist Party of China is like the bright sun!

Ling: How true, Aunt Sha!

Aunt Sha (*continues, singing "erh huang yao pan"*):
Without the Party my whole family would have died
long ago!

Wang: But we have the Communist Party, Aunt Sha, so we poor people are not afraid of them any more!

Aunt Sha: That's right!

(*Enter Ah-fu with a bowl of glutinous rice cakes.*)

Ah-fu: Aunt Sha!

Aunt Sha: Yes, Ah-fu?

Ah-fu: Ma told me to bring some rice cakes for the instructor.

Aunt Sha: I've already steamed some.

Ah-fu: Ma says this is just to show our love for our army-men.

Aunt Sha: Well said! Put the cakes in this basket. I'll fry them for the comrades later.

Ah-fu: Young Wang, Aunt Li's waiting for you to bring her the sacks to fill with rice so she can hide the grain.

Wang (*aroused from deep thought of Aunt Sha's bitter past, wants to settle accounts with Tiao*):   Aunt Sha, where is that bloodsucker Tiao you just mentioned?

Aunt Sha: Still thinking about that, eh? He's dead already. But he had a son. It's said he was studying in Japan a few years ago. We don't know where he is now.

Ling: Aunt Sha, Young Wang is never satisfied until he knows everything. (*Turns to Wang.*) Young Wang, Aunt Li is waiting for those sacks to hide the grain.

Wang: Oh, yes.

Ah-fu: Let's go together. (*Exit with Wang.*)

(Aunt Sha picks up a basket to go and wash clothes. Ling notices.)

Ling: Aunt Sha, washing clothes again! Let me do that.

Aunt Sha: The instructor's been helping with our harvesting all night. Why shouldn't I wash a few clothes for him?

Ling: Then let me go with you.

Aunt Sha: All right. Let's go. *(Exit with Ling.)*

(Kuo and Yeh enter in a boat, unload basket after basket of grain.)

Yeh: Take care, instructor.

Kuo: Don't worry. Platoon Leader Yeh! *(Points to the baskets of grain.)* Go and hide Aunt Sha's grain in the jar buried behind her house, quick.

Yeh: Right. *(Carries the baskets to the back of the house.)*

(Kuo picks up a broom and starts sweeping the courtyard. Looking at the beautiful landscape of the south after a night's work, he is full of feeling, longing for his comrades-in-arms and eager to return to the battlefield as soon as possible.)

Kuo *(sings "hsi pi yuan pan")*:
The glory of the morning is mirrored in Lake Yangcheng,
The reeds in full bloom, the paddy so sweet,
Neat rows of willows line the shore.
By their own hands, the working people
Have carved out a lovely landscape
In this southern region teeming with fish and rice.
Not one inch of our fair land will we surrender,
Nor will we tolerate the brutality of the Japanese invader.
I left the battlefield wounded
And came to Shachiapang to recuperate.
For a fortnight I've been thinking

Of my comrades (*changes to* "*erh liu*") *and command-
ers,*
(*Changes to* "*liu shui*")
And I wonder where they are.
(*Changes to* "*kuai pan*")
*Our armymen and the people stand ready
To crush the enemy's* "*mopping-up*" *campaign,
Longing for the day to raise our swords and kill the
wolves.
Day and night our wounded yearn to get fit for battle,
So we can return to the front soon!*

(*Enter Aunt Sha with Ling.*)

Ling: Instructor!
Aunt Sha: Instructor!
Kuo: Aunt Sha!
Ling: Instructor, Aunt Sha helped wash our clothes again.
Aunt Sha: Why mention it, lass? Isn't it only natural for
     me to wash a few clothes?
Kuo: Ha . . . ha. . . .
Aunt Sha (*to Kuo*):   Are all the comrades back?

(*Ling hangs up the laundry.*)

Kuo: Yes, they're back. We've finished harvesting the rice.
     We've hidden your share for you.
Aunt Sha: That's fine. You must be tired.
Kuo: Not at all, Aunt Sha.
Aunt Sha: Come and have a rest. Look, instructor, here
     are some rice cakes Ah-fu brought you.
Kuo: The people here are so good to us!

(*Enter Szu-lung with two fish and some crabs and
shrimps in his hand.*)

Szu-lung: Ma, I've caught two fish, and some crabs and
     shrimps, too.
Aunt Sha: Did you go fishing, Szu-lung, straight after
     work?

Szu-lung: Yes. To give the instructor something to go with his rice.

Kuo: Ha . . . ha. . . .

Aunt Sha: Fine. Give them to me. I'll clean them.

Kuo: Let me do it.

Szu-lung: Don't bother, Ma. Leave it to me. (*Goes into the house.*)

Kuo: Sit down, please, Aunt Sha.

(*Yeh comes out from behind the house.*)

Yeh: Instructor, several of our comrades have asked to rejoin their units. (*Hands him applications.*)

Kuo: How impatient they are! (*Reads the applications.*) Well, Platoon Leader Yeh, I think those who have recovered might leave first.

Yeh: Right.

Aunt Sha: Leave? Where would you go?

Kuo: To look for our units.

Aunt Sha: To look for your units? How can you!
(*Sings "hsi pi pao pan"*)
You comrades were wounded in battle,
So Shachiapang is your home;
If anyone doesn't look after you well,
Just tell me and I'll criticize him.

Yeh: Aunt Sha. . . .

(*Kuo stops him with a gesture.*)

Kuo: Aunt Sha's asking for our opinion. Ah . . . Aunt Sha, there's a point I'd like to raise.

Aunt Sha: Raise a point with me? (*Candidly.*) Fine. Out with it.

Kuo: All right. Listen, Aunt Sha.
(*Continues the singing*)
The other day the comrades had a chat,
They all talked about you, Aunt Sha.

Aunt Sha (*seriously*): What did they say?

Kuo (*continues singing*):

Once their tongues began wagging
There was no stopping them. . . .

Aunt Sha: They must have a lot of complaints.

Kuo (*continues singing*):
Everyone raised his thumb and praised you.

(*Kuo, Yeh and Ling chuckle.*)

Aunt Sha: I haven't done anything worth talking about.

Kuo: Aunt Sha.
(*Warmly, sings "hsi pi liu shui"*)
You treat our comrades like your own sons,
Nurse us with the best care,
You never stop mending and washing our clothes,
And cook us three fine meals a day with fish and
shrimps.
Our comrades say: If we stay here long
We will be too fat and lazy to walk or climb,
Not to speak of fighting at the front.

Aunt Sha (*to Yeh and Ling*):   Look, what nonsense he's
talking!

(*Kuo, Yeh and Ling chuckle.*)

Kuo (*continues singing*):
When the comrades have fully recovered—

Aunt Sha (*continues the singing*):
Even then (*Affectionately.*) *I won't let you go.*
I want you to have three good meals a day
And sleep until the sun is in the west.
I want everyone of you to be healthy and strong, like an
iron tower.
And then you'll mount your horses—

Kuo (*continues the singing*):
And gallop south to kill the enemy,
Cleaning out all traitors and bandits
And driving out the Japanese pirates.
When the sun scatters the clouds

And a red flag hangs before every house,
We'll come back to see you, our revolutionary mother!

(*Sister Ah-ching, Chao, Fu-ken and Ah-fu rush in. On hearing the noise, Szu-lung comes out of the house.*)

Sister Ah-ching: Instructor!

Kuo: Sister Ah-ching.

Sister Ah-ching: The Japanese gangsters have started "mopping up." They're moving fast. The county Party committee wants you to hide in the marshes for a while. I've got a boat and provisions ready.

Kuo: Sister Ah-ching, Comrade Chao! Ask the militia to help people evacuate and rush to hide as much grain as possible. If there's any you can't hide right away, bring it along!

Sister Ah-ching and Chao: Right!

Sister Ah-ching: Don't worry about us, instructor. Go and take cover at the agreed spot. When the coast is clear, I'll go to get you. Aunt Sha, how about Szu-lung and Ah-fu taking the comrades there?

Aunt Sha: Good! (*Goes into the house to take the rice cakes and rice crusts.*)

Szu-lung: Where's the boat?

Ah-fu: At the northwest corner of the town.

Kuo: Platoon Leader Yeh, tell the comrades to assemble at the northwest corner.

Yeh: Right!

(*Ling takes down the laundry and goes off with Yeh.*)

Sister Ah-ching: Szu-lung, mind you keep under cover. Don't let anyone see your boat.

Szu-lung: Yes.

(*Enter Aunt Sha with a basket.*)

Aunt Sha: Take these rice crusts and cakes along with you. (*Hands the basket to Szu-lung.*) There's no shelter in the marshes. How can the wounded comrades stand it?

Kuo: Aunt Sha, we have Chairman Mao's wise leadership and the tradition of the Red Army men who crossed snow-covered mountains and swamps. No difficulty can stop us.

(*Guns rumble in the distance.*)

Sister Ah-ching: It's best to go now, instructor.

Kuo: Sister Ah-ching, Town Head Chao and Aunt Sha, you must be very careful too!

Sister Ah-ching, Aunt Sha and Chao: We will.

Kuo: Ah-fu, Szu-lung, let's go. (*Exit with Szu-lung and Ah-fu.*)

Sister Ah-ching (*to Chao and Fu-ken*):   Do as Instructor Kuo said, quick!

Chao: I'll look after evacuating our people.

Fu-ken: I'll get some people and hide the rest of the grain.

Sister Ah-ching: Be quick!

Chao and Fu-ken: Right. (*Go off.*)

Sister Ah-ching: Aunt Sha, you'd better get your things ready too. I'll go and see to the comrades.

Aunt Sha: All right.

(*Sister Ah-ching goes up a slope. Aunt Sha removes the tea-set and enters the house.*)
(*Lights fade. The gunfire draws closer. Flames shoot up in the distance. Lights come up gradually. Sister Ah-ching and Chao help the elderly people and children and direct the masses along the evacuation route. Japanese troops shoot into the crowd. People rise in furious resistance. Fu-ken bravely kills a Japanese gangster and carries a wounded peasant on his back; Szu-lung seizes a rifle. They go off. Enter Tsou, interpreter for the Japanese troops. Enter Kuroda, the Japanese colonel, with his troops.*)

Tsou: Reporting! No New Fourth Army men here, nor their wounded.

Kuroda: Go find the "Loyal and Just National Salvation

Army." Order them to catch all the sick and wounded New Fourth Army men.

Tsou: Yes, sir.

Kuroda: Get going!

(*Curtain*)

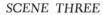

SCENE THREE

COLLABORATION

Three days later. Headquarters of the puppet "Loyal and Just National Salvation Army."

(*As the curtain rises, Tiao and Tsou are conferring in whispers.*)

Tiao: I'm sure there'll be no problem. This bandit chief is in a fix, caught between the New Fourth Army and the Imperial Army. If he wants to have a good time, wining and dining, he'll have to attach himself to the Imperial Army.

Tsou: Attach himself to the Imperial Army? I don't think this Commander Hu has made up his mind to that yet. In his gang, what he says still goes.

Tiao: What he says goes? In a little while, it'll be what I say goes.

Tsou: You're really smart!

(*Enter Liu.*)

Liu: Reporting! The commander is here.

Tiao: Good.

(*Enter Hu, arrogant and fierce.*)

Hu (*sings "hsi pi san pan"*):
In troubled times heroes spring up everywhere,
Any man with a few guns can be a chief;

I get along by keeping in with three sides:
Chiang Kai-shek, the Japanese and secret societies.

Tiao: Let me introduce you. This is Hu Chuan-kuei, commander of the newly reorganized "Loyal and Just National Salvation Army." Commander, this is Mr. Tsou
Yin-sheng, interpreter for Colonel Kuroda of the Japanese Imperial Army.

Hu: Fine. Sit down, sit down.

(Hu shakes hands with Tsou nonchalantly.)

Tiao: Commander, Mr. Tsou has come with a proposal
from the Imperial Army.

Hu: Well, out with it.

Tsou: Commander Hu, last time Chief-of-Staff Tiao and
I agreed that in this mopping-up campaign we'd cooperate in attacking the New Fourth Army. But we
failed to wipe them out. The Imperial Army is not at
all pleased with you.

Hu: So what? The New Fourth Army men have legs and
they keep on the move. If the Imperial Army can't
catch up with them, how should I? Frankly, I'm not
such a fool as to strike an egg on a rock. In this force,
I'm the boss.

Tsou: It's true you are the boss in this force, but the
Imperial Army wants to be your boss.

Tiao: Commander, Colonel Kuroda wanted to destroy our
troops. We should thank Mr. Tsou for helping us out.

Hu: Helping us out? What's the use of fine talk? What
our troops need is money, guns and ammunition.

Tiao: They've got all that ready for us.

Tsou: If we come to terms, the Imperial Army will station
you in Shachiapang.

Tiao: That's a rich district, commander, with plenty of
fish and rice.

Hu: Old Tiao, Shachiapang is a Communist-controlled
area. And the New Fourth Army can make things hot
for us there.

Tsou: So can the Imperial Army, commander.

Tiao: Whoever suckles me is my mother, commander. With the Imperial Army to back us up, let's have a go at the Communists! Have you got the guts?

Hu: All right. That's settled then. (*Shakes hands with Tsou.*)

Tsou: But there's a small condition.

Hu (*to Tiao, displeased*): Why so many conditions?

Tsou: The New Fourth Army has a number of sick and wounded soldiers hidden in Shachiapang. The Imperial Army wants Commander Hu to capture them without fail.

Tiao: That's easy. I'll see to it.

Hu: Since we are fighting the Communists together, that's nothing. Orderly!

(*Liu and Hsiao-san enter.*)

Liu and Hsiao-san: Here, sir.

Hu: Pass on my orders: March into Shachiapang this afternoon.

Liu and Hsiao-san: Yes, sir. (*Go off.*)

Tiao: Well, commander, now you've attached yourself to Chiang Kai-shek in the open and to the Japanese in secret. You can take advantage of both and save the nation by a devious path.* You're really a hero of our time.

Hu: Open or secret, this is all thanks to you, the go-between. And you'll be going back to your old home. You can restore your family fortune and bring glory to

---

* This refers to the dastardly practice of capitulating to Japan and fighting communism followed by the Kuomintang reactionaries during the War of Resistance Against Japan. The Kuomintang reactionaries directed part of their troops and government officials to surrender to the Japanese invaders and then, as puppet troops and officials, to join the Japanese troops in attacking the Liberated Areas, which were under the leadership of the Communist Party of China. This was what they cunningly named "saving the nation by a devious path."

your ancestors. I may be a dragon here, but I'll be no match for you, a snake in its old haunts.

Tsou: You're both doing all right.

Tsou, Hu and Tiao: Ha, ha, ha. . . .

(Curtain)

≍

SCENE FOUR

A BATTLE OF WITS

After a three-day "mopping-up" raid on the market town of Shachiapang, the Japanese troops have left. The Spring Tea-house by the roadside near the wharf. A table and two stools on either side of the stage. The Japanese troops have smashed some of the tables, stools and crockery and knocked the awning askew. Some broken bricks and tiles on the ground, among them the shop sign of the Spring Tea-house.

(As the curtain rises, enter Sister Ah-ching, helping the old and guiding the young.)

Sister Ah-ching: Mind your step.

Old Man: Thank you, Sister Ah-ching, for all your help on the way.

Sister Ah-ching: It was nothing, the least I should do.

Old Man: What a wreck they've made of the place!

(Another group of peasants enter.)

Peasants: Sister Ah-ching!

Sister Ah-ching: So you're back.

Peasants: Yes.

Old Man: Let's help clean the place up.

Sister Ah-ching: Don't bother. I can do it myself.

(Sister Ah-ching picks up the shop sign and puts it on a table. The others set the tables and stools to rights, remove the broken crockery, bricks and tiles and pitch up the awning.)

Young Woman: Sister Ah-ching, I must be going on home.
Old Man: Sister Ah-ching, we have to go, too.
Sister Ah-ching: Be careful, don't fall.
Old Woman: We're also going.
Sister Ah-ching *(to a young girl)*: Give your mother a hand, won't you?

(The peasants go off.)
(Sister Ah-ching dusts the shop sign, holds it up for the audience to see the inscription and hangs it up, and then opens the cupboard for tea-sets.)

Sister Ah-ching *(sings "hsi pi yao pan")*:
   The enemy raids lasted three whole days,
   Bloodstains remain on broken walls.
   All our neighbours who fled are coming back,
   I must send a boat to fetch our wounded comrades.

(Aunt Sha and Szu-lung enter.)

Aunt Sha and Szu-lung: Sister Ah-ching!
Aunt Sha: I see you're back.
Sister Ah-ching: Yes, I'm back.
Szu-lung: Now that the Japanese have gone, we should bring the wounded comrades back.
Sister Ah-ching: Right, Szu-lung. Let's go straight away.
Szu-lung: Let's go.

(Voice offstage: "Hu Chuan-kuei's troops will soon enter the town!")
(People run in and tell Sister Ah-ching: "Hu Chuan-kuei is coming!" They hurry off.)
(Chao and Fu-ken enter.)

Chao: Sister Ah-ching, Hu Chuan-kuei's troops will be here very soon.

Sister Ah-ching: Hu Chuan-kuei, eh? The Japanese have just left and he comes hot on their heels. How could he arrive so fast? (*To Fu-ken.*) Did you see his men?

Fu-ken: Yes. Scores of them.

Sister Ah-ching: Scores of them?

Fu-ken: They have Kuomintang insignia on their caps and the "Loyal and Just National Salvation Army" on their banner.

Sister Ah-ching (*thinking*): "Loyal and Just National Salvation Army"? . . . And Kuomintang insignia? . . .

Chao: They say Tiao Teh-yi is back, too.

Aunt Sha: Tiao Teh-yi is the son of the bloodsucker Tiao.

Sister Ah-ching (*to Fu-ken*): Go and have another look.

Fu-ken: Right. (*Exit.*)

Sister Ah-ching: Is Hu Chuan-kuei just passing through or has he come to stay? It's not clear. We shouldn't bring back the wounded comrades at this moment. We must find some way to send provisions to them.

Chao: I'll prepare some food.

Szu-lung: I'll get the boat ready.

Sister Ah-ching: Be vigilant!

Chao and Szu-lung: Yes.

(*Szu-lung gives Aunt Sha a hand and they go off, followed by Chao.*)
(*Sister Ah-ching goes into the house.*)
(*Voice offstage: "Halt!"*)
(*A woman cuts across the stage.*)
(*Voice offstage: "Halt!" Enter Hsiao-san in pursuit of a girl holding a bundle.*)

Hsiao-san: Halt! We heroes are fighting the Japanese to save the country and we've driven the devils away for you. You ought to give us something in appreciation!

(*Hsiao-san snatches the girl's bundle.*)

Girl: What right have you to grab my things?

Hsiao-san: Grab things, did you say? Why, I even grab people! (*Pounces on her.*)

Girl (*in the face of danger, shouts for help*):   Sister Ah-ching!

(*Sister Ah-ching rushes out of the house and protects the girl.*)

Sister Ah-ching: Enough, enough. We're all neighbours here, so what's the fuss. Come and sit down. Have a cup of tea.

Hsiao-san: What are you trying to do? Get in my way? . . .

(*Enter Liu.*)

Liu: Tiao Hsiao-san, the commander will be here any minute. What are you doing here?

Sister Ah-ching: Why, it's Old Liu!

Liu (*preening himself*):   Sister Ah-ching, I'm an adjutant now.

Sister Ah-ching: Oh, so you're now an adjutant. Congratulations.

Liu: It's been a long time since I saw you. How are you?

Sister Ah-ching: Very well, thank you.

Liu: We're among friends, Tiao Hsiao-san. What have you been up to?

Sister Ah-ching: That's true. I don't seem to know this brother. We've never met. He's having a little trouble with me here.

Liu: Tiao Hsiao-san, this is Sister Ah-ching. She once saved the commander's life. If he knew you'd kicked up a row here, do you think you could get away with it?

Hsiao-san: How was I to know? Sister Ah-ching, I have eyes, but can't see Mount Tai, while you have the heart of a statesman, big enough to hold a boat. I'm sure you won't let yourself sink to my level.

Sister Ah-ching (*having discovered that they are enemies, acts diplomatically with them*):   That's all right. The first time strangers, the second time acquaintances. I'm not the sort to count on powerful connections to put somebody on the spot behind his back. Isn't that true, Adjutant Liu?

Liu: Sister Ah-ching is an honest sort.

Sister Ah-ching (*to the girl*): Go home now.

Girl: He's taken my bundle.

Sister Ah-ching: Your bundle? He surely doesn't want your bundle. (*To Hsiao-san.*) That was just joking, wasn't it? (*To Liu.*) Well?

Liu: Yes. (*To Hsiao-san.*) Find the right place if you want to joke.

(*Unwilling but helpless, Hsiao-san hands the bundle to Sister Ah-ching.*)

Sister Ah-ching (*hands it to the girl*): Take it and say thanks. Off you go home.

(*Exit the girl.*)

Liu: Tiao Hsiao-san, go and meet the commander and chief-of-staff. Go now!

Hsiao-san: See you later, Sister Ah-ching.

Sister Ah-ching: See you then. Come back later and have a cup of tea.

(*Exit Hsiao-san, glowering and disgruntled.*)

Liu: Sister Ah-ching, he is a cousin of our chief-of-staff. I hope you'll make allowances for him.

Sister Ah-ching: That's all right. Please sit down, Adjutant Liu. When the water boils I'll make you some tea. You're a rare guest. It's not often we have such company in our small teahouse.

(*Sister Ah-ching is about to go into the house when Liu calls her back.*)

Liu: Don't go to any trouble, Sister Ah-ching. I was sent in advance to have a look around. The commander will soon be here himself.

Sister Ah-ching: The commander?

Liu: Well, I mean Old Hu!

Sister Ah-ching: Ah, Old Hu is a commander now?

Liu: That's right. He's got lots of men and guns too. Quite different from what he was when he came here last. He's a big shot now! Times change. Bird guns have been replaced by artillery!

Sister Ah-ching: I see (*Makes up her mind to find things out.*) Isn't that grand! Adjutant Liu, how time flies! You've been away quite some time. (*Watches Liu while wiping the table.*)

Liu: Yes, quite a while.

Sister Ah-ching (*sounding out Liu*):   You'll stay longer this time, won't you?

Liu: This time we've come to stay.

Sister Ah-ching: . . . I see. (*Having found out they are to stay, simulates welcome.*) That'll be fine.

Liu: We'll be stationed in Shachiapang for good. Our headquarters will be housed in Chief-of-Staff Tiao's home. We've sent men to fix it up. The commander said he would drop in at your tea-house first.

(*Footsteps offstage.*)

Liu: The commander has come.

(*Liu hurries to meet the newcomers. Sister Ah-ching considers how to deal with them.*)
(*Hu, Tiao and Hsiao-san enter. Four puppet soldiers walk past the slope.*)

Hu: Well, Sister Ah-ching!

(*Hu takes off his cloak. Liu takes it and goes off.*)

Sister Ah-ching (*turns to greet him*):   I hear you're a commander now. Congratulations!

Hu: How are you?

Sister Ah-ching: Very well, thank you. What good wind blows you back?

Hu: How's business? You must be doing well.

Sister Ah-ching: Not too bad, it all due to your kindness.

Hu: Ha, ha, ha. . . .

Sister Ah-ching: Please take a seat, Commander Hu.

Hu: Thanks. Let me introduce you. This is my chief-of-staff, Tiao Teh-yi, son of the late honourable Mr. Tiao, the wealthiest man in town.

(Tiao scrutinizes Sister Ah-ching.)

Sister Ah-ching (*senses that Tiao is a treacherous and cunning foe and so acts diplomatically*):   Chief-of-staff, I have the honour of borrowing a piece of your worthy land to settle on and make a living. You are a big tree with deep roots. I'm looking forward to your help.

Hu: Yes, indeed, you must help her.

Tiao: You're being too polite.

(Tiao takes off his cloak. Hsiao-san takes it and goes off.)

Sister Ah-ching: Please sit down, chief-of-staff.

Hu: Where's your husband?

Sister Ah-ching: That wretch! We quarrelled and he cleared out.

Hu: He's such a restless fellow, he can't sit quietly at home. Where did he go?

Sister Ah-ching: Someone saw him trading in Shanghai. He said he wouldn't come back and see me till he'd made something of himself.

Hu: That's it! A real man must have such ambitions.

Sister Ah-ching: How can you stick up for him!

Hu: Sister Ah-ching, last time I escaped death in a great calamity, I owe my present position to that. I ought to really thank you.

Sister Ah-ching: It's all because you were born under a lucky star. Look, here I chatter without offering you two gentlemen any tea. Sit down a while. I'll get you some tea. (*Goes into the house.*)

Tiao: You seem to know her very well, commander. Who is she?

Hu: You mean Sister Ah-ching?
   (Sings "hsi pi erh liu")
   When I started raising troops,
   I had barely a dozen men, half a dozen rifles.
   (Changes to "liu shui")
   Pursued by the Imperial Army, I fled hurry-scurry.
   As luck would have it, Sister Ah-ching hid me in a water vat;
   She went on serving the customers without turning a hair.

   (Sister Ah-ching, kettle and cups in hand, listens carefully. Noticing that the enemies have seen her, she comes out of the house as if nothing happened.)

Hu *(continues singing)*:
   The Japanese were fooled and went away,
   And so I escaped a great calamity. (Turns to Sister Ah-ching.)
   I shall always be grateful to you for saving my life.
   As a believer in brotherhood,
   I must repay you some day.

Sister Ah-ching *(deliberately humbles herself before the enemies)*:   Why make so much of a small thing, Commander Hu? The idea just came to me on the spur of the moment. You know, after it was all over, I was really scared.

   (While pouring tea, Sister Ah-ching scrutinizes them.)

Sister Ah-ching: Have some tea, chief-of-staff. *(Suddenly remembers.)* I forgot to bring cigarettes. I'll get some. *(Goes into the house.)*

Tiao *(watching her as she goes away)*:   Commander, I was born here, but I never saw this woman before.

Hu: She and her husband came here after the fighting started in Shanghai.* You were studying in Japan then.

---

* On August 13, 1937, the Japanese aggressors launched a major attack on Shanghai.

Of course you don't know her.

Tiao: She's no simple creature.

Hu: What's that, have you suspicions about her?

Tiao: Oh, no, no. Not if she's the commander's benefactor.

Hu: Come, come, the same Old Tiao.

Tiao: Ha, ha, ha!

(Sister Ah-ching comes out of the house bringing cigarettes, a box of matches and a kettle.)

Sister Ah-ching: Chief-of-staff, have one of these poor cigarettes.

(Tiao takes a cigarette that Sister Ah-ching offers him. As Sister Ah-ching is about to light it, he declines and lights it with his lighter.)

Sister Ah-ching: Commander Hu, please have a cigarette.

(Hu takes a cigarette. Sister Ah-ching lights it.)

Tiao (*watching Sister Ah-ching from behind her, sings "fan hsi pi yao pan"*):
This woman is quite out of the ordinary.

Sister Ah-ching (*continues the singing*):
What dirty tricks is Tiao Teh-yi up to?

Hu (*sings "hsi pi yao pan"*):
This fellow Tiao simply gives me no face.

Sister Ah-ching (*continues the singing*):
This silly fool is useful for keeping off the wind.

Tiao (*thinks a while, then opens his cigarette-case and offers Sister Ah-ching a cigarette*): Have a smoke?

(Sister Ah-ching declines with a wave of her hand.)

Hu: What's the idea? She doesn't smoke.

Tiao (*continues the singing*):
She's neither humble nor pushy.

Sister Ah-ching (*sings "hsi pi liu shui"*):
He's both sinister and crafty.

Hu (*sings "hsi pi yao pan"*):
    What can Tiao Teh-yi be driving at?
Sister Ah-ching (*sings "hsi pi liu shui"*):
    *Whom are they working for, Chiang or Wang?**
Tiao (*sings "hsi pi yao pan"*):
    I'll sound her out in a roundabout way.
Sister Ah-ching (*continues the singing*):
    I must watch his every move and not fall into his trap.

(*Sister Ah-ching turns to enter the house. Tiao calls after her.*)

Tiao: Sister Ah-ching!
    (*Sings "hsi pi liu shui"*)
    I've just heard about you from the commander,
    Sister Ah-ching, you are out of the common run.
    I admire your coolness, cleverness
    And the courage you had to fool the Japanese;
    Unless you are truly patriotic,
    You wouldn't have risked your life for another without fear.
Sister Ah-ching (*continues the singing*):
    Please don't praise me so, chief-of-staff,
    Risking my life for another is a compliment I hardly deserve.
    I keep a tea-house and hope for good business,
    So I must observe the code of the brotherhood;
    The commander was a frequent customer,
    A big tree, and I wanted to enjoy its shade.
    What's more, he was born lucky
    So that catastrophe turned into fortune.
Tiao (*continues the singing*):
    The New Fourth Army stayed here a long time,
    That's a big tree with fine shade,
    You had plenty of dealings with them,

---

* Chiang Kai-shek was then the ringleader of the capitulationists hiding in the anti-Japanese ranks, while Wang Ching-wei, an arch traitor, openly surrendered to the Japanese.

152

I'm sure you served them with special care.
Sister Ah-ching (*continues the singing*):
 My stove is built for business,
 My kettle doesn't ask where the water comes from,
 My tables are used by travellers from everywhere;
 Whoever comes here is a customer
 And I have to be pleasant to him;
 I greet all comers with a smile,
 And once out of sight, out of mind.
 When the customer leaves, the tea grows cold—

(*Sister Ah-ching throws out the tea remaining in Tiao's cup and Tiao is taken aback.*)

Sister Ah-ching (*continues singing*):
 There is no question of giving anyone special care.
Hu: Ha, ha, ha. . . .
Tiao: Ha, ha, ha. . . . Sister Ah-ching is just the right person to run a tea-house. However much you may say, nothing ever leaks out. My compliments to you!
Sister Ah-ching: What does he mean, Commander Hu?
Hu: He's like that, a queer bird. Never mind what he says, Sister Ah-ching.
Sister Ah-ching: It's all right with me. (*Takes the kettle and goes into the house.*)
Hu: Old Tiao, Sister Ah-ching once saved my life. When it comes to the question of face, we must let things ride easy. If you kept bombarding her with questions like that, how can I save face? What are you up to, anyway?
Tiao: Don't misunderstand, commander. She's a shrewd, fearless and level-headed woman. Since we intend to stay on here to save the country by a devious path, she could be very useful to us. But we still don't know whether she's for us or not.
Hu: Sister Ah-ching? She's for us.
Tiao: Then let's ask her for the whereabouts of the New

Fourth Army and its wounded. She's bound to know.
But she might not say, even though she knows.

Hu: I'll handle it. You'd only get snubbed.

Tiao: That's true. You have great influence with her.

Hu: Ha, ha, ha. . . .

(*Sister Ah-ching warily but calmly comes out of the house with a plate of melon-seeds.*)

Sister Ah-ching: Commander Hu, chief-of-staff, try some melon-seeds.

Hu: Thanks. . . .   (*Drinks tea.*)

Sister Ah-ching: . . . . The full flavour of the tea is coming out now.

Hu: That's right. The full flavour. Sister Ah-ching, there's something I'd like to ask you.

Sister Ah-ching: Well, if it's something I know. . . .

Hu: It's about the New Fourth Army. . . .

Sister Ah-ching: The New Fourth Army? Oh, of course.
    (*Sings "hsi pi yao pan"*)
    You don't have to ask, commander,
    Many New Fourth Army men were stationed here.

Hu: Stationed here, eh?

Sister Ah-ching: Yes.

Hu: Any wounded?

Sister Ah-ching: Yes.
    (*Continues, singing "hsi pi liu shui"*)
    There were a few wounded men,
    Some light cases, some serious.

Hu: Where did they stay?

Sister Ah-ching (*continues singing*):
    Here in our town,
    Billeted in each household;
    They also came to my small tea-house
    To drink tea, fetch hot water or have a wash.

Hu (*to Tiao*):   Well?

Tiao: Where are they now?

Sister Ah-ching: Now?
(*Continues singing*)
Once the order came to muster
They all set out in mighty formation.
Hu: The wounded, too?
Sister Ah-ching: The wounded?
(*Continues, singing "hsi pi san pan"*)
The wounded, too, vanished without a trace,
Only heaven knows where to find them.
Tiao: All gone?
Sister Ah-ching: All gone. If they hadn't they would surely
have been found by the Japanese who combed the town
for three whole days in a "mopping-up" operation.
Tiao: The Japanese don't know this place, they blunder
blindly. Nothing is easier than to hide a few men in a
big place like Shachiapang. Take the case of Commander Hu. Didn't you hide him in your water vat
right under the noses of the Japanese?
Sister Ah-ching: Oh, I suppose Chief-of-Staff Tiao means
that I am hiding the wounded men of the New Fourth
Army. Really, when you listen to someone talk, you must
judge by his tone; when you listen to drums and gongs,
you must catch the rhythm. If that's the case, I shouldn't
have saved you, Commander Hu, for it's become a
handle for gossip.
Hu: Now, Sister Ah-ching, don't. . . .
Sister Ah-ching: No. . . .
Hu: Oh, don't. . . .
Sister Ah-ching: No, no, no! Today, before your eyes,
Commander Hu, have your men search my small tea-
house inside and out. Otherwise I'll be under suspicion
and hard put to it. (*Throws the duster on a table, flicks*
her apron, and sits down with her arms folded, head
erect and looking angry to hit back at the enemy.)
Hu: Now see what you've done, Old Tiao.
Tiao: I was only joking. Why take it so seriously?
Hu: That's right, he was only joking.

Sister Ah-ching: How am I to bear the consequences of such jokes, Commander Hu? (*Goes into the house.*)

Tiao (*watches the marshes on the other side of the lake, then turns to Hu*): Commander, the wounded men of the New Fourth Army haven't gone far. They're about.

Hu: Where are they?

Tiao: Look! (*Points to the marshes.*) Most likely they are in the reed marshes there.

Hu: In the reed marshes? (*Suddenly enlightened.*) Right. Orderly!

(*Liu and Hsiao-san enter.*)

Hu: Go and search the reed marshes!

Tiao: Hold on a minute. We can't make the search, commander. You are not a local man, you're not familiar with the terrain. The marsh area is large and complicated. If we go in blindly, it would be like fishing a needle out of the ocean. Besides, they are hidden while we're in the open. They'd just pick us off. If we want to do the job for the Imperial Army, that's no way to go about it. We'd be the losers.

Hu: What do you suggest then?

Tiao: I'll make them come out themselves.

Hu: You're raving in broad daylight. Why should they come out by themselves?

Tiao: I can make them do it. Orderly!

Liu and Hsiao-san: Here!

Tiao: Summon all people to the Spring Tea-house. I'll give them a talk.

Liu and Hsiao-san: Yes, sir! (*Go off.*)

Hu: Why are you sending for them?

Tiao: I want them to go to Lake Yangcheng to catch fish and crabs.

Hu: Catch fish and crabs? What's the big idea?

Tiao: We'll put some of our men in civilian clothes in every boat. Seeing people fishing in the lake, the New

Fourth Army men will think the coast is clear and they'll come out. Then we'll fire at them from all boats. And then. . . .

Hu: You're marvellous, Old Tiao! Ha, ha, ha. . . .

(*Offstage, people's voices draw nearer. Liu and Hsiao-san enter.*)

Liu and Hsiao-san: Reporting! All present.
Tiao: Good, I'll talk to them.

(*Voices of protest offstage.*)

Liu and Hsiao-san: Stand in order! . . . Hey, stand in order!
Hsiao-san: The chief-of-staff is going to speak to you.
Tiao: Fellow countrymen! We are the "Loyal and Just National Salvation Army," a unit fighting against the Japanese. Now, we've come here. We know you're too poor to give us much of a welcome. That's not your fault. But we'd like you to catch some fish and crabs in the lake. We'll pay you the market price.

(*Voices of protest offstage. Fu-ken: "No, officer! We'd be killed if we ran into Japanese motorboats!" . . . .*)

Hsiao-san: Quiet, there!
Tiao: Don't worry. We'll put three of our men in each boat to protect you.

(*Voices of protest offstage: "No, we're not going! We don't dare go!" . . . .*)

Hu: Damn it! Who dares to refuse? I'll shoot anyone who refuses to go!

(*Hu, Tiao, Liu and Hsiao-san go off.*)
(*Sister Ah-ching hurries out of the house.*)

Sister Ah-ching (*sings "hsi pi san pan"*):
    Tiao Teh-yi, that dirty scoundrel
    Poisonous snake, vicious wolf!

He is setting a trap
And our comrades may be fooled.
Once the fishing boats row out,
There's going to be trouble.

(*Voices of protest offstage.*)

Sister Ah-ching (*continues singing*):
If our people refuse to go,
There will be bloodshed and death;
How I wish I had wings to fly to the marshes!
I'm burning to find a way out.

(*Hsiao-san shouts offstage:* "You won't go? Then I'll
shoot!")

Sister Ah-ching: Shoot?
(*Sings "hsi pi liu shui"*)
If a shot rings out here,
It'll be a warning to the marshes;
Knowing something has happened in the town,
Our comrades will hide deep in the reeds. (*Leans
forward to watch, notices a broken brick and a straw
hat and hits upon an idea.*)
Steady on, and be calm,
A trick will get the enemy to open fire.

(*Sister Ah-ching picks up the broken brick at the foot
of the wall, covers it with the straw hat and hurls them
into the lake, then hurries into the house.*)
(*Hsiao-san runs in.*)

Hsiao-san: Someone's jumped into the water!

(*Hu and Liu rush in.*)
(*Liu and Hu open fire. Hearing the shots, Tiao rushes
in.*)

Tiao: Stop! . . . Good Heavens! Stop shooting!

(*Sister Ah-ching approaches the threshold to watch.*)

Hu: Why?

Tiao: Do you expect the New Fourth Army men to come out after hearing all this firing?

Hu: Why didn't you say it sooner? Tiao Hsiao-san!

Hsiao-san: Here!

Hu: Arrest those who stirred up the trouble!

Tiao: Adjutant Liu!

Liu: Here!

Tiao: Detain all the boats! I'll starve them out.

(*Hu and Tiao go off, followed by Liu and Hsiao-san.*)
(*Sister Ah-ching comes out of the door, deep in thought, deliberating what should be the next step in the fight. A dramatic pose.*)

(*Curtain*)

≍

SCENE FIVE

HOLDING OUT

Immediately after the previous scene. In the marshes. The sky is dark, a storm is brewing.

(*As the curtain rises, Kuo and some soldiers are gazing towards Shachiapang. Enter a soldier.*)

Soldier: Reporting! No new enemy movements after the shots.

Kuo: Keep on watching in the direction of Shachiapang.

Soldier: Right. (*Exit.*)

Kuo: Comrades, mend the reed-sheds first and move the seriously wounded in. Tell Platoon Leader Yeh I'm going to the outpost to have a look.

All: Right!

(*Exit Kuo.*)

Lin: Comrades! What was that shooting from Shachiapang?

A Soldier: It means there are enemy troops there, either
Japanese or traitors.

Hsiao-hu: Then our people there are in for a hard time
again.

Chang: If the enemy is still in Shachiapang, we'll have to
stay where we are for the time being. But we've run
out of food and medicine. This is quite a problem.

(*Kuo enters, observes the mood of the soldiers.*)

Hsiao-hu: Why did we come here anyway? Much better
if we'd stayed in Shachiapang to fight the enemy!

Other Soldiers: That's right.

Squad Leader: That would have been downright fool-
hardy. If we want to fight, we'll have to wait for orders.
Hasn't the instructor told us to mend reed-sheds?
Come on, let's do that first.

All: Let's go and mend the reed-sheds. (*Go off.*)

(*Kuo gazes at the soldiers going off, turns back, lost in
thought.*)

Kuo (*sings "erh huang tao pan"*):
Shots from the opposite shore ring through the marshes.
(*Changes to "hui lung"*)
*For several days, we've been watching the changing
situation*
And trying to figure out what's going on;
The tide in my heart rises and falls like the Yangtze.
(*Changes to "man san yen"*)
In the distance, Shachiapang is lost in mist and clouds.
Why are there no boats sailing the lake?
Why hasn't Sister Ah-ching come to see us?
There seems to be much behind all this.
Chiang Kai-shek, Wang Ching-wei and the Japanese
Have been making secret deals for a long time.
The people of Shachiapang are bound to face disaster.

(*Changes to "kuai san yen"*)
*Our fighters are ready to risk leaving the marshes to kill
the enemy,
One by one they've expressed their resolve to fight.
Their feelings are easy to understand—
Class hatred and national wrath burn in their hearts.
I must try to curb their impatience,
Get them to think of the overall situation,
Watch the enemy moves and wait for orders,
Gripping tight their guns.*
(*Changes to "yuan pan"*)
*Chairman Mao and the Party Central Committee guide
us forward;
Encouraged, we are keeping up the fight around this
lake town.
We must be patient and hold out among the reeds,*
(*Changes to "tuo pan"*)
*Take the initiative and be flexible,
So we can defeat a stronger foe.
Rivers, lakes and estuaries are good battlegrounds,
This region south of the Yangtze is a natural granary.
Do not say the marshes are locked in dense mist and
clouds,
Nothing can block out the radiance of* (*changes to free
rhythm*) *the red sun.*

(*Hsiao-hu shouts offstage: "Instructor!" Runs in.*)

Hsiao-hu: Young Wang has fainted!

(*Enter Squad Leader, carrying Wang on his back, with
Yeh, Ling and other soldiers following.*)

All: Young Wang! Young Wang. . . .
Kuo: Little Ling, quick, take a look at his wound and see
if it's any worse.
Ling: Instructor, I've just looked at it. It's a little worse
but not too serious. His trouble is a high fever from
malaria, and he's weak from hunger.

Kuo: Has he had any medicine?

Ling: We've run out of quinine.

Kuo: How are the seriously wounded?

Ling: A little worse. And the medicine is running out.

Yeh: Instructor, medicine and food are a big problem.

Kuo: Well, we must find a way out.

All: Young Wang, do you feel any better?

Wang: Look, comrades, there's nothing wrong with me. (*Tries to walk a few steps, staggering.*)

Squad Leader: Young Wang, you're hungry. I've a rice cake here. Take it.

Wang: No!

All: Eat it, Young Wang.

Wang (*deeply moved*): Comrades, our instructor has given his ration to the badly wounded. You take it, instructor!

Kuo: Young Wang! (*Waves it away and, with warm class feelings, urges Wang to eat.*) Comrades, though medicine and food are a big problem, I'm sure the local Party organization will try in every way to help us, and so will the people here. But it seems that right now the Party and the people have difficulties, so they can't come to our help straight away. What are we to do? We are fighters trained in the old Red Army tradition. Are we to be daunted by a little hardship?

All: No, we're not!

Squad Leader: On the Long March our Red Army men climbed snow-capped mountains and crossed swamps, overcoming every kind of difficulty. We can hold out just as they did.

Other Soldiers: That's the spirit.

Kuo: Right!

(*Chug of a motorboat. Enter a soldier.*)

Soldier: Reporting! We've spotted a motorboat on the lake.

Kuo: Oh! Keep it under observation!

(*Exit the soldier.*)

Kuo: Platoon Leader Yeh, take two comrades with you to guard the outpost.

Yeh: Right! Come with me!

(*Yeh, Chang and a soldier go off.*)

Kuo: You two, go and take care of the seriously wounded.

Squad Leader and Ling: Right! (*Go off.*)

Kuo: Comrades!

All: Here!

Kuo: Get ready for battle!

All: Right.

(*All gaze in the direction of the motorboat. The sound of its engine grows fainter.*)
(*Yeh, Chang and a soldier enter.*)

Yeh: Instructor! The motorboat's heading for Shachiapang.

Kuo: Judging from what's happened, the Japanese must have withdrawn. A moment ago there were pistol shots in Shachiapang. Now a motorboat on the lake. . . .

Yeh: Only the Japanese have motorboats.

Kuo: My idea is to send two comrades across the lake to scout.

Yeh: Right!

All: Let me go! I'll go!

Kuo: Lin Ta-ken and Chang Sung-tao, you two take a boat and row over. Go to see Sha Szu-lung or Ah-fu. Don't call on Sister Ah-ching, she must be in a tough spot herself. After you get information about the enemy, try to find some medicinal herbs. Be careful when you enter the town and don't let anybody spot you on your way back.
(*Sings "hsi pi erh liu"*)
The two of you row to the opposite shore in disguise,
Moor your boat under a tree west of the town.
Get some herbs for the sick and wounded,

And come back with information about the enemy,
All the comrades have full confidence in your success,
And look forward to the triumphant return of our scouts.
(Changes to "liu shui")
Once we are clear about the enemy situation,
Our judgment will be sound.
Then the initiative will be in our hands;
We'll be free to advance, withdraw, attack or take cover,
And tackle the enemy with flexibility.
Our wounds healed, we'll rejoin our units and ask for action,
And swing eastwards to wipe out the enemy forces.
With battle drums rumbling and the red flag unfurled,
We'll recapture the region south of the Yangtze at one stroke.

Lin and Chang: We'll accomplish our mission without fail.

Kuo: Go and get ready.

Lin and Chang: Right!

(Lin and Chang go off.)
(Squad Leader shouts offstage: "Instructor!" Some underground stems of reeds and seeds of a wild water plant in hand, he runs in. Ling and a soldier follow.)

Squad Leader: Look, instructor! Underground stems of reeds and these water plants seeds, aren't they edible?

Kuo: Yes, they are! Comrades, when all of us rack our brains to find ways and means we can overcome difficulties, however great! Chairman Mao has taught us: "Frequently a favourable situation recurs and the intiative is regained as a result of 'holding out a little longer.'" Comrades!
(Sings "hsi pi san pan")
No difficulties can daunt heroes,
The Red Army's tradition is passed on from generation to generation.

Chairman Mao's teachings are imprinted in our minds,
Persevering in the struggle, we will seize victory tomor-
row.
Comrades! (*Jumps onto an earthen terrace.*) These
marshes are the front, our battlefield. We must wait for
orders from above, and hold out till victory.

All: Yes, we must wait for orders, fear no difficulties and
hold out till victory.

(*A sudden rainstorm.*)

Hsiao-hu: What a big rainstorm!
Kuo (*inspires the soldiers' fighting morale heroically and,*
in powerful tones, sings "suo na hsi pi tao pan") :
We must be like the pine on the summit of Mount Tai!

(*Lightning and thunder. Kuo jumps off the earthen ter-*
race and joins the soldiers in fighting against the storm.)

All (*sing in chorus while dancing*):
We must be like the pine on the summit of Mount Tai,
Standing tall and proud against the sky.
No hurricane can blow it down,
No thunderbolt can split it asunder;
The fiery summer sun cannot wither it,
It grows greener and fresher in winter's snow and ice.
That pine, scarred and ravaged, has stood the harshest
trials
And become stronger, tougher and more vigorous than
ever,
Its branches as of iron, its trunk as of bronze.
Everyone admires its noble qualities.
Let us eighteen sick and wounded soldiers
Stand as firm as eighteen pines!

(*The soldiers stand in the teeth of the storm, steady and*
firm, forming a tableau of heroes.)

(*Curtain*)

SCENE SIX

A RESCUE PLAN

The next day. The Spring Tea-house. A storm has just passed, but the sky is still dark and louring.

(*As the curtain rises, there is nobody outside the house. The clatter of mah-jong tiles being shuffled can be heard indoors now and then.*)
(*Sister Ah-ching comes out of the house.*)
(*Enter a young man.*)

Young Man: Sister Ah-ching, were you looking for me?
Sister Ah-ching: Are Town Head Chao and Szu-lung back yet?
Young Man: I haven't seen them.
Sister Ah-ching: If Szu-lung is back, ask him to come here.
Young Man: All right. (*Exit.*)

(*Enter Liu.*)

Sister Ah-ching: Adjutant Liu.
Liu: Sister Ah-ching, is Chief-of-Staff Tiao inside?
Sister Ah-ching: Yes, he's there watching the game.
Liu: I see.

(*Liu walks straight inside. After thinking for a moment, Sister Ah-ching follows him briskly.*)
(*Liu and Tiao come out of the house.*)

Tiao: What is it?
Liu: The interpreter, Mr. Tsou, is looking for you.
Tiao: Oh!
Liu: The Imperial Army has phoned to ask about the sick and wounded of the New Fourth Army.
Tiao: What slave-drivers! All those people we've seized say they know nothing. What a hard job it is to find those sick and wounded men!

Liu: I think that fellow Wang Fu-ken. . . .

Tiao: Wang Fu-ken?

Liu: The one who kicked up the row the other day.

Tiao: That's right! Let's work him over.

Liu: You'd better hurry. The interpreter, Mr. Tsou, is leaving right away. The motorboat is waiting for him.

Tiao: Hey, you stay here and keep your eyes open. I'll be right back.

Liu: Chief-of-staff, I'd better keep out of the way. The commander has kept losing his temper with me these past few days. And he's having no luck at mah-jong today, so he'll make things hot for me again. . . .

Tiao: You think it's you he's angry at? I know better. You can count on me!

Liu (*obsequiously*): Right! I'm at your service, chief-of-staff!

Tiao: Go inside and see if he wants anything.

Liu: Yes, sir.

(*Exit Tiao. Liu goes inside.*)
(*Sister Ah-ching comes out and scans the sky and the lake, deep in thought.*)

Sister Ah-ching: Tiao Teh-yi keeps running about, and Hu Chuan-kuei is playing mah-jong inside. I can't go out or leave the place. Old Chao and Szu-lung took food to the comrades and aren't back yet. This is the fifth day our comrades have been in the marshes. What can I do to get them out of danger?
(*Engrossed in thought, sings "erh huang man san yen"*)
The wind is howling, dark clouds hang low in the sky,
And I'm restless with anxiety.
Our men have run out of food and medicine, and we've lost touch;
How they have suffered in the marshes in the violent storm!
(*Changes to "kuai san yen"*)
The eighteen men are precious to the revolution,

They are our flesh and blood.
As a liaison worker I now have a heavy task,
Secretary Cheng stressed this again and again on parting.
In the face of danger, how can I be at a loss
After all these years of nurturing by the Party!
Last night Town Head Chao and Szu-lung took food to
the marshes,
What can be keeping them so long?
I should have gone myself to see our comrades,
But I'm spied on here and can't leave;
Tiao Teh-yi has posted guards and seized the boats.
What's to be done? What can be done?
What a trying situation! . . .

(*The strains of "The East Is Red" seem to ring in her ears and she is filled with confidence.*)

Sister Ah-ching (*continues singing*):
Chairman Mao!
With your teachings and the wisdom of the masses,
I can certainly meet this test and beat the enemy.

(*Enter Aunt Sha with Szu-lung.*)

Szu-lung and Aunt Sha: Sister Ah-ching.

Sister Ah-ching (*startled*): Szu-lung, so you're back. Did you get the food to them?

Szu-lung: No. Town Head Chao and I hadn't rowed far last night when we were spotted by the enemy. We jumped into the water and got away, but they seized our boat.

Sister Ah-ching: Where's Town Head Chao?

Szu-lung: In bed with a high fever. Last night when we got into the water, he had an attack of malaria. And he has a bad cold. So he sent me to report to you.

Aunt Sha: Sister Ah-ching, what do you think we ought to do?

Sister Ah-ching: We must get hold of a boat somehow and send them some food.

Szu-lung: Suppose I try to make off with a boat to-night. . . .

Sister Ah-ching (*hearing steps approaching, quickly stops Szu-lung; judging from the footsteps it is Liu coming*): Here comes Adjutant Liu. Let Szu-lung pretend to be ill. Then we'll ask him for a boat to send Szu-lung to the county town for treatment.

(*Szu-lung leans over a table as if he were ill. Liu comes out of the house.*)

Sister Ah-ching: Adjutant Liu.

Liu: Sister Ah-ching. (*Sees Szu-lung.*) Hey, who's that?

Sister Ah-ching: Aunt Sha's son.

Liu: What's he doing here?

Sister Ah-ching: He's ill.

Aunt Sha: The lad's sick, Adjutant Liu. We hope you'll lend us a boat to take him to the county town to see a doctor.

Liu: Lend you a boat? Out of the question.

Aunt Sha: Sister Ah-ching, please put in a good word for me.

Sister Ah-ching: Yes, Adjutant Liu, see how sick the lad is! We don't have a doctor here. Please do us this small favour.

Liu: It's not that I don't want to help, Sister Ah-ching, but it's not in my power. There are plenty of boats over there, but they're not to be touched. That's Chief-of-Staff Tiao's order. You'd better let it be, Sister Ah-ching, or you'll find yourself in trouble.

Sister Ah-ching: Poor boy, he's in a bad way.

(*A roving doctor's bell rings offstage. A puppet soldier shouts:*
"Halt! Who goes there?")
(*Cheng replies offstage: "I'm a doctor."*)
(*Sister Ah-ching and Aunt Sha are overjoyed, but look calm.*)

Aunt Sha: Ah! A doctor's come!

Sister Ah-ching: What a piece of luck! He'll be able to cure the boy. (*Calls towards offstage.*) Don't let the doctor go! (*To Liu.*) Adjutant Liu, please let the doctor examine the lad.

Liu: No, it can't be done.

Aunt Sha: Adjutant Liu, since you won't lend us a boat, at least allow the doctor to examine my boy!

Liu: It can't be done!

Sister Ah-ching: But, Adjutant Liu, since the doctor's already here, must we really send him away? Please let him examine the boy!

Liu: You know very well, Sister Ah-ching, that I wouldn't be able to account for this to Chief-of-Staff Tiao. He's given explicit orders that no stranger is to come here.

Sister Ah-ching: Is this so important? Even Commander Hu himself would grant us this small favour, let alone the chief-of-staff.

Liu: Very well, the commander is inside. Please go and ask him.

Sister Ah-ching: Do we have to trouble him about such a small thing?

Liu: But it's not in my power to decide.

(*Hu comes out of the house.*)

Hu: What's the matter?

Liu: Commander! A doctor has come. Sister Ah-ching wants us to let him examine this lad.

Hu: Examine this lad?

Sister Ah-ching: It's like this. The boy is sick, and a doctor happens to be passing by. So I put in a word and suggested that he should examine the lad. Adjutant Liu said you wouldn't mind granting us this favour, but that it would put you in an awkward position if Chief-of-Staff Tiao came to know of it. After that, I didn't dare ask you.

Hu (*to Liu*): If Chief-of-Staff Tiao breaks wind, does it

smell sweet? Don't treat an utterly worthless thing like an order from on high!

Sister Ah-ching: Actually, Adjutant Liu's not to blame. He told me you were a generous, kind-hearted man. I was afraid that it might be unpleasant for you, commander, if Chief-of-Staff Tiao were to take the matter seriously. So, we'd better let the doctor. . . .

Hu: Examine the lad!

Liu: Yes, sir! (*Towards offstage.*) Hey! Please come over here, doctor!

Sister Ah-ching: Thank you, commander, on behalf of the boy.

Aunt Sha: Thank you, commander.

(*Enter Cheng.*)

Sister Ah-ching and Aunt Sha: Doctor!

Cheng: How are you all?

Sister Ah-ching and Aunt Sha: Very well, thank you.

Aunt Sha: Please come here and feel his pulse, doctor.

Cheng: All right.

(*Cheng comes face to face with Hu. Hu studies him. Cheng behaves with great composure.*)

Sister Ah-ching (*to divert Hu's attention*):   How's your luck now, Commander Hu?

Hu: Terrible. I didn't win a single game in four rounds. That's why I came out to take a walk.

Sister Ah-ching: After this rest, you'll be able to turn the tables on them. When you go back, I'm sure you'll win three games in a row with a full house.

Hu: Good! Since you've wished me luck, I'll stand you a treat if I win.

Sister Ah-ching: Then I'm certain you'll have to stand me a treat. Now go inside. They're all waiting for you to win the game!

Hu: Oh, ha, ha, ha! . . . (*Goes into the house.*)

Liu (*to Cheng*):   Where are you from?

Cheng (*calmly*): From Changshu county town. My family has practised medicine there for three generations.

Liu: Got your identification papers?

Cheng: Yes.

Liu: Let's have a look.

(*Cheng produces his identification papers and hands them to Liu.*)

(*Sister Ah-ching brings over two cups of tea.*)

Sister Ah-ching: Adjutant Liu, you and your men have really had a tiring job the past few days: guards posted along the lake shore, boats seized, and people not allowed to go out fishing. What's really happened?

Liu: Nothing, really. It's just that New Fourth Army men are said to be in the marshes. . . .

Sister Ah-ching: New Fourth Army men? Then why don't you send troops to track them down?

Liu: The chief-of-staff says the marshes are too big. We'd never find them. But let's change the subject. (*Turns to Cheng.*) Hurry up!

Sister Ah-ching: Doctor, the lad is suffering from. . . .

Cheng: I know my patient's symptoms and the cause of the trouble without being told. If what I say tallies with the facts, take the medicine I prescribe. If not, I'll not ask you for a single cent.

Liu: Now then, don't boast. We'll soon see how good you are.

Cheng: This illness is owing to some obstruction in the stomach. The patient must feel a stifling sensation.

Liu: Wait a moment. (*To Aunt Sha.*) Does that fit?

Aunt Sha: Yes, just now he complained of a tightness in the chest.

Liu: So he does know his job.

Cheng: Let me see your tongue. (*Examines Szu-lung's tongue.*) There's a hot humour in the stomach. Not eating properly, lacks nourishment.

Aunt Sha: That's right, lacking food.

Cheng: The liver is encumbered. That's liable to make him restive.

Aunt Sha: Yes, very restive.

Liu: Just a bit under the weather, that's nothing to fret about.

Cheng: Don't worry. I'll make out a prescription. I guarantee one dose will set him right.

(*Liu fixes his eyes upon Cheng. Sister Ah-ching and Aunt Sha look anxious. After thinking for a moment, Sister Ah-ching goes into the house.*)

Cheng (*sings "hsi pi erh liu"*):
Don't worry! The case isn't serious;
Composure leads to ease of mind.
Let someone take good care of him at home. . . .

(*Sister Ah-ching returns.*)

Sister Ah-ching: What are you looking at, Adjutant Liu?

Liu: I'm interested in medicine. (*To Cheng.*) Be quick with your prescription.

Cheng: It's ready.
(*Continues singing*)
One dose of medicine will put him right.

Liu: Give that to me! (*Takes the prescription.*)

Cheng: Well, well.

(*A puppet soldier comes out of the house.*)

Puppet Soldier: Adjutant Liu, the commander wants you. (*Exit.*)

Liu: Right! (*Puts the prescription on the table.*) Sister Ah-ching, please keep an eye on things here for me. I'll be back in no time.

Sister Ah-ching: All right.

(*Liu goes into the house. Sister Ah-ching hurriedly signals to Szu-lung and Aunt Sha to keep a look-out. Cheng and Sister Ah-ching confer in whispers.*)

Chinese open-air stage—once a village temple, Shensi

Guerilla Theatre

On the Docks

The White Haired Girl

The Red Lantern

Red Detachment of Women

Taking Tiger Mountain by Strategy

Shachiapang

Shachiapang

Sister Ah-ching: Quite a few people here have been arrested.

Cheng: I see. From the information we have, Hu Chuan-kuei has gone over to the Japanese invaders body and soul.

Sister Ah-ching: What's to be done then?

Cheng: We must remove this nail. Our main force will be here very soon.

Sister Ah-ching: Good.

Cheng: Find out the disposition of the enemy forces. I'll send for the information in a couple of days.

Sister Ah-ching: What about those sick and wounded comrades?

Cheng: Move them at once to Red Stone Village.

Sister Ah-ching: All right.

(*Szu-lung coughs as a signal. Liu comes out of the house.*)

Liu: Sister Ah-ching, the commander has won the game and says you've asked him to stand you a treat, so I'm to go shopping for him.

Sister Ah-ching: That's fine.

Liu (*to Cheng*): Hey, why are you still here?

Cheng (*packing his medical kit*): I'm going now. Mind he takes the medicine promptly, not later than this evening.

Liu: Get going, hurry up!

Cheng: All right, I'm leaving.

Aunt Sha: Doctor, the sky's overcast and the road is slippery. Be careful!

Sister Ah-ching: Yes, do be careful! The road's rough.

Cheng: Don't worry about me. Take good care of the patient.

Liu: Off with you, hurry up!

(*Exit Cheng, followed by Liu*).

Sister Ah-ching: The county Party committee wants us to move the comrades to Red Stone Village. We've got to get a boat.

Szu-lung: I have an idea.

Aunt Sha: What is it?

Szu-lung: I'll slip away into the water, cut the moorings of a boat and push it out. I won't use a pole or oars. The boat will be empty, and it won't make much noise. If I can push it out half a *li*, it will disappear into the mist on the lake. As things stand now, that's the only way.

Aunt Sha: He's a good swimmer, Sister Ah-ching. Let him go.

Sister Ah-ching: That's all we can do now. Take that path, Szu-lung, and find a quiet spot to slip into the water. But you must be very careful.

Szu-lung: Sister Ah-ching!
(*Sings "hsi pi kuai pan"*)
A good swimmer since childhood,
I dare to ride the highest waves.
Across the lake, I'll meet the comrades—
Ma! Sister Ah-ching!
Please set your minds at ease!

(*Szu-lung and Aunt Sha go off. Enter Ah-fu.*)

Ah-fu: Sister Ah-ching!

Sister Ah-ching (*surprised, turns round*): Anything important, Ah-fu?

Ah-fu: Last night the instructor sent Lin Ta-ken and Chang Sung-tao to my house.

Sister Ah-ching: What did they want?

Ah-fu: Information about Hu Chuan-kuei, and medicinal herbs. When they'd got those, they left.

Sister Ah-ching: Didn't you find them any food?

Ah-fu: Yes, I did. They took it with them.

Sister Ah-ching: That's good. You can go back now.

Ah-fu: Right! (*Exit.*)

(*Sister Ah-ching looks across the lake.*)

Sister Ah-ching (*sings "hsi pi san pan"*):
The boat is disappearing through the mist,
I'm sure the comrades will reach Red Stone Village.

(*Sister Ah-ching goes into the house. Enter Liu.*)

Liu: Sister Ah-ching, here are my purchases. (*Follows her into the house.*)

(*Tiao and Hsiao-san enter. Liu returns.*)

Liu: Chief-of-staff, where's the interpreter, Mr. Tsou?

Tiao: He's gone. Adjutant Liu, the commander is getting married.

Liu: Getting married? Who's the bride-to-be?

Tiao: Mr. Tsou's sister.

Liu: Needless to say, chief-of-staff is the go-between.

Tiao: Say, I've got a good job for you, a trip to the Chang-shu county town to buy something for the wedding.

Liu (*most grateful*):   Very good, sir. Thank you, chief-of-staff!

(*Tiao, thoughtful, walks up a slope on the shore and looks across the lake through binoculars.*)

Tiao (*suddenly shouts out*):   Hey! There seems to be a boat on the lake.

Liu (*astonished*):   A boat! There's been a strong wind all day. Maybe it snapped the moorings, so an empty boat has drifted out.

Tiao: No, that can't be it. An empty boat with a broken rope would drift with the wind and the current towards the shore. How can it go out against them? Someone must be in the water pushing it.

Liu: Someone in the water?

Tiao: Get a few men and give chase!

Liu: Yes, sir.

(*Curtain*)

———

SCENE SEVEN

DENOUNCING THE ENEMY

Shortly after the previous scene. Tiao's house.

> (*As the curtain rises, Liu and Hsiao-san, offstage, are torturing people and shouting: "Out with it, quick! Speak up!"*)
>
> (*Hu, in a temper, gulps down some wine. Tiao staggers in with a leather whip, ferocious and upset, his tunic unbuttoned at the neck and the sleeves rolled up.*)

Tiao (*declaims*):   *The New Fourth Army men have moved out of the marshes safely.*

Hu (*declaims*):   *How am I to cope with this high-handed pressure from the Imperial Army?*

> (*The torturers can be heard conducting an interrogation offstage.*)

Tiao (*declaims*):   *We've seized some riff-raff to find out who the Communists are.*

Hu (*declaims*):   *Hours of questioning, and we've got nothing out of them! Has anyone confessed?*

> (*Liu and Hsiao-san answer offstage: "No one."*)

Hu: Say, Old Tiao, why not shoot a few of them?

Tiao: Yes, I'm wondering whom to start with. Orderly, bring in Wang Fu-ken!

> (*Liu and Hsiao-san answer offstage: "Yes, sir."*)
>
> (*Liu and Hsiao-san drag in Fu-ken.*)

Hu: Speak up! Where have the wounded New Fourth Army men gone?

Tiao: We'll set you free when you tell us who the Communists are in the town.

(*Fu-ken furiously points at Hu and Tiao. The two step back in panic.*)

Fu-ken: You traitors and stooges riding roughshod over the people!

Hu: Orderly!! Have him shot for the other riff-raff to see!

Fu-ken: Traitors! Stooges! Down with Japanese imperialism! Down with traitors and stooges! . . .

(*Fu-ken is taken off.*)
(*Fu-ken shouts offstage: "Long live the Chinese Communist Party!" "Long live Chairman Mao!"*)
(*A volley of shots.*)
(*Liu and Hsiao-san yell offstage: "Did you people see? You'll be shot like him if you don't speak up! Speak up! Quick!"*)

Tiao: Tiao Hsiao-san, have that old gaffer Liu shot too. His son is in the New Fourth Army.

(*Offstage Hsiao-san yells: "Old gaffer Liu, step forward!"*)
(*Loud shouts offstage: "Down with all traitors!" The masses angrily shout slogans.*)
(*A volley of shots.*)

Hu: Orderly!

(*Enter Hsiao-san.*)

Hu: Have that old woman Sha shot too!

Tiao: Wait! Lock her up!

Hsiao-san: Yes, sir! (*Exit.*)

Tiao: We just can't shoot that old woman, commander. The Imperial Army wants her confession, not her life. By sparing her, we'll be able to find out who the Communist working behind the scenes is.

Hu: Communist? We wouldn't know him even if he were sitting right in front of us!

Tiao: Commander, there is one very suspicious person.

Hu: Who's that?

Tiao: Where did Adjutant Liu start shooting so rashly that day? Where did we lose one of the boats we'd seized? Both happened near the Spring Tea-house!

Hu: You mean to say. . . .

Tiao: Sister Ah-ching!

Hu: . . . .

Tiao: It's very suspicious.

Hu: What do you mean? Arrest her?

Tiao: Oh, no, no! She saved your life, commander. Haven't you sent for her?

Hu: I invited her to help me with my wedding.

Tiao: Let's ask her a few questions when she comes.

Hu: Questions? What questions?—"Are you a Communist?"

Tiao: Certainly not. (*Whispers in Hu's ear.*) How about that?

Hu: All right, as you like. Orderly!

(*Enter a puppet soldier.*)

Hu: When Sister Ah-ching comes, report immediately!

Puppet Soldier: Yes, sir (*Exit.*)

(*Hu and Tiao go off.*)
(*A puppet soldier reports offstage: "Sister Ah-ching is here."*)
(*Sister Ah-ching enters, inspects the surroundings.*)

Sister Ah-ching (*sings "hsi pi san pan"*):
The New Fourth Army is marching back east to smash the "mopping up,"
The sun will soon shine again over Shachiapang.
Hu Chuan-kuei has sold out to the Japanese
And is wreaking havoc on our people.
(*Changes to "liu shui"*)
This debt of blood must be kept in mind.
On instructions we've reconnoitred
All enemy positions except this headquarters,

Now I have a chance to enter the tiger's den
To see what's going on here. . . .

(Hu and Tiao enter, tidy and neat.)

Hu: Sister Ah-ching!

Sister Ah-ching: Commander Hu! Chief-of-staff!
(Continues to sing, changing to "san pan")
Congratulations, commander, on your coming wedding!

Hu: So you know everything?

Tiao: You're well informed indeed.

Sister Ah-ching: Why, the whole town is agog with the news. Adjutant Liu has told every family to send "voluntary" gifts.

Tiao: Well, sit down. Tea!

(A puppet soldier brings tea in. Exit.)

Sister Ah-ching: Commander, they say the bride is very pretty.

Hu: Oh! You've heard that too?

Sister Ah-ching: Of course I have. She's a well-known beauty in the county town of Changshu, with an excellent character, very talented, and unusually good-looking. A girl in a hundred!

Hu: Ha, ha, ha. . . . Sister Ah-ching, you put things well. I sent for you today to ask you to help with the wedding. You must come and lend a hand on that day!

Sister Ah-ching: Of course. That's the least I should do. I'll come early in the morning. I think I can handle such things as making tea and waiting on the guests. . . .

Hu: No, no! I wouldn't think of troubling you with such chores. But when the bride arrives in her sedan-chair, I hope you'll see to it that we do things right and don't bungle the business.

Sister Ah-ching: Right you are! As soon as she arrives, you leave everything to me. I'll see that she observes all the proprieties, so that none of your relatives or friends can find fault with her. Don't you worry, commander.

Hu: Fine. She has a whole pack of fault-finding relatives. But with you here to help, I won't worry.

Sister Ah-ching: Where's the bridal chamber?

Hu: In the back court. When everything is ready tomorrow, I'll ask you over again to have a look.

Sister Ah-ching: Good, I'll certainly come.

Hu: Come early.

Tiao (*bangs the table with a cigarette tin and asks sternly*): Has that old woman Sha owned up?

(*Liu and Hsiao-san answer offstage: "No, not yet."*)

Tiao: Bring her in!

Sister Ah-ching: You're busy, commander, so I'd better go. I don't want to be in the way.

(*Sister Ah-ching turns to go. Tiao stops her.*)

Tiao: Sister Ah-ching, you can stay while we get on with our business.

Hu: Yes, stay a little longer, since the chief-of-staff asks you.

Sister Ah-ching: All right. (*To Hu.*) Then I'll stay for a bit.

(*Sister Ah-ching ponders a little, self-assured, walks calmly to the table and sits at it with perfect composure.*)

Tiao: Bring her in!

Aunt Sha (*offstage, sings "hsi pi tao pan"*):
I'm so thankful our men are out of danger. . . .

(*Enter Aunt Sha.*)
(*Sister Ah-ching, Tiao and Hu look at her with different feelings and expressions.*)
(*Liu and Hsiao-san enter.*)

Aunt Sha (*sings "hsi pi san pan"*):
Even if they break my bones, I wouldn't care!
Shoulders back, I face the foe—(*Startled to see Sister Ah-ching sitting there.*)

What's Sister Ah-ching doing here? (Thinks for a mo-
ment and the truth dawns on her.)
It's most likely the enemy's putting her to test.
I must protect her and face everything myself!

Hu: Well, old woman, are you going to speak or not?

Aunt Sha: What do you want me to say?

Hu: Did your son row the New Fourth Army men out of
the marshes?

Aunt Sha: I don't know.

Hu: Where is he now?

Aunt Sha: I don't know.

Hu: Who got you and your son to do this? Who was behind it?

Aunt Sha: I don't know.

Hu: Damn you! "I don't know." "I don't know." I'll teach
you to say you don't know.

(Before he can lash her with a whip, Tiao intervenes.)

Tiao: Hold on, commander. Sit down, sit down. Ho, ho,
ho. . . Old lady, you've been wronged. Well, sit down
and listen to me.
(Sings "hsi pi yao pan")
Don't be so stubborn, old lady,
Let me put it to you straight;
You're old and never leave the town,
How could you have made such a cunning scheme?
You must have acted at someone's bidding,
She pulled the strings, while you played on stage.
Look how you've been tortured,
Yet she just sits back and looks on indifferently.
Just tell me who she is,
And I guarantee you'll never be short of firewood or rice.
Do you understand, eh?

(Aunt Sha remains silent with her head high.)

Tiao: Sister Ah-ching, won't you try to persuade her?

Sister Ah-ching: Me?

Tiao: Yes. You're neighbours. Why not make her see reason? (*To Hu.*) Right?

Hu: Right. Sister Ah-ching, please reason with her.

Sister Ah-ching: All right. Since Chief-of-Staff Tiao thinks so highly of me, I'll try. But I know this old lady's character. I don't expect anything better than a rebuff. (*Goes over to Aunt Sha, planning while walking; folds her arms on her chest as she stops near Aunt Sha.*) Aunt Sha, the chief-of-staff says your son has sent a boat to the New Fourth Army men. Is that true?

(*Aunt Sha stares angrily at the three.*)

Sister Ah-ching: Aunt Sha, he's your only son. How could you bear to part with him?

Aunt Sha: The boy's grown up. He's free to choose his own way.

Hu: Tell me, has the New Fourth Army done you any good?

Aunt Sha: Well, I'll tell you.
(*Angrily denounces the enemy, singing "erh huang yuan pan"*)
On August 13, the Japanese attacked Shanghai,
And the land south of the Yangtze was overrun by the aggressor;
Our people were plunged into a bloodbath, corpses piled up high,
Flames scorched the dear earth far and wide.
Led by the Communist Party, the New Fourth Army has resisted Japan;
Braving hardships, it marched east, deep into the enemy's rear,
And liberated villages and towns.
Where the red flag flies, people sing as they see the sun again.
You call yourselves the "Loyal and Just National Salvation Army,"

Then why haven't you fired a single shot at the Japanese invaders?
Tell me, which country do you want to save?
Why not save China, why collaborate with the Japanese?
Why insist on fighting the Communists?
To whom are you loyal and just?
You are stooges of the enemy, a bunch of traitors,
Without shame or conscience!

Hu: Shut up!

Liu and Hsiao-san: Nonsense!

Aunt Sha (*continues singing*):

I dare you to justify yourselves and tell people the truth,
Then you can cut me to pieces for all I care!
The day will come when Shachiapang is free,
And we will see how you traitors (changes to free rhythm) meet your end!

Hu: Take her out! Have her shot!

Liu and Hsiao-san: Come on!

(*Tiao immediately motions to Hsiao-san not to carry out the order. Hsiao-san takes the hint.*)
(*Aunt Sha walks off, head high; followed by Liu and Hsiao-san.*)

Sister Ah-ching: Commander Hu!

Tiao: Wait a minute. Sister Ah-chiang has something to say.

Sister Ah-ching (*rises calmly, and casually*): . . . It's time I left.

(*Tiao and Hu register disappointment.*)

Sister Ah-ching: It's not for the likes of me to meddle in your official business.

Hu: Oh, no, we'd like to hear what you have to say.

Tiao: That's right. The commander wants to have the old

lady shot. As a neighbour of hers, how can you bear to see her die without trying to save her?

Sister Ah-ching: Others will come to save her.

Hu: What others?

Sister Ah-ching: Well, if her son Szu-lung took a boat to the New Fourth Army men, he's bound to save his mother. What's more, the New Fourth Army men will surely come to rescue her.

Hu: If I have her shot now, what can they do for her?

Sister Ah-ching: Exactly. If you have her shot now, no one will come. If no one comes, you won't catch anyone.

Hu: Ah, you mean we should keep this woman as bait for bigger fish?

Tiao: So you think we'd better not shoot her?

Sister Ah-ching: You are the man with the gun. It's for you to decide. I was just thinking for the commander's benefit.

Hu: Quite right.

Tiao: Good. Sister Ah-ching is really on our side. All right. We'll set that old lady free at once. Will you please take her home?

Sister Ah-ching: Of course I will, chief-of-staff, since you have so much trust in me.

Tiao: Good. Orderly! Set the old woman free.

(*Liu offstage: "Right. Come on!"*)
(*Enter Aunt Sha, followed by Liu.*)

Aunt Sha: Put me to death at once. None of your dirty tricks!

Hu: Old woman, we're setting you free. You should have some sense.

Tiao: You're free now, old lady. Sister Ah-ching, won't you see her home?

Sister Ah-ching: Aunt Sha, let's go.

(*Exit Aunt Sha, followed by Sister Ah-ching.*)

Tiao (*to Liu*): Follow them and listen to what they talk about.

Liu: Right. (*Exit.*)

Hu: Old Tiao, what tricks are you up to?

Tiao: If they start whispering together, it'll prove that they're in collusion. Then we'll arrest them at once and question them both.

(*Liu offstage: "Reporting!" Hurries in.*)

Liu: Reporting! Chief-of-staff, they've come to blows!

Tiao: Who?

Liu: That old woman Sha and Sister Ah-ching.

Hu: Put the old woman in jail again.

Liu: Right! (*Exit.*)

(*Enter Sister Ah-ching, her hair slightly in disorder and one shoe half off.*)

Sister Ah-ching: O my! What a fierce old woman! As soon as we were outside, she threw herself on me and started calling names—"traitor," "stooge" and the like. Look at me! My clothes torn. (*Sits down.*) My mouth bleeding. Just look! (*Puts on her shoe.*)

Hu: Old Tiao, don't think you're so clever. Are you convinced now? Sister Ah-ching, I hope it's not serious? My wedding. . . .

Sister Ah-ching: I'll see to your wedding all right. My, that old creature's out of her mind, imagining she could get the better of me. She's no match for me. I soon put her in her place.

Tiao: I hope you aren't suspicious, Sister Ah-ching?

Sister Ah-ching: Humph! If I were that suspicious, I'd take good care to steer clear of suspicious types.

(*Sister Ah-ching dusts her shoes with a handkerchief and sits back, head erect. Hu stares at Tiao who looks crestfallen.*)

(*Curtain*)

═

SCENE EIGHT

TO THE ATTACK

Three days later, before dawn. In the fields.

(As the curtain rises, Szu-lung and Yeh enter. After scouting around, they go off.)

Kuo *(offstage, sings "hsi pi tao pan")*:
The moon lights our road to battle,
Breezes cool us on our way. . . .

(Enter Kuo. With one hand on his pistol, he strikes a dramatic pose, brave and forceful, and looks round with bright eyes. Then he turns around, waves towards off-stage and strikes a dramatic pose, sideways. Soldiers of the commando platoon enter.)

Kuo *(sings "hsi pi yuan pan")*:
We cross rivers and hills,
And march past slumbering villages.
Our detachment has cast a net
To wipe out the Japanese and the traitorous bandit gang.
The commando platoon has just been organized,
(Changes to "kuai pan")
Advancing rapidly, we'll spring a surprise attack on Shachiapang.
Like a sharp dagger thrusting into the enemy's heart,
We will take him unawares.
His whole line will be thrown into confusion,
Like an ant-hill flooded with hot water (changes to free rhythm) or a beehive set on fire!

(Szu-lung and Yeh enter.)

Yeh: An enemy patrol!

Hsiao-hu: Let's finish them off!

Kuo (*stops Hsiao-hu and gives order*): Take cover!

(They take cover.)
(A patrol of puppet soldiers crosses the stage.)
(Szu-lung and Yeh stand up, look round and then wave their hands. Kuo and others jump out from behind a mound in a "hu tiao"—cartwheel—style.)

Kuo: Platoon Leader Yeh and Sha Szu-lung!

Szu-lung and Yeh: Here.

Kuo: Look! (*Performs the Peking opera dance movements "kua tui" and "ti tui"—poses on one leg and then strides forward, then kicks one leg up and turns—and strikes a dramatic pose, sideways.*) Shachiapang is in front of us. You two go reconnoitre!

Szu-lung and Yeh: Right. (*Go off.*)

Kuo: Forward march!

(Soldiers of the commando platoon straighten their uniforms.)

Kuo (*sings "hsi pi kuai pan"*):
The blockade line is doted with sentries and pillboxes,
To us they are nothing but paper fortresses.
We've sighted Shachiapang (changes to free rhythm) in the distance,
There we'll destroy the bandits' den and capture their chieftain.

(Kuo performs the Peking opera dance movements "sao tang tui" and "hsuan tzu"—squats on one leg and makes a complete circle with the other leg extended, then jumps into the air and makes a complete turn in a horizontal position. He and the others form a tableau of marching soldiers.)

(Curtain)

⹀

SCENE NINE

BREAKING THROUGH

Immediately after the previous scene. Outside the back courtyard of Tiao's house.

(As the curtain rises, a puppet soldier is on sentry duty.)

Puppet Soldier: The commander has invited the Japanese to his wedding, so he's ordered more of us to stand sentry. Ah! Just my rotten luck!

(Yeh and others enter, capture the puppet soldier and drag him away.) (Kuo and Sister Ah-ching enter, followed by soldiers of the commando platoon and militiamen.)

Sister Ah-ching: Instructor, go over this wall and you'll be in Tiao Teh-yi's back courtyard!
(Sings "hsi pi kuai pan")
The enemy disposition remains unchanged,
As shown on the map we sent you.
Their main force is posted east and west of the town,
With only one squad left at the gate to the house.
The militia has just cut their telephone line,
So they can't call up reinforcements from their flanks.
The men inside are having a wedding feast,
Playing drinking games and acting like rowdies;
Climb over this wall, push into the courtyard,
And you'll wipe out all these monsters (changes to free rhythm) at one stroke!
Kuo: Sha Szu-lung!
(Sings "hsi pi san pan")
You lead the assault group to the gate
And wipe out the enemy guards!

(Szu-lung leads off two soldiers.)

Kuo (*continues singing, to Sister Ah-ching*):
You go to the end of the town to meet our main
force. . . .

(*Sister Ah-ching leads off the militia.*)
(*Kuo vaults up onto the wall, looks round and waves
back. Then he somersaults off the wall.*)
(*The soldiers somersault over the wall.*)

(*Curtain*)

SCENE TEN

WIPING OUT THE ENEMY

Immediately after the previous scene. Tiao's courtyard.

(*As the curtain rises, Kuroda, Hu and Tiao enter, followed by two Japanese soldiers. Tsou enters from the
opposite direction.*)

Tsou: The motorboat is ready!
Kuroda: The telephone line has been cut. The situation's
not good. Be careful!

(*Gunfire.*)

Kuroda: Where's the firing?
Hu: I don't know.

(*Enter a puppet soldier.*)

Puppet Soldier: Reporting! The New Fourth Army's in
the back courtyard!
Kuroda: Delay them, block them! (*Dashes off in panic.*)

(*Fighting. Soldiers of the commando platoon wipe out
the Japanese and puppet troops. Kuo accurately picks
off one enemy soldier after another. Finally, he stands
with Kuroda under his foot in a dramatic pose.*)

(Soldiers of the commando platoon cross the stage with captured enemy soldiers.)
(Enter Cheng with soldiers from the main force.)
(Sister Ah-ching and Chao enter with the militia.)
(Kuo enters, shakes hands with Cheng and Sister Ah-ching and others.)
(New Fourth Army soldiers enter, with Kuroda, Tsou, Hu and Tiao under arrest.)
(Enter Aunt Sha, supported by Szu-lung.)
(Crowds enter, including people who have just been freed from prison.)
(On seeing Hu, Tiao and others, those just set free raise their shackles in anger to strike them, but are stopped by Kuo.)

Kuo: Fellow countrymen! We'll hand these traitors over to the Anti-Japanese Democratic Government for trial!

Sister Ah-ching: Right! We'll surely put them on public trial!

Hu: You are. . . .

Sister Ah-ching: I'm a member of the Chinese Communist Party! You Japanese imperialists! You traitors!

Kuo: Take them away!

(Hu, Tiao, Kuroda and Tsou hang their heads in dismay and are led off.)
(Kuo, Sister Ah-ching and others meet Aunt Sha. The people of Shachiapang, under the leadership of Chairman Mao and the Communist Party of China, are rid of the Japanese and puppet troops and once more see the light of day.)

(Final curtain)

Red Detachment of Women

The White Haired Girl

Peasants and Soldiers in Ballet Shoes

BALLET IN CHINA IS DIFFERENT FROM BALLET anywhere else in the world. The plant is classic Russian; a vigorous Chinese graft has produced the uniqueness.

Instead of an imitation of Russian or Western ballet, an original, socialist, proletarian art—a condensation and amalgamation of old and new—was born. Today's post-Cultural Revolution "model" ballet is an intense dramatization in dance of the Chinese people's violent and victorious fight for emancipation.

Classic ballet, little known in China before the revolution, began in the late 1920s as the almost-exclusive concern of White Russians refugeed in Shanghai. One of the teachers was George Goncharoff, who fostered two outstandingly talented young dancers: Hong Kong-born Margot Fonteyn and Trinidad-born Tai Ai-lien. Both went on to England, Tai Ai-lien to study with Anton Dolin, Marie Rambert, and Kurt Joos at Dartington Hall. Returning to China, she founded her own dance group in wartime Chungking. Later Madame Tai Ai-lien became a deputy to the People's Congress, a position she no longer holds. Goncharoff died in 1954, little realizing where his beginning ballet footwork would lead.

China's first full-scale experience with ballet occurred after Liberation. In October 1950, a group called The Central Dramatic Academy Ballet Corps staged *Doves of Peace,* a ballet largely choreographed by Tai Ai-lien. She subsequently became head of the Peking School of Ballet after it grew out of the Peking School of Dance in 1954. It was China's first regular ballet school. In 1956 the students presented a public concert which included excerpts from *The Nutcracker Suite, Raymonda, Coppélia,* and the waltz from *Sleeping Beauty;* P. A. Gusev, a Russian ballet master at the school, directed full-length productions of *Le Corsaire* and *Swan Lake. Giselle, Esmeralda, Fountains of Backchiserai,* and a new ballet, *The Maid of the Sea,* based on traditional Chinese dance forms, were also produced. Dimitri Saplain of the Bolshoi taught the company *La Fille Mal Gardée* (which the Chinese translated as *Useless Precautions*). The ballet ensemble eventually toured Moscow and Warsaw.

Chinese dancers traveled to the Soviet Union for training, and Russian instructors came to teach in China, some of the best in the Soviet Union arriving in 1954. Leningrad and the Bolshoi brought their classics, and in 1957 the New Siberian Ballet danced *Giselle* alongside Britain's Ballet Rambert's presentations of Sir Frederick Ashton's *Facade* and Anthony Tudor's *Gala Performance.*

The Magic Lotus Lantern, a dance drama without dialogue, based on a Chinese legend, combined Western ballet technique and traditional dance forms. It was performed in Peking in the late fifties and was made into a film in Shanghai.

The Royal Swedish Ballet toured in 1960, introducing George Balanchine's *Symphony in C* and *Four Temperaments* to apparently pleased audiences. Chinese attempts were admirable, though perhaps not up to the technically brilliant, elegant foreign productions. As Chen Chiang-ching, vice director of the Peking School of Dance in 1960, explained to my husband when he visited China that year, Chinese dancers had been doing ballet for six years, the Bolshoi for a hundred.

The school then had 340 students, some specializing in ballet, some in folk and social dancing. Children began at around age eleven to spend six to eight years as boarding students, with a schedule of ten to twelve hours of study and technique daily. A similar school of ballet started in Shanghai in March 1960.

For all the applause and admiration, this foreign entertainment appeared odd—except to urban sophisticates—and unrelated to Chinese culture. Think of classic Peking opera, with its stylized conventions, being presented to average spectators in Mississippi or in Maine. When the break occurred between the Soviet Union and China, culminating in 1960, imported classic ballet received its dismissal notice, though it wasn't all that apparent at the time. British ballerina Beryl Grey accepted an invitation by the People's Republic as late as 1964 and appeared in Chinese productions of *Les Sylphides* and *Swan Lake* in Peking and Shanghai. In the few weeks she was there, Miss Grey lectured and taught as well.

"I was extremely impressed by the beautifully trained bodies and sensitivity of the performers," writes Miss Grey.* "I had not expected to see such good limbs and well arched feet. Their backs were unusually supple and their extensions high without any apparent forcing . . . I found it difficult

* *Through the Bamboo Curtain*, by Beryl Grey, Collins, London, 1965.

to realize they had been learning Western ballet for only ten years. Their dancing had a definite Soviet style to which they were already adding their own characteristics, artistry and sensitivity. I was tremendously excited at the prospect of working with them for a whole month."

Impressed by the "poise, the quiet composure and concentration" of the young dancers, Miss Grey said, "They all appeared to have a highly developed sense of dignity and responsibility, and I never saw any display of temperament. In classes and rehearsals, the dancers and musicians were serious, composed, and completely absorbed in their work. After the performance there was no dashing off home or out for dinner and amusement. None of them had the time for that."

Chinese ballet by this time had made great strides, had become more independent and able to take its own road of development, striving to transform itself into revolutionary shape "to meet the needs of modern times and give a better class education to the masses."

Still, the repertoire of the Peking School of Ballet was composed mainly of foreign works. Beryl Grey mentions that "ballet, along with all other artistic companies in China, received a directive to concentrate on contemporary themes." This was the reason, she explains, for the absence in 1964 of some of the dancers and choreographers. "They have gone to the countryside of Hainan to draw inspiration for a new modern ballet, *Red Women's Army*, I was told. They were proud of this project, the first full-length ballet of their own."

Mao Tse-tung had given warnings of the coming Cultural Revolution; in culture-conscious China the battle lines were drawn early in the backstage world of the arts. Opposition to revolutionary reform was deep. The theatre people we met in 1970 told us that leaders of the highest rank—Liu Shao-chi, Chairman of the People's National Congress and constitutional head of state; Chou Yang, Deputy Director of the Chinese Communist Party's Propaganda Department; and Lin Mo-han, also of the Propaganda Department, among others—had been and were firm sponsors of pure foreign ballet and theatre. Chou En-lai had attended and enjoyed the foreign ballet, but the Premier was a staunch advocate of a revolutionized theatre serving the people, not an elite group. However, some of the Party members in authority kept up a demand for more of the old and foreign ("wholesale Westernization" was the term used to describe this), doing their utmost to ridicule and harass the creation of the new art aimed at the masses. Failing to stop it, they threw various well-aimed monkey wrenches into production plans, rehearsals and scheduled performances.

Those on the side of "bourgeois" art are mainly defeated today, but the battle took a toll in the cultural ranks. The ideological targets were "foreign to the exclusion of things Chinese; the ancient against the contemporary; and interest in the dead instead of the living."* Chiang Ching, dedicated to principles her husband had expressed in 1942 when Mao spoke on literature and art at the Yenan Forum, supported the revolutionary-minded comrades of theatre, dance and music. Through her encouragement and advice the first full-length revolutionary ballet on a contemporary theme— *Red Detachment of Women* (title changed from *Red Women's Army*, mentioned earlier by Beryl Grey)—was presented on October 1, 1964, in Peking.

Only two ballets made up the repertoire until 1971: *Red Detachment of Women* and *The White Haired Girl*. (A third, *Yi Meng Sung—The Song of Yi Meng Mountain* —was added in August 1971.) Both deal with the liberation of a peasant slave girl. The dominant theme ("the red line") is "Wherever there is oppression, there is resistance and struggle"; the resistance is that of the peasants against the exploiting class and their success in a revolutionary struggle based on the principles of Marxism-Leninism-Maoism. Mao Tse-tung Thought "guides the enslaved people's

* *Chinese Literature*, Peking, February 1970.

anger and hatred against the landlord class onto the revolutionary road to destroy the old world and emancipate mankind."*

The action of *Red Detachment of Women* occurs during the Second Revolutionary Civil War (1927–37) on Hainan Island, off the southern coast of China. In brief, this is the history of that terrible period. The year 1927 marked a permanent parting of the ways between the allied Nationalist (Kuomintang) Party of Chiang Kai-shek and the Chinese Communists. On April 12, 1927, the workers of Shanghai organized a massive demonstration for labor reforms in the belief that they had the support of both parties. In the Kuomintang betrayal, remembered as the Shanghai massacre, thousands of youths were slaughtered, including many Communists and socialists (left-wing Nationalists); Chou En-lai was captured, sentenced to death, but escaped; and the Communists, until then united with the Kuomintang, went underground. Mao's followers survived by building bases among the poor peasants in the countryside. They built a Red Army, undertook the Long March (1934–35), built up grass-roots support throughout the country, increased in strength from year to year, until in 1937 Chiang Kai-shek was obliged to join them against the Japanese invaders.

Before 1937 the island of Hainan was the stage of intense civil war. In the countryside many able-bodied poor peasants joined the Red Army. The women also banded together, using farming tools to defend themselves. With the help of the Communists they acquired weapons and guerrilla technique. Out of this a Women's Detachment developed; the story of these Hainanese women guerrillas has become legendary.

Against a tropical island setting, among the Li people whose Five Fingered Mountain is seen in the background, *Red Detachment of Women* focuses on the political awakening of the slave girl Wu Ching-hua, and her libera-

* *China Reconstructs*, Peking.

tion from a wealthy Hainan landlord during the midst of the struggle. The ballet begins with her flight from the tyrant's prison and torture, her capture and merciless beating, after which she is left for dead. Rescued by Hung Chang-ching, Communist Party representative of the Women's Company of the Red Army and directed by him to their base, Ching-hua joins the soldier-women. During an attack on the landlord's home the emotional girl is unable to control her hatred and fires without orders, thus upsetting battle plans. Through political guidance by the partisan women and Hung Chang-ching, Ching-hua comes to understand revolutionary tactics and discipline. She matures into a model soldier, behaving with great courage and responsibility during a Kuomintang assault. Victory ensues, though Hung Chang-ching has been captured and executed by the traitor landlord. Ching-hua subsequently kills the despot and pledges herself to follow in the footsteps of the martyred Hung. He has given his life, but the peasant women who have been set free by the Red Detachment join the ranks, and the revolution goes on.

The White Haired Girl deals, in eight acts, with a village peasant youngster in northwest China. Hsi-erh's father, unable to pay his debts, is beaten to death and she is taken by force to work in the home of the landlord, Huang Shih-jen. Her fiancé joins the People's Army, determined to liberate the village and rescue the girl. Hsi-erh, menaced by the landlord, beaten by his mother, and ever defiant, flees to the mountains, intent on survival and revenge. In the course of time she endures such suffering that her long black hair turns white. The Eighth Route Army frees the village, and Hsi-erh's fiancé finds the nearly wild girl in a cave. Reunited with her people, she has the triumph of seeing her oppressor liquidated, his account books, title deeds, and forced-labor bonds burned. Along with the young villagers, Hsi-erh joins the army and goes forth to carry on the revolution.

Both stories have their life-size counterparts in not-so-long-ago Chinese history. Theatre audiences include middle-aged "Hsi-erhs" and "Wu Ching-huas" reliving their pasts as their children learn about it.

The story of a white haired girl goes back to before 1940 in the Shansi-Chahar-Hopei Border Region in the northwest.* The term "border region" applied to territory recovered from the Japanese, where local puppet regimes were dissolved by Communist partisans who, together with the peasantry, set up administrative areas in the enemy's rear. My husband remembered being with Chou En-lai in a cave town north of Yenan in 1936 when a crazed woman appeared on the edge of a bluff "hurling epithets into the courtyard. . . . She was very fierce, would let no one near her, wore no clothes winter or summer, and lived like a wild beast in a cave in the hills . . . her whole family had been destroyed in a famine and pestilence which had left her a demented orphan. Soldiers and villagers used to put out food at night and she would come down, snatch it, and run off to her lair."**

Stories spread about a "white haired goddess." Two members of the Lu Hsun Academy of Literature and Art in Yenan, Ho Ching-chih and Ting Yi, wrote a folk opera on the tale in 1945. It was awarded a Stalin Prize in 1951. This version is about superstitious villagers who place offerings in the local temple to placate "the goddess." Determined to get to the bottom of the myth, two cadres from the district hide in the temple and confront the apparition. Giving a wild shriek, she dashes off and is found by the cadres hiding with her child in a cave. She pours out her story, crying bitterly.

Nine years before the war against Japanese aggression broke out and before the Eighth Route Army reached this district, a wicked landlord had cruelly oppressed the vil-

---

* A similar tale occurs in Szechwan province. Possibly one would find it in other areas as well.

** *The Other Side of the River*, by Edgar Snow, Random House, New York, 1962, p. 76.

lagers. An old tenant had a pretty daughter of seventeen who took the landlord's fancy. On the pretext of collecting rent, he drove her father to suicide, carried off and raped the girl. She became pregnant and he decided to murder her. His plot was discovered by a household servant, who helped the girl to escape. Hidden in a mountain cave she bore a child, and there she remained, full of hate and bitterness. Her hair turned white from suffering. She knew nothing of the Eighth Route Army nor of the changes that had occurred in the world outside.

People came from considerable distances to see the play. The songs became known, and in the street members of the cast were pointed out. This is reported by Ho Ching-chih in the preface to the published opera:

"That's the white haired girl!" "There's Tenant Yang!" "The running dog Mu is here!" "Landlord Huang, you bad egg!"

"It's all true to life," said country folk discussing the story. "We've all come from the old society. Who wouldn't cry at the dreadful things that happened to that girl!"

Ho continues: *"The White Haired Girl* was constantly revised as a result of suggestions and criticisms. When we sat with the audience . . . we often heard the most unrestrained, genuine and valuable comments. The people are our teachers, and it was they who taught us how to work. The new art serves the masses and reflects their lives, and the masses are the characters and the critics, sometimes the creators too, of this art."*

In 1947, Jack Belden was in a village five or six miles from the Kuomintang lines. On the eve of the International Women's Day he saw a play called *The White Haired Woman* given in an open field close to the battle area. It must have been a later treatment of Ho's opera. At the end the girl "is adopted by guerrillas who eventually free her home village and bring the landlord's son before a Speak Bitterness Meeting. The villagers debate what to do with

* *The White Haired Girl,* by Ho Ching-chih and Ting Yi, 1945.

the son. At this juncture, to my utter surprise," writes Belden, "many members of the audience stood up in great excitement, shouting 'Sha! Sha! Kill him! Kill him!' . . . The bitter reality of the play was not lost on the women in the audience, many of whom, as I found out, had undergone similar experiences. At several points in the play I saw women, old and young, peasant and intellectual, wiping tears from their eyes with the sleeves of their jackets. One old lady near me wept loudly through nearly the whole play. Frankly, I was almost as much affected by this play (or by the audience's reaction to it) as were the women."*

A day I spent at a dance school in Shanghai in the winter of 1970 revealed more steps in the long history of *The White Haired Girl*'s development from peasant opera to current model ballet, via Yenan, Jack Belden's front-line fire experience, early film versions, a Japanese ballet shown in Peking in 1957 and again in 1960–62—and the three-stage expansion of the present production, whose beginnings date from 1964.

In November sunlit suburbs, the Shanghai Dance School's buildings were in a pleasantly tree-clustered setting behind a garden area given over to flourishing vegetables. A hundred thirty dancers and teachers, an orchestra of 56, and 45 PLA members and staff live in this state-supported compound. It has been home, school, and work place for most of them the last ten years.

After tea and background briefing we were escorted to a large bright practice hall to watch a demonstration that included Peking opera technique: tumbling, cartwheeling without touching the floor, high back-somersaulting, mid-air double turns, etc. Later the young dancers (the average age is twenty-four) talked about their experiences living and working with the peasants for whom they also perform, and about their own reeducation and remolding. They were

* *China Shakes the World*, by Jack Belden, Monthly Review Press, New York, pp. 210–11.

eager to explain themselves and their new-found revolution to two heretofore rarely available Americans.

Dedication and devotion are words synonymous with ballet dancers, regardless of race or place. Without both these qualities there would be little incentive for the grueling practice that must continue even after mastery of the art. There is a world of difference in the meaning of these two words, however, as applied to the sophisticated, egotistical (and often brilliant) dancers I have known in the West, and to these ballet children of the Chinese revolution. For the latter, these words apply to the use of talent with a political formation that has little to do with *self-*expression.

Lin Pei-hsin, a bright young man who dances various "second roles," recounted his experiences in the countryside:

"We were thirteen and fourteen when we first came here in 1960; we didn't know much about 'the struggle between two lines.' Before the Cultural Revolution we only paid attention to vocational studies and not to politics at all. Technique was uppermost. Once we went to the countryside and put on *Swan Lake*, expecting praise from the peasants. Some people left; some fell asleep; some said, 'It's ugly.' We thought it was because they knew nothing about art. Later on, we realized it was just the opposite—*we* who didn't know the art of the workers, peasants and soldiers. They want art forms that unite them with the socialist revolution. There was a great ideological difference between us and them. So we began to rehearse *The White Haired Girl*. When we went back to the countryside the situation was completely different. Twenty thousand people came to see us perform on the threshing ground. Some stood on the back of the stage and said they were happy even if they could only see the backs of the dancers. They stood on roofs, in trees, all over. They brought friends and families. We express their love and hatred; we speak for them. Some cry. We feel very excited because they support us so thoroughly.

"Ballet is no longer 'court art' or bourgeois art. Once we played on an airfield for the PLA. Once in a factory the workers welded a big steel plate for us to use as a stage—such conditions for dancing would have been unthinkable for former ballet dancers.

"At Heng Sha Island we ate, worked and lived with the peasants. They put up bamboo poles for us to use as practice bars on the threshing ground. They welcomed and encouraged us. In daytime we worked with them and gained deep feelings—every crop is hard to cultivate. We have been supported by the sweat of the laboring people; we must support *them*. In the evenings we hung lights on bamboo poles. They all arrived early, eager to see a ballet that Chairman Mao has seen. An eighty-year-old lady who had never seen a performance in her life insisted on coming. A blind person said, 'Even if I hear the sound of the music it will be enough.'

"Last November it was cold, but we felt warm in our hearts when we performed for the peasants. We get clay on our ballet shoes—this shows we are serving our socialist society, that our stand is correct."

The role of Hsi-erh in *The White Haired Girl* is shared by several ballerinas, since the strenuous dancing, lasting more than two hours, would be too exhausting for one. Diminutive, sweet-faced T'sai Kuo-ying, who plays Hsi-erh in the first half, spoke after Mr. Lin. By chance, an evening later, we sat next to her at a Peking opera, *On the Docks*, and had an opportunity to talk. I found her straightforward, intelligent and charming.

"Working with the peasants is not only good for our own thinking, it's good for the characters we play," she said earnestly. "For example, in the first scene when father brings back the red string as a gift. [The ballet opens on New Year's Day, when presents are exchanged, and also when all debts were traditionally due.] I come from a worker's family, but I grew up in the new society and it's commonplace for me to get a piece of string. I couldn't express Hsi-erh's happiness at receiving this little piece of thread as a gift.

"Then we went to the countryside—we all go in busy seasons, usually at autumn harvest—and I heard about the past bitterness. One woman told me that when her child was born she had nothing to clothe it in. She had to leave it alone in the house when she went to the fields. It never had decent food or clothes. I heard many such stories. I began to understand that piece of thread. Before the Cultural Revolution we paid no attention to the problems of society. Now all this is changed. At Heng Sha Island it was cold, and I became sick. The peasants sent boiled eggs and different dishes to me just like I was their own child.

"To work with the peasants does away with the delicateness and fragility of the dancers. We used to need naps and were afraid to work because it might hurt us. We thought we were special people. We *can't* do the same work as the peasants; we do the work of the aged and the children. After two hours of cotton-picking we have to kneel down. They work for eight hours. We are not as good as they in many respects. In capitalist society the artists feel a head taller than others, but we feel ordinary now when we work with peasants and workers."

Envy stole over me as I listened to these young people who belong to a society that has gained their wholehearted dedication. I remembered stories told of the treatment of China's talented children in the not-too-distant past, of discipline achieved through daily beatings of theatrical trainees, of the harsh and rigid life devoted to the cause of commercialism. These youngsters reflected dignity, confidence and service to a common cause of country and mankind. There was no doubt they meant what they were so earnestly saying.

A young choreographer we met that November day at the school summarized best the meaning of the effects of the Cultural Revolution on ballet. Lithe, articulate, poised, and an excellent technician, Lin Yang-yang enlightened and entertained as he outlined the "struggle" to create *The White Haired Girl* according to Mao Tse-tung's teachings, against opposition from the Liu Shao-chi oriented Establishment.

(Lin looked a bit like a youthful Truman Capote. Chinese names were often difficult for me to remember. I made it a practice to note feature resemblances to people I knew personally or as public figures. Thus: Wang Kuei-fu, woman on left with glasses, looks like Jean White, Li Ching-mei, man with gray shirt, looks like Fernandel—or somebody like my niece Katcha, or Christiane, or Jean Louis Barrault, etc. It surprised me that so many Chinese looked like so many Westerners. Later, sorting through hundreds of pictures, I was glad for this method of identification.)

Lin Yang-yang told us the following: "The creation of *The White Haired Girl* here at the school is a revolution in proletarian ballet. Liu Shao-chi wanted a capitalist ballet; he pushed what we call the black line—anti-Party and anti-socialist ideas. We were performing both classic and modern ballet. Teaching materials came from the Soviet Union. When we did *Don Quixote* or *Swan Lake*, people often marched out of the hall. Once a mother of a student here came and saw her son playing a prince. She was angry and wanted him to come to work in the fields. This shocked us into thinking. We studied Chairman Mao's teaching, 'For whom is fundamental and a question of principle.' We realized we should be serving the 700,000,000 people. If we don't carry out revolution in art the socialist revolution will not be carried out.

"Revisionists in the city Party Committee at that time came to see us. They said, 'Don't hurry, learn from foreigners first.' They said foreign ballet couldn't reflect the present life in China. We weren't even allowed to see revolutionary performances playing in the theatre here in Shanghai. When Ko Ching-shih (the mayor of Shanghai) organized a festival of plays depicting socialist construction, the black line people tried to undermine it. This was reflected in our school—rehearsals for *Swan Lake* or *Giselle* were always scheduled to prevent us from attending the festival.

"It was Chiang Ching who supported us here, and Mayor Ko. We presented a half-hour version of *The White Haired Girl* in June 1964. Chiang Ching fully approved. With her help, a one-hour production was given on National Day of that year. Even after that the struggle went on against those in the school who opposed the new ballet. The main point was whether we would *extol* the workers, peasants, and soldiers, or *distort* the workers, peasants, and soldiers. We decided to show the *resistance* of Hsi-erh and her father. We made the father *fight* the landlord. The father no longer commits suicide; he is killed while resisting. We made Hsi-erh fight; we had her throw an incense burner at the landlord. We showed him in collaboration with the Japanese; this exposes his savageness and deceptiveness. The revisionists here talked about 'truthful writing' and 'middle characters'; they said there were always mediocre and backward people everywhere, peasants who are afraid to fight the landlord, for instance. They didn't approve of the father being killed—it makes the landlord look like a bandit.

"The revisionists wanted to give prominence to love as 'the eternal theme of ballet.' When the home village is liberated we show the soldiers and civilians joined together to defeat Japanese imperialism and the landlord collaborator. Chairman Mao said, 'Without a people's army we have nothing.' But the revisionists said, 'Too much smell of gunpowder; the young hero should first of all look for Hsi-erh, his love.' But this would distort the heroic image of the army man. Stanislavsky says, 'The theme of struggle between male and female is eternal.' New China wouldn't be able to establish itself on the basis of male and female struggle! This idea abolishes the struggle of *classes*. We do not oppose love, but love between the people is lofty. If the hero looked for the girl first it would mean his class consciousness is low. The ending should be the girl picking up her gun, joining the army and marching out to fight for the revolution."

Lin Yang-yang's face was serious, the boy and girl dancers were in obvious agreement—I felt a million miles away from New York City.

"In order to depict heroic images of workers, peasants, and soldiers," explained the choreographer, "we have cast away unnatural, artificial dances. We use formal ballet conventions but we have given them revolutionary content. For example, typical in ballet: *ying feng chan chih*—to spread one's wings in the welcoming breeze [here Lin demonstrated with knowing eloquence an arabesque in a languid and lyrical movement] when instilled with revolutionary content changes from litheness to fervor [his body became firm and charged with force and *Swan Lake's* decadent princess became a revolutionary].

"Sudden standing on points is used to express the ecstasy of love in *Romeo and Juliet*. Hsi-erh used this to express triumph as she escapes from the landlord's house. It is also to show heroic revolutionary defiance.

"Our ballet calls for a whole new set of dance language. When Hsi-erh is taken by the landlord, her boyfriend picks up an ax and dances solo, but this is very different from the bourgeois male solo which is an egotistical display for applause. A pas-de-deux is used when Hsi-erh fights off the landlord; when turns are used, it is in a different nature and context from the old ballet."

Lin Yang-yang provided other examples showing the assimilation of the old and foreign into the new, indigenous ballet. National dance steps like the *yang ko*, the north China peasant dance associated with harvest time and liberation, and the folk-dance steps of the Li people of Hainan in the south, as well as Peking opera gestures and acrobatics, unite in flexible harmony with alien ballet movement. Sudden pointing with widespread legs is very Chinese looking and very dramatic, as is walking or spinning on the knees (*kuei chuan*). Peking opera technique side by side with conventional ballet is startling and exciting; often the two are combined in one movement, usually with the classic Chinese gesture or posture taking command of the upper part of the body.

The Shanghai Dance School has an excellent company. Western critics could pick out choreographic limitations resulting from cultural insulation, but the gains made by dancers with a totally different heritage are impressive. However, many of what the Chinese consider their own innovations are to be found way back in the history of our ballet, when it did away with classic restrictions. Western ballet is full of breakthroughs in content and form. To mention Jerome Robbins is to bring up only one relatively recent tradition-smasher. *Fancy Free* may not have been a "proletarian" ballet, but it was a far cry from *Swan Lake*, one of the chief "decadent" offenders to the Chinese.

Agnes DeMille made ballet understandable to the uninitiated throughout the United States when she burst ballet barriers with *Oklahoma*, triggering a new concept of dance for those who did and those who didn't appreciate the classic. Edgar Y. Harburg's *Finian's Rainbow* created leaps forward many years ago. Some workers and "peasants" went on points in the United States before they did in China. Couched in its music and dance *Carousel* dealt poignantly with working people's lives, though certainly not on revolutionary terms. Western heroes too have changed. But it is understandable that the Chinese have come to regard our ballet and theatre as "reactionary," given the ideological differences between the two countries and the absence of exchange which would have enabled the Chinese (and us) to be more in the know. Perhaps if *West Side Story* or *Man of La Mancha* were shown in China this dark concept of our theatre would be modified to some extent. *The Trial of the Catonsville Nine* might seem bizarre with its priests and ex-nuns, but the cry of its content would have to be given recognition. These outstanding examples (different as they are) vividly demonstrate that theatre in the "bourgeois" world does not consist only of *Oh! Calcutta!s* and decadent dance.

Meanwhile the great gap exists, and the Chinese are finding their own way. Though it may be premature to state that they have really revolutionized ballet, they are creating a unique art. For the masses to whom entrechats and arabesques used to mean nothing, a proletarian tale depicted with great beauty in now-understandable content and form is a moving and educational experience. It is to be judged principally by the laboring people of a new world "for whom" it has been created and there is no doubt of that judgment when one sees the rapt attention paid to theatrical offerings by the Chinese audiences.

The productions of *The White Haired Girl* that we saw in Sian and Shanghai were danced with skill and spirit— zeal is the word—by slim, light-footed ballerinas in the demanding part of Hsi-erh, and an attractive hero and a highly disciplined corps de ballet. Songs in the background (a singer and chorus are discreetly placed to the side of the orchestra in the pit) accompany the dancing. The music is sweeping; the words are searing. Hsi-erh's soprano solo vocally expresses her danced rebellion and fury when tortured by the landlord and his mother:

> Whips lash me, needles stab me,
> I care not how savagely you beat me.
> I will escape this house . . .
> Hatred heaped on hatred,
> Ever deeper is my hatred.

Hsi-erh vows:

> I will become a storm!
> I will become thunder that
> Shakes the nine heavens!

And indeed she does. Seeking food in the mountain temple, she encounters Huang the landlord and his lackey, Mu, who are fleeing from the Eighth Route Army. In a shriek of music Hsi-erh leaps from the high altar and hurls a heavy incense burner at the cringing men. The audience responded with an audible gasp—Women's Liberation was on stage.

I was especially touched when Hsi-erh returns to her village and meets the friend who had helped her escape from the landlord's house. I often found a moment of deep feeling revealed more strikingly in dance than in opera— lack of words results in total body expression that conveys pure and keen emotion. The audience was with it when the landlord met his fate. They *wanted* Hsi-erh to join the revolution—and she did. I could understand any kids out front going right out the next morning to sign up with the PLA—but it's not that easy; they're very selective. In other words, we in the audience all connected, and what more could anyone want?

The production of *Red Detachment of Women* that we saw in Peking was more polished than that of *The White Haired Girl*. It was also more interesting visually: the island setting, the light-heartedness and play by the water's edge, the unexpected sight of short-panted, gun-bearing ballerina soldiers drilling on full point, and the contrast of lovely native costuming. The China Ballet Troupe of Peking danced that August evening. This fine company's style and spirit would be hard to equal.

Red Detachment of Women went through a struggle similar to that of the other model offerings. As early as 1959 it was prepared as an opera in Tung Tza, in central Hainan. A film dramatization claimed a prize at the International Festival in Moscow in 1961. The scenario, written by Hsieh Chin, contained some ideological errors and was subsequently revised. This version continued to be shown until 1966—the beginning of the Cultural Revolution—and has now been replaced by the beautiful new film that millions of viewers saw in the United States on television in early 1972. By 1964 Chiang Ching had chosen the story to be converted into a ballet in Peking. It is said that there was powerful opposition to its creation even after Premier Chou En-lai intervened in support of the troupe. In spite of disapproval, work progressed. The whole company went to Hainan Island to become familiar with the revolutionary areas and to meet former members of the women's detachment. Later, during rehearsals in Peking they went again to improve their military bearing and to learn from the army the proper handling of weapons.

The work is beautiful in presentation, moving not only for the workers and peasants for whom it has been made, but for anyone, occidental or Oriental, Communist or bourgeois, who cares about a budding, original theatre.

Red Detachment of Women

(MAY 1970 SCRIPT)

REVISED COLLECTIVELY BY THE CHINA BALLET TROUPE

≈

CAST OF CHARACTERS

Hung Chang-ching: *male, Party representative in the Women's Company*

Wu Ching-hua: *soldier in the Women's Company, later its Party representative*

Company Commander: *leader of the Women's Company*

Pang: *boy messenger in the Red Army*

The Tyrant of the South: *despotic landlord, commander of counter-revolutionary "civil guards"*

Lao Szu: *his bailiff, head of the "civil guards"*

PROLOGUE

The Second Revolutionary Civil War Period (1927–1937). Hainan Island. Night. The Tyrant of the South's dungeon.

(*The curtain rises.*)

Chained to a post is Wu Ching-hua, daughter of a poor peasant. She hates being a bondmaid, a slave. Several times she has run away, but each time she has been caught, brought back and cruelly beaten. She stands with head and chest high, her eyes blazing with hatred. If only she could smash the bloody shackles which bind her and wreck the lair of these man-eating beasts!

With her in the dungeon are two other peasant women, locked up by the Tyrant because they have been unable to pay their land rent. They too have been beaten savagely. Fists clenched, they pour out their hatred.

(*The two women dance.*)

Lao Szu, the Tyrant's bailiff and bullyboy, enters with a guard. He has been ordered to take Ching-hua out and sell her.

He unlocks the shackles, releasing Ching-hua. Strong class feeling makes her forget her painful injuries and rush to her cellmates. She urges them to fight the Tyrant to the end.

Lao Szu comes after her and menaces her with his whip, pushing her towards the dungeon door.

Catching him off guard, Ching-hua seizes the whip and kicks him to the ground. (*At the door, she does "kung chien pu." Her arms forcefully spread, she glares at Lao Szu, and performs the "liang hsiang."**)

He starts to rise. The two women throw themselves on him and the guard and hold them fast.

Ching-hua watches in concern. The women urge her to flee.

She dashes out of the tiger's maw with determination.

---

* A term in traditional Chinese opera. It is a still, statuesque pose assumed for a brief moment by the principals and others while entering or leaving the stage, sometimes after a dance or an acrobatic feat, in order to bring out sharply and concentratedly the spiritual outlook of the characters.

⌣̄

SCENE ONE

Immediately following the prologue. Late at night in the dark cocoanut grove.

(*Lanterns marked "South Manor" gleam.*)

Lao Szu and a gang of guards are in pursuit of Ching-hua. Carrying whips and ropes, they prowl like beasts of prey among the cocoanut trees, but in vain. Lao Szu is fuming with rage. He orders his men to scatter and search.

(*Dance of Lao Szu and the guards.*)

Ching-hua is hidden behind a tree. After the gangsters leave, she emerges quickly. (*She does "tsu chien kung chien pu liang hsiang."*)

(*Solo dance.*)

She advances swiftly in big strides. (*Then she rapidly does "tsu chien sui pu—pas couru," and "pi cha tiao—pas de chat," followed by "pu pu."*) Separating small trees with her hands, she cautiously peers in all directions, then runs deeper into the grove. The enemy's chase intensifies her hatred. If they don't catch her, she'll flee. If they do, she'll fight. Rather death than slavery! (*She does "ping chuan— chaîne," "yeh tui chuan—tour en dedans," "hsien shen tan hai—attitude basse" and "tao ti tzu chin kuan."*)

Discovering guards coming her way, Ching-hua nimbly hides behind a tree.

Two of the men furtively search.

She cleverly eludes them but in the darkness bumps into Lao Szu. They grapple in a desperate struggle.

(*Struggle dance.*)

Ching-hua turns and jumps up. Flinging off his arms, she swings one leg in a sweeping kick. Lao Szu leaps to avoid it. She turns and runs. Pursuing, he grabs her left arm. She angrily pushes down on him. Neither give way. (*They do "hsi tui la chuan—tour lent à deux."*)

She breaks loose. Again he pounces on her. She fights fiercely. (*She does "pi cha," "chiao chu," and "chien shih pien shen tiao—jeté entrelacé," then performs the "liang hsiang."*)

"You're coming back with me," Lao Szu yells.

She furiously raises her head. "I'll die first!" Lao Szu is weakening. Ching-hua's courage doubles. She twists his arm, bites him fiercely and kicks him to the ground.

She runs, but the vicious guards catch up and surround her. They are too many for her. She again falls into their clutches.

The Tyrant of the South rushes in, followed by guards and bondmaids. The sight of Ching-hua's stubborn resistance enrages him. He cruelly presses her temple with the tip of his cane. She is adamant and refuses to bow her head. He strikes her savagely. She seizes one end of the cane. She will fight even if it costs her life. (*They do "chuan fan shen."*) The Tyrant trembles with rage. He orders his guards to drag Ching-hua aside. "Beat her to death!" he howls.

Whip blows are heard. The hearts of the bondmaids, who share the same suffering and hatred as Ching-hua, burn like fire. They are torn by anxiety for her. The tearing cuts of the whips seem to be ripping their own flesh. If only they could save their class sister!

(*The bondmaids dance.*)

The Tyrant decides to make Ching-hua an example to cow the others. He orders that she be dragged in and beaten to death before their eyes.

Ching-hua refuses to yield. She continues to fight courageously as the lackeys rain blows on her with their whips. (*She does "tan hai fan shen" and "kuo pao."*) She struggles, chest high and fists raised, until they beat her unconscious.

Lao Szu announces that she is dead. "Anyone who resists or tries to escape," the Tyrant grates threateningly to the bondmaids, "will meet the same fate."

Thunder rumbles. A storm is brewing. The Tyrant, Lao Szu and other lackeys hastily leave. Heartbroken, the bondmaids rush towards Ching-hua. The guards drive them away.

Lightning flashes, thunder rumbles. A violent storm shakes the cocoanut grove.

In the deluging rain, Ching-hua slowly revives.

(Solo dance.)

Her body a mass of excruciating wounds, weak from hunger and cold, where can she go in this dark night? Is there no end to the cocoanut grove? (She does "tsu chien sui pu—pas suivi.") Is there no road open to oppressed slaves? Haltingly, she stumbles forward, forward. . . . Then the pain overcomes her and she falls in a faint.

The rain passes, the sky clears. Dawn breaks through the mist. Sunlight slants into the cocoanut grove.

Red Army cadre Hung Chang-ching and his messenger Pang enter, disguised as peasants. They are on a scouting mission.

(Hung and Pang dance.)

Bold, steady and alert, a bamboo hat in hand, Hung advances, examining the surroundings. (He does "chi pu yuan chang," inclined forward to look around, then performs the "liang hsiang.") He peers everywhere with flashing eyes. (Lightly he does "chien yueh—sissonne ouverte," "tso pu—chassé," "shang pu fan shen," and performs the "liang hsiang.")

He and Pang discover Ching-hua. They run over and lift her up. She gradually comes to. On seeing two strangers, she struggles to run away.

"Don't be afraid," they say kindly. "We're poor working people just like you."

Dizzy from her exertions, Ching-hua nearly falls. Hung

quickly supports her. He sees the bloody weals on her arms. Shocked, he gently pats them with the towel from around his neck.

Class hatred flames in his heart. "Who beat you like this?"

His simple, earnest manner dispels Ching-hua's suspicions. She angrily points towards where the Tyrant has gone. "That fiend who kills without blinking an eye—the Tyrant of the South!"

"The Tyrant of the South," Hung and Pang repeat in fury. "That butcher! We'll make him pay for his countless bloody crimes."

In concern Hung asks: "Where will you go now? Where is your home?"

"Home? I have no home. . . ."

Hung is filled with deep proletarian feeling for this poor peasant's daughter who has suffered so bitterly. He points and says: "Beyond the cocoanut grove, on the other side of the mountain, red flags wave in the bright sun. The armed forces of us workers and peasants are there. Go to them, become a soldier and get revenge."

Ching-hua, though lacerated and bruised all over, is greatly inspired. "No matter how many hardships and dangers, that's the road I will take."

She wipes her hands on the front of her tunic and, trembling, accepts the silver. She gives Hung a deep bow, then flies off in the direction he has indicated.

Hung and Pang watch till she is out of sight. Then, alertly scanning the dense grove, they continue scouting. (*They perform the "liang hsiang."*)

(*Curtain*)

⪤

SCENE TWO

(*Vigorous, ringing, the "March of the Women's Company."*)

Forward, forward!
Important the soldiers' task, deep the women's hatred.
Smash your shackles, rise in revolution!
We're the women's company, taking up arms for the people.
Forward, forward!
Important the soldiers' task, deep the women's hatred.
Communism is the truth, the Party leads the way.
Slaves will arise, slaves will arise!
Forward, forward! . . .

A morning several days later, on the drill field in a Red base.

(The curtain rises.)

(Fleecy white clouds dot the clear blue sky, coloured flags flutter in the breeze, songs fill the air. A lofty kapok tree is in bloom with a profusion of red flowers.)

A happy crowd of local people have gathered by the kapok tree to celebrate the formation of the Red Army Women's Company. There are young and old, Red Militia, girls of the Li nationality. . . .

(Group dance.)
("March of the Women's Company" again rings forth.)

Bright and brave, the Red women soldiers, with Party Represenative Hung and the Company Commander at their head, march briskly to the drill field. The peasants are over-joyed, children jump merrily, welcoming cheers resound.

Hung and the Company Commander solemnly proclaim the formal establishment of the Red Company of Women of the Chinese Workers' and Peasants' Red Army!

The Company Commander orders a practice drill. The

girls perform a spirited rifle drill *("tsu chien sui pu—pas suivi")* to the commands of their leader.

(Target practice dance.)

Hung brandishes a sword vigorously with the fearless heroism of revolutionary soldiers.

(Sword dance.)

He advances with firm, broad steps. *(He does "tao hua," and performs the "liang hsiang" with sword raised.)* He leaps into the air boldly. *(He does "sheh yen ta tiao," "pei tao fei chiao," "yen shih tiao," "hsiao peng tzu—série de renversés" and "la tui peng tzu—grand jeté en tournant," and performs the "liang hsiang" with a sword slash.)*

Women soldiers, also flourishing swords, fly back and forth on the stage, steel blades flashing, militant cries ringing.

(Women's sword dance.)

A little girl soldier, sturdy and nimble, spiritedly practices with hand grenades.

Women soldiers, bright and bold, do a bayonet drill. It ends with shouts of fierce class hatred.

(Bayonet dance.)

Five brawny Red Militia men dash out from the crowd with a five-inch dagger in each hand. They perform a dance full of leaps and twists, brave and clever, manifesting the great strength of the people's forces.

(Dagger dance.)

The soldiers and civilians are of one heart. Everyone is stirred. Children perform a mime in dance showing the overthrow of the Tyrant of the South. The whole place is in a ferment.

(Dance by the entire ensemble.)

Suddenly, a Children's Corps sentry rushes in and announces: A girl who has run away from Cocoanut Grove Manor is here.

She's arrived at last! Ching-hua, having overcome severe hardships, walks stumbling forward. Everyone surrounds her in concern and supports her. Kids in the Children's Corps tell her: "This is a Red base. See, the red flag!"

Red flag! Ching-hua stares at the rippling banner with deep emotion. She staggers forward and presses it against her cheek. Tears roll down her face.

"Red flag, oh, red flag, today I've found you! . . ."

Soldiers and peasants crowd around. In agitation she looks at the women soldiers in their new uniforms, at the red star on their caps, the red tabs on their collars, their red armbands. . . . She excitedly touches the girls by the hand.

"I want to be a women soldier too!"

Hung, the Company Commander and Pang the young messenger come forward. Ching-hua immediately recognizes her benefactors and is very excited. Hung enthusiastically presents her to the Company Commander and the peasants. "This class sister has been cruelly oppressed and her hatred is strong. She was nearly killed several times, but finally managed to escape from the hellish Cocoanut Grove Manor."

All the soldiers and peasants give Ching-hua a hearty welcome.

The Company Commander hands her a bowl of coconut milk. "Drink. This is your home now. We are all your class sisters."

Cocoanut milk! The cool sweet liquid is infused with deep class feeling. For more than ten years Ching-hua had been a bondmaid, a slave. No one treated her like a human being. But today beneath the red flag, how warm the sunshine, how friendly the people! She raises the bowl with both hands and drinks.

The Company Commander notices the weals on her

arms and asks her about herself. For generations Ching-hua's family suffered bloody oppression. Fury wells up in her heart. She pours out the story of the crimes of the Tyrant of the South.

(*Solo dance.*)

She pulls up her sleeves and reveals the whip marks covered with blood. (*She does "tse shen hsi tui," "chan chih tun chuan" and "pei shen kuei pu."*) She tells of the tortures she endured in the Tyrant's dungeon. (*From "pang yueh pu—jeté fermé" she turns to "tsu chien ping li—soutenu en tournant." In the "tsao hsing" she shows how she was chained in the Tyrant's dungeon.*) She tells how she was nearly beaten to death by the Tyrant in the cocoa-nut grove. (*She does "tan hai fan shen" and expresses her fury in the "liang hsiang."*)

Hung points out the cruelties inflicted on Ching-hua's family for generations as a lesson to the soldiers and peasants, saying:

"Her suffering is ours. Her hatred is ours. Slaves must arise. But only by taking up guns and waging revolution under the guidance of our great leader Chairman Mao and the Chinese Communist Party can we win a new world and liberate hundreds of millions of suffering people." (*He does "hsi tui ta tiao," and "kung chuan—tour en l'air" and performs the "liang hsiang" with an arm extended.*)

Tremendously aroused, the masses hold up banners reading: "Down with the tyrants! Share out the land!" "Capture the Tyrant of the South." They are determined to overthrow the Tyrant and liberate Cocoanut Grove Manor.

Hung and the Company Commander approve Ching-hua's request to join the army. The Company Commander hands her a rifle.

Ching-hua excitedly accepts it. Chest high, she takes her place in the fighting ranks of the Red Company of Women.

(*Curtain*)

≕

SCENE THREE

Dusk. The courtyard of the Tyrant's manor.

(The curtain rises.)

It is the Tyrant's birthday. The manor is a scene of hectic activity. Guards carry pots of wine, platters of meat, expensive gifts. Some noisily drive across the yard a number of Li nationality girls they have seized. Local tyrants, evil gentry, Kuomintang scoundrels and bandit chieftains arrive to join in the festivities.

The Tyrant emerges from the manor house to greet his guests. Local tyrants and Kuomintang scoundrels present gifts, bow and offer birthday greetings. Highly elated, the Tyrant invites them into the banquet hall.

His wife orders the bondmaids to serve fruit and cakes.

(The bondmaids dance.)

Guards with whips compel the Li girls to dance for the birthday banquet. Filled with loathing for the Tyrant and his despotic landlord and gentry guests, the girls are forced to comply.

(Li nationality dance.)

A guard hurries in with a red calling card which he hands to the Tyrant, announcing: "An important guest has arrived."

The Tyrant looks at the card. A big merchant from overseas! He doesn't know him. What brings him here? The gentry discuss this, but cannot agree on a reason. Dizzied by the prospect of lavish gifts, the Tyrant is not willing to let the opportunity slip by. He orders his guards to line up and present arms in welcome to the important guest.

The "important guest" is none other than Hung, Party representative in the Women's Company. After several days of scouting he has learned the enemy's situation and has worked out a plan. That is, he will take advantage of the confusion created by the Tyrant's birthday party and enter the enemy's lair disguised as a big merchant, accompanied by Pang and other fighters, also in disguise. At midnight, shots will be fired as a signal for the Red Army to attack from the outside while he and his group strike from within. In this way they will wipe out the Tyrant and his gang.

Calm and dignified, Hung strides into the courtyard. (*Loftily, he performs the "liang hsiang."*)

The Tyrant hastily comes forward to greet him. Hung orders his "retainers" to present the gifts. The Tyrant stars greedily. With excessive courtesy he bids his guest take a seat of honour.

To impress Hung, he directs Lao Szu and the guards to put on military display.

> (*Guards dance with halberds. Lao Szu executes a boxing dance.*)

Hung flings them a handful of sliver. They scramble avidly for the rolling coins. The Tyrant, embarrassed, invites Hung into the banquet hall.

It is now late at night. The manor looks exceedingly gloomy.

Ching-hua and another girl soldier steal in, disguised as bondmaids. They want to make contact with Pang. At the doorway, they quietly dispose of the sentry, then look around carefully. Ching-hua explains the layout of the manor to the other girl.

Footsteps are heard approaching. The girls turn quickly and alertly hide behind a rockery.

Two guards pursue and savagely beat a little bondmaid. She falls senseless to the ground. They carry her off.

> (*Dance of guards and little bondmaid.*)

Ching-hua watches in a fury. She charges out to save her suffering class sister. (*She does "ying feng chan chih—arabesque," "chien shih pien shen tiao—jeté entrelacé" and "pi cha tiao—pas de chat."*) The other girl stops her.

Pang cautiously approaches in the dark. He gives the secret signal Ching-hua has been waiting for. (*He does "kua yeh tui kung chuan," and "tsan pu," landing in a "pu pu" followed by a "kuo men kan."*)

(*Pang solo.*)

China-hua hears his signal and goes to him. He tells her there has been no change in the enemy situation. They will proceed according to plan, and strike when Hung fires the shot. Pang swiftly returns to his own post.

Loud voices in the banquet hall. The Tyrant and the guests come out. He is seeing them off.

At the sight of the Tyrant, Ching-hua's whole being cries out for vengeance. She has only one thought: "Kill the Tyrant of the South! Get revenge! Revenge!"

(*She and her companion dance.*)

Ching-hua leaves her companion and rushes out. (*She does "tao ti tzu chin kuan" and "pien tui chuan."*) The girl tries to hold her back. Ching-hua is in an uncontrollable rage. (*She does "hsien shen tan hai—attitude basse" and "ying feng chan chih—arabesque."*) Pushing her companion aside, she turns abruptly and fires two shots, wounding the Tyrant. Ching-hua has prematurely given the signal.

The startled enemy come swarming out. Ching-hua's companion pulls her into cover.

Shots crackle on all sides. The Red Army unit has surrounded the bandit lair. Terrified, the wounded Tyrant jumps into a concealed tunnel with Lao Szu and flees.

Hung swiftly emerges from the hall and calmly prepares to cope with the unexpected change. He makes a rapid appraisal, then orders Pang and the others to kill the guards in co-ordination with the Red Army's assault from the outside.

The guards break and scatter in cowardly flight.

The flag of victory waves over the manor. Tears in their eyes, the peasants surge into the courtyard. Hung and the

Company Commander tell them: "We've opened the Tyrant's granary. All that grain was produced by the sweat and blood of the poor. It's now going to be distributed to you."

Cheering, the peasants race towards the granary.

Pang comes forward with the Tyrant's cane. "The bandit chieftains, big and small, have all been wiped out," he says. "Only the Tyrant and Lao Szu are missing." The Company Commander and Pang go to search the rear courtyard.

The peasants, on receiving grain, are overjoyed. Hung carries in a big basketful. Warmly, fondly, he delivers it into the hands of an old farmhand. With uplifted bags of golden grain, the peasants cheer again and again: "Long live Chairman Mao!" "Long live the Communist Party!" "We thank our dear ones—the Workers' and Peasants' Red Army!"

(A grain distribution dance by the masses.)

Pang and the Company Commander bring in an old despotic landlord they have found in the rear courtyard. In response to Hung's stern queries, he tremblingly reveals the Tyrant's tunnel.

Ching-hua realizes that the Tyrant has escaped. Enraged and impatient, she tries to plunge, gun in hand, into the tunnel, but Hung stops her.

The Company Commander severely criticizes her for breaching discipline, and relieves her of her gun. Ching-hua is very upset.

Concerned about her, Hung comes over and questions her in detail.

⚌

SCENE FOUR

Early morning. Rosy clouds fill the sky. A Red Army camp by the Wanchuan River.

(The curtain rises.)

On a blackboard beneath the cocoanut trees is written: "Only by emancipating all mankind can the proletariat achieve its own final emancipation." Hung is conducting a political class for the women soldiers.

(Hung solo.)

With grand sweeping gestures he points to the distance, indicating the great goals of the proletarian revolution and the responsibilities of revolutionary fighters. "Revolution is not simply a matter of personal vengeance," he says. "Its aim is the emancipation of all mankind." *(He does "yi ti hsi tui kung chuan—saut de basque," "to ni," "pang tui kung chuan—grand temps levé en tournant à la seconde," and performs the "liang hsiang.")*

Revolutionary truth illuminates the fighters' hearts like the sun. Standing before the ranks, Hung encourages them to unite closely, shoulder to shoulder and hand in hand, under the leadership of Chairman Mao and the Chinese Communist Party, and join in the revolutionary torrent which will sweep away the old world.

Class is dismissed. Ching-hua remains behind. She studies the shining words on the blackboard, then walks and sits on a stump.

(Ching-hua solo.)

She rises again slowly, her mind in ferment, and tries to grasp the significance of what the Party representative has just said. *(She takes "tsu chien sui pu—pas suivi," followed by a "sheh yen" stance in a kneeling position.)*

Regretfully, she recalls her mistake in opening fire without permission in Cocoanut Grove Manor. "In the whole world is there any proletarian who hasn't been steeped in blood and tears? Why do I think only of vengeance for myself?" *(With a quick succession of "tsao hsing" on points, she demonstrates how she shot at the Tyrant of the South.)*

She runs to the blackboard, reads it carefully. Suddenly, she understands. (*She turns forcefully, does "ling kung yueh —grand jeté," "ho li shih—attitude" and "hsien shen tan hai—attitude basse."*) She strides resolutely to greet the rising sun. Fist raised she vows: "I will follow Chairman Mao and the Chinese Communist Party forever and be a conscious proletarian vanguard soldier fighting all my life for the liberation of mankind!"

The Company Commander, returning from target practice, fondly hails her. Ching-hua, ashamed, walks over and criticizes herself. Pleased to see Ching-hua maturing poltically, the Company Commander cannot restrain her affection for the stubborn new fighter. She urges Ching-hua to continue raising her proletarian consciousness and to channel her hatred for the class enemy into proficient skill at annihilating them. Under the Company Commander's instructions, Ching-hua practises shooting and grenade throwing.

(*They dance.*)

Hung arrives and is happy to see Ching-hua determined, militant and in high spirits. He tells the Company Commander to return Ching-hua's gun. Greatly moved, the girl expresses her revolutionary determination to the Party representative and the Company Commander.

In the sunshine of the revolutionary base, the heroic Red Army Women's Company is united, alert, earnest and lively. It has a flourishing and youthful spirit.

Soldiers return from drill with captured enemy rifles and report to Hung. He chats with them and urges them to capture still more weapons and wipe out still more of the foe.

Several women soldiers enter, carrying fish and vegetables they have grown themselves. Hung goes to work with the soldiers.

A girl soldier mends an army tunic for one of the men. A man soldier is exchanging absorbedly experiences of target practice with a girl. A group of soldiers patrol along the bank of the river, vigilantly guarding the Red base.

A few girl soldiers, washing vegetables by the river, notice the head cook approaching with a pair of buckets on a shoulder pole. They mischievously block him, snatch the buckets and cheerfully fetch water for him.

(Dance of the girls and the head cook.)

Merry songs of approaching peasants can be heard in the distance. Hung and the Company Commander go with soldiers to meet them.

Peasants enter with bamboo hats they have woven and lichee they have picked, and present them to the Workers' and Peasants' Red Army.

Holding the hats, the peasant girls dance and sing of the close ties between the soldiers and the civilians.
(Song:)

The river water is clear, oh clear,
Hats we weave for the Red Army dear,
Our armymen love the people, we support them delighted,
As one family we are with them united.

The river water is clear, oh clear
Hats we weave for the Red Army dear,
Our armymen love the people, we support them delighted,
Together we strike the foe benighted.

Our Red base is beautiful, we closely cohere,
The river water is clear, oh clear,
Hats we weave for the Red Army dear,
Together we'll march ever on, no fear.

Hung thanks the peasants on behalf of the army for their warm support. He says the fighters will win more victories to manifest their gratitude.

In response to the peasants' enthusiastic welcome, the Company Commander and Ching-hua lead the women soldiers in a joyous dance.

Hung and the Red Army men dance boldly, staunchly, with vigorous strides and powerful arm movements, with soaring leaps and stalwart gestures. (*They do "hsi tui tiao —temps levé, jambe repliée," "pien shen tiao—grand fouetté," "kung chuan—tour en l'air" and perform the "liang hsiang."*) These show the all-conquering power and invincible courage of the Workers' and Peasants' Red Army.

(*Dance of Hung and Red Army men.*)

Happy soldiers and civilians, close as one family, gaily dance and sing.

(*Dance of the entire ensemble.*)

Suddenly they hear the approaching beat of galloping hoofs. Pang the messenger enters with an order from headquarters.

Cannon booms in the distance. The Kuomintang troops have launched a major offensive against the base area.

It is a tense situation. Hung and the Company Commander decide that they should set out immediately.

The fighters of the Red Army and Red Militia are promptly assembled. They march with firm strides, bidding farewell to dear ones as they hasten to the battlefield.

≈

SCENE FIVE

Shortly before dawn. A battle position in a mountain pass.

(*The curtain rises. Racing clouds, towering cliffs, rolling gun smoke, leaping flames.*)

In order to wipe out the enemy effectives, the main force of our army is rapidly sweeping around to their rear. The Company Commander is leading a group from the Women's Company in this manoeuvre. An intercepting platoon of Red Army soldiers and Red Militia men under

Hung is holding the mountain pass to give our army time to complete its move in safety.

Heavy fire is heard at the foot of the mountain, as the crafty enemy attempts a pincers assault. Hung sizes up the situation and decides to take a few comrades to protect the flank. He orders Ching-hua to command the holding action in the pass.

"We will complete our mission," Ching-hua and the soldiers vow.

The enemy charges the pass. Making use of the favourable terrain, Ching-hua and her comrades give the enemy a head-on blow. Their hate-laden bullets angrily pour down, their hand grenades burst amid the enemy. The fighters are brave and staunch. Solidly united, they give each other cover. (*They do "hua cha" and "kuei chuan."*) They beat back the enemy's frenzied assault.

(*Dance of Ching-hua and the fighters.*)

The little girl soldier is hit, but she continues to fight. Ching-hua hurries over and bandages her wound.

Having defeated the enemy's flanking attempt, Hung leads the soldiers back to the position. He shows warm concern for the wounded girl. She vows she will not leave the firing line.

Again the enemy is stirring. They gather additional soldiers and attack once more. The Red Army men tell Hung: "Our ammunition is nearly finished."

Outnumbered, running out of bullets, Hung calmly calls the fighters together and says: "Now is the time to prove our worth to the Party. When our bullets are gone, we'll still have our swords and rocks. We must defend the position with our blood and lives!"

The fighters whip out their swords and lift up rocks. Grimly, they wait.

The enemy swarm up the slopes, snarling and brandishing their claws. Hung and his comrades swing their swords, heave their rocks, and send the foe reeling.

Ching-hua, who suffered much and has strong class hatred, is firm and courageous, thanks to the education the Party has given her. She hotly battles the attacking die-hards.

(Dance fight of Ching-hua and a guard.)

Gripping her sword with both hands, she slashes. The guard hastily wards off the blow. In the heated duel Ching-hua's blade flies out of her grasp. Fearless, she rushes him, empty-handed, and grabs him by the neck. (*She does "ying feng chan chih—arabesque," lands in "shuai cha," then rises and performs the "liang hsiang."*)

She fights with growing strength. One kick sends the guard's halberd sailing, and they grapple. She nimbly trips him down. (*Ching-hua does "chien chiao," and trips the guard, landing him in a "ko tzu." Pressing down on him, she does "hsuan tzu."*)

The guard weakens. She steps on him, seizes his dagger and stabs the scoundrel to death.

Red Army soldiers and Red Militia men battle shoulder to shoulder, striking terror in the hearts of the enemy.

(Dance fight of two soldiers and two guards.)

Amid a hail of bullets and rolling smoke, Ching-hua, Pang and the fighters beneath the fluttering red flag vali-antly fight the foe. Their courage is enormous. It grows as they battle, and soon the red flag of victory waves on high.

(Red flag dance.)

The enemy forces have scattered and retreated, and the heroes remain in control of the position.

Hung looks at his watch. Excitedly, he announces: "By now our main force has moved out according to plan. Our intercepting platoon has successfully completed its delaying action." Smiles of triumph appear on everyone's face.

As the platoon prepares to leave, the enemy springs

another assault. Hung decides to remain behind and cover the withdrawal of his troops. He orders Ching-hua to lead the comrades out immediately.

She pleads that she be allowed to stay. Ching-hua has already been admitted to the Communist Party on the firing line. Hung solemnly unstraps his dispatch case and gives it to her. "If we should lose contact, deliver this to the battalion Party committee."

He peers down at the enemy at the foot of the mountain. Ching-hua again goes to him and begs that he let her stay and fight. Hung waves a resolute hand. "Carry out orders!" She reluctantly leads the comrades from the position.

Only Hung, a Red Army fighter, and a Red Militia man are left. They steadfastly hold out against the foe.

The enemy feverishly attack. Completely in command of the situation, Hung battles the foe furiously on every side. (*He flings a grenade.*)

The Red Army soldier is hit, wounded. Hung orders the militiaman to support him. The Red Militia fighter spots a bandit soldier aiming at Hung. He rushes him and takes the bullet in his chest.

Two enemy soldiers charge. Hung, now alone, fights valiantly, with the typical courage of a proletarian revolutionary soldier who has an indomitable spirit and is determined to vanquish all enemies.

(*Dance fight of Hung and the two enemy soldiers.*)

Swinging his sword, he fights the die-hards. (*One enemy soldier falls in "kao pu hu." Hung whirls and puts his foot on him.*)

The other enemy soldier attacks. Hung jumps up and slashes at them with his sword and kills them. (*Hung does "yen shih tiao" and "shuang peng tzu—double spirale." He slashes left and right and then performs the "liang hsiang" with his sword raised.*)

More enemy soldiers swarm in and surround Hung.

He pulls out his last hand grenade, yanks the firing string and raises it menacingly. The attackers scramble and flee. Hung flings the grenade after them. It explodes and they topple to the ground, dead.

Supporting his two comrades, Hung starts moving out through the pass. They are met by a fusillade of bullets. Hung is severely wounded. His two companions are killed. With his remaining strength, he gently lowers them to the ground. Holding himself erect by sheer force of will, he gazes after the departing Red Army platoon. A smile of satisfaction appears on his face as the platoon reaches safety.

His wound gives a sharp stab of pain, and he falls in a faint.

Dark clouds gather. Thunder rumbles.

The Tyrant of the South and a Kuomintang army officer enter with a gang of bedraggled-looking soldiers. Trembling, they crawl to the top of the rise, where they discover Hung. They fearfully surround him.

Hung revives. He indignantly pushes the enemy soldiers aside and rises before the clifftop like a towering pine. Lightning rips across the cloudy night sky, illuminating Hung's militant figure. His angry piercing gaze quells his attackers. Terrified, they dare not look up.

Thunder and lightning rock the firmament.

INTERLUDE

(*The curtain rises.*)

With the force of an avalanche the main force of the Red Army advances swiftly in pursuit of the enemy troops.
(*Dance of the Red Army men.*)

Preceded by a flame-red battle flag, the Red Army units, powerful and courageous, cross over mountains chasing the foe.

They press forward as irresistibly as molten steel, speeding like arrows from a bow. (*They do "pi cha ta tiao—grand pas de chat."*)

≍

SCENE SIX

Dusk. Rear courtyard of the Tyrant of the South. Oppressive overcast sky. Dim and gloomy. A huge banian tree, tall and spreading.

News of one victory after another by the Red Army creates panic in the enemy lair. Lao Szu runs in and threatens the guards with his gun, trying desperately to halt the collapse.

A Kuomintang army officer, who has been knocked dizzy by the blows of the Red Army, refuses to heed the pleas of the Tyrant that he remain. He runs for his life, followed by the beaten remnants of his troops.

The Tyrant's wife is frantically busy, ordering the servants to move her valuables. She stumbles about, ready to flee.

Seeing his power slipping away, the Tyrant beats his chest, stamps his feet and roars in frustration. Lao Szu lyingly vows that he will go with his master and fight to the end. They snarl and brandish their claws for a last-ditch struggle.

(The Tyrant and Lao Szu dance.)

The guards keep running in to report the approach of the Red Army. Trapped, the Tyrant decides on a last resort. "Put the manor on full alert," he orders. "Pile brushwood beneath the banian tree, and bring in Hung."

Four guards push Hung into the courtyard.

Head and chest high, Hung is calm. He looks contemptuously at the enemy die-hards. (*He performs the "liang hsiang."*)

The Tyrant holds out a sheet of paper. In a vain attempt to save himself from total defeat he orders Hung to write a "recantation."

Hung throws off the guards with a shake of his arms. The rascals fall back in alarm.

Hung glances scornfully at the brushwood and torches beneath the banian tree. He steps forward with firm strides, his strong arms outstretched. He looks at the sky and surrounding countryside, his determination soaring: How beautiful is our native land! How fertile and vast. For the past hundred years, fiends have been running amok, spreading ruin. But now the building of a revolutionary base in the Chingkang Mountains has opened new vistas. Chairman Mao has pointed the way to victory—armed revolution, the wresting of political power. No one can stop a spreading prairie fire!

Raising his right arm, he stands in the middle of the execution grounds thinking, listening, his mind far away. He seems to hear the battle song of the Red Company of Women, he seems to see the people's armed forces mowing down the enemy. His tightly clenched right fist waves slightly in rhythm to the battle song, his eyes shining.

The execution grounds are a battlefield. As if with a weapon in his hand Hung marches straight up to the Tyrant. The landlord and Lao Szu cringe before his piercing gaze and fearless manner. (*Hung does "chien shih pien shen tiao—jeté entrelacé," sailing scornfully over the Tyrant who kneels in a frightened crouch.*)

Swinging his arms, Hung sweeps across the execution grounds like a whirlwind, terrorizing the foe. (*He does "fei chiao," "pien tui—grand rond de jambe en dehors," and "kung chuan—tour en l'air." Furiously he does "ping chuan —chaîne in a rapid movement, then turns sideways to perform the "liang hsiang."*) With the utmost contempt and hatred for the class enemy, he grabs the sheet of paper, rips it to shreds, and flings it in the face of the Tyrant.

What does death matter? The communist creed is the truth! Hung points at the villains in a rage. "Communists are not afraid to die! You'll never escape the people's punishment!" He soars over the heads of the foe like an eagle in the sky. (*He does "hsuan feng kung chuan—grand assemblé en tournant," "yen shih tiao," "pang tui chuan—grande pirouette à la seconde" and performs the "liang hsiang" with an arm in the air.*) The bandits fall prostrate and trembling in the face of the Communist's splendid courage and heroism.

To the grand strains of the *Internationale*, Hung angrily shakes off the guards who try to seize him and with majestic calm mounts the pyre beneath the banian tree. He extends his left hand, as if to caress the beautiful motherland. Gazing far, he sees the glorious, triumphant New China that is to come. Standing in the flames, he raises his right fist and shouts: "Down with the Kuomintang reactionaries! Long live the Chinese Communist Party! Long live Chairman Mao!"

Hung, the Communist, towers above the blaze, his spirit magnificent as the mountains and rivers.

(*Dark change.*)

Rosy dawn streaks the sky. Dark clouds scatter, revealing a glowing sun rising in the east.

Red flags waving, bugles blaring, the Red Army surges into Cocoanut Grove Manor.

Lao Szu, clutching the money box of the Tyrant's wife, runs into the fleeing Tyrant. They battle ferociously. Lao Szu kicks the landlord to the ground and tries to escape.

Ching-hua rushes in and kills Lao Szu with one shot. She whirls and kicks down again the Tyrant who is trying to rise, threatening him with her gun.

Pretending to be subdued, the kneeling Tyrant begs for his life. Stealthily, he pulls out a dagger and swings a vicious blow at Ching-hua. She dodges and sends the dagger flying.

He runs in haste. With two shots she ends the life of the depraved criminal and counter-revolutionary chieftain.

Red Army soldiers rush in. They pour a volley of bullets into the Tyrant's body, avenging the labouring people he had oppressed.

The rising sun lights up the land. Liberation has come to the long-suffering people of Cocoanut Grove. They and the soldiers joyously congratulate one another.

The Red Army men free peasants who had been immured and beaten in the Tyrant's dungeon, and knock off their shackles. A white-haired grandfather is re-united with a grand-daughter the Tyrant had snatched away. Peasants angrily relate to the Red Army the Tyrant's evil deeds. With tears of happiness in their eyes, they express from the bottom of their hearts their boundless love for and gratitude to our great leader Chairman Mao, the Chinese Communist Party and the Workers' and Peasants' Red Army.

Ching-hua and the Company Commander inquire everywhere about Hung. A bondmaid from the manor sorrowfully points to the banian tree and tells of Hung's heroic death. This news comes as a terrific blow.

Grief-stricken, Ching-hua runs to the tree.

(Ching-hua and Company Commander dance.)

Wiping away their tears, clenching their fists, they call on the fighters to convert sorrow into strength, to carry on the cause of the fallen hero and wage revolution until final victory. (*They do "pan feng shih—écarté" "ling kung yueh —grand jeté" and "ho li shih—attitude" and end by performing the "liang hsiang" with their heads raised.*)

The powerful strains of the *Internationale* swell forth. Red Army soldiers and the liberated labouring masses gather before the banian tree and bid sorrowful farewell to their beloved comrade-in-arms: Comrade Hung, you shall live forever in our hearts!

The battalion commander announces that Ching-hua has been appointed Party representative of the Women's Company. Ching-hua solemnly accepts Hung's dispatch case which the battalion commander hands her. "Oh, Party, you rescued me from an abyss of bitterness," she says, "you raised me to maturity in the flames of class struggle. I pledge to model myself after Comrade Hung. I shall be a revolutionary and never leave the battlefield until the red flag waves over the Five Continents and Four Seas!"

Hung has given his life, but millions of new revolutionaries rise. Beneath the red battle flag, the hard-working women who have just been freed step forward to join the ranks of the Red Company of Women.

The people's army grows in size and strength. Revolution's torrent cannot be stemmed. In the bright sunlight, the swelling ranks stride forward along the path crimson with the blood of the fallen.

Onward, onward! Under the banner of Mao Tsetung, onward to victory!

≍

THE RED LANTERN–
AND THE THEATRE TO BE

≋ FALLING MIDWAY BETWEEN *Taking Tiger
Mountain* and *Shachiapang*—more realistic in style than
the former, less intricate in plot than the latter—*The Red
Lantern* is probably the favorite of the Chinese. Posters of
its family trio adorn more household walls and amateur
groups choose more excerpts from its score than from any
of the other operas. It is a classic "Past Bitterness" story,
reaching the hearts of the many Chinese who relive, first
or second hand, a similar experience. Moments of drama
strike profoundly. If I were a young actress I would aspire
to the role of Tieh-mei if only for the aria she sings alone
in her murdered family's home toward the end of the play.
In the factories and schools we visited we were often entertained by "propaganda teams"—amateur theatrical groups;
almost always Tieh-mei, in the body of a teen-aged Red

Guard, or a young woman worker, or even a mini-model ripening in a primary school, appeared "on stage" to sing the solo in which the heartbroken girl conquers her pain and vows to carry out her martyred father's charge.

Li Yu-ho, a railway switchman, lives with his mother and his daughter Tieh-mei. They are all actually members of different families brought together through tragic circumstances. Tieh-mei's real parents were murdered during the massacre of the Peking-Hankow railway strikers by the northern warlord Wu Pei-fu in Febraury 1923, and she, a babe in arms, was brought by her father's close friend, the young apprentice Li, to his adopted mother and home. On stage we see the small North China home where seventeen years later, the girl has grown up in the care of the "granny" and the "father" she loves as her own. Japanese have invaded the country. Li, a seasoned underground Party member, has just been entrusted with a secret code he must deliver to the guerrillas in the Cypress Mountains.

A railway worker's red signal lantern is the identifying liaison sign for the comrades engaged in this dangerous task. It has become a symbol of the Communist Party, and is particularly dear to the Li family, as it originally belonged to Tieh-mei's grandfather.

Before Li Yu-ho can carry out his charge, he is betrayed to the enemy by Wang Lien-chu, an underground Communist who turns traitor under torture. Hatoyama, the Japanese gendarme chief, tries persuasion, bribery and threat on Li, then tortures him. Enraged by his refusal to hand over the code, Hatoyama arrests Granny and Tieh-mei and threatens them as well as Li with execution. The family stands firmly together, accepting death as small sacrifice for the cause of the revolution. Finally Hatoyama puts the grandmother and Li Yu-ho to death in front of Tieh-mei, freeing her at the last minute in order to trap her into revealing the code's whereabouts. The young girl, alone and filled with bitter sorrow, returns home where, with the help of neighbors, she outwits the police spies. Clutching her only possession, the red lantern, Tieh-mei gets to the mountain guerrillas and delivers her martyred father's secret code.

Tieh-mei is a young "successor" to the revolution, determined to be like her father and grandmother:

> I realize I should act as they do,
> And be the same kind of person.
> I am seventeen, no longer a child,
> I should share my father's worries
> If he's carrying a thousand-pound load,
> I should carry eight hundred.
>
> My father is as steadfast as the pine,
> A Communist who fears nothing under the sun.
> Following in your footsteps I will never waver.
> Generation after generation we shall fight on,
> Never leaving the field until all the wolves are killed.

Granny Li's "storm-tossed years" have made her into as strong a revolutionary as her son; "when the heavy burden of revolution falls on you," she tells her granddaughter,

> Don't cry, don't break down, be brave and staunch
> Learn from your father his loyalty, courage and iron will.

Li Yu-ho has unyielding strength in the face of death. When Hatoyama's "request" to join him in a feast is presented to Li by the police, he sings

> A poisoned arrow is hidden in the invitation card,
> A sudden change in the weather means a traitor lurks.
> I laugh at his feast spread among swords and axes,
> With true revolutionary spirit in my heart,
> I coolly face the enemy, firm as a mountain.
>
> We have hundreds of millions of heroes
> Fighting Japan to save our country.
> Your reliance on traitors is as useless
> As fishing for the moon in the lake.

It's sure-fire for the audience. Tears slip down many a cheek when the Li family occupies the stage, or when Tieh-mei's haunting, defiant solo is sung in a school auditorium or on a communal threshing ground. At one performance I sat next to a woman who had left her family and joined the Eighth Route Army in the northwest at the age of twenty-odd, and who is now a responsible Party member in her fifties. She cried quietly in the seat beside me, wiping her eyes unashamedly; she had probably seen the play many times before. The music is beautiful; the story is compact, taut and as simple as a police thriller, with the outlaws (the revolutionaries) the heroes. *The Red Lantern* is a model of a model Peking opera.

The play depends mainly on the characters, not so much on what they do—there is no suspense or surprise in their behavior—but on who they are, and in this respect the opera seems closer to our concept of modern theatre. With the exception of the swift, short battle scene when the guerrillas ambush and annihilate the Japanese gendarmes, there is little use of acrobatics, though Peking opera gestures are employed throughout. It is drama on a heroic scale, peopled by selfless human beings whose lives personify the bitter past imposed by an imperialist foe, and who voice implacable faith in the socialist future.

The people are the chief interest. I was most moved when they acted as plain human beings, and they do this without diminishing the revolutionary integrity of the char-acterizations—promising a more dimensional theatre-to-be. The combining of two levels—the prosaic and the heroic —is not incongruous; there is harmony between the realistic person and the idealized symbol, just as there is between the naturalistic and the stylized acting, once one gets accus-tomed to it. This is what is meant by "the creative method of combining revolutionary realism with revolutionary ro-manticism."

An example of this combination is in the scene after Li Yu-ho has been tortured and awaits execution. He is a

Chinese Prometheus bound. The scenery echoes his heroism: "A high wall, a steep slope, a sturdy pine reaching the
sky. In the distance a mountain pierces into the clouds."
Li is heard offstage:

> At the jailer's bloodthirsty cry . . .

He enters, strikes a dramatic pose with chest extended and
sings:

> I stride forth from my cell.

The Japanese guards push him and he performs some
Peking opera dance movements: sideways on both legs,
backing a few steps on one leg, a pause (*liang hsiang*),
turning around on one leg and then swinging the other and
advancing boldly, forcing the guards to retreat. The aria
Li sings is strong and defiant. Soon after, Tieh-mei is
brought in; she is a frightened, shocked child. Li, all father,
steels himself as he gently encourages his daughter. It is a
scene of human value that contrasts, but does not jar with,
the previous sheerly heroic episode.

When Granny tells Tieh-mei the story of her true parents, how they were killed in the strike and how she was
brought to her present home as a baby by her father's best
friend, warmth and grief blend, and we see the girl grow
up before our eyes. Li's pleasure in his foster-daughter estab-
lishes a sympathetic relationship early in the play:

> She's a good girl!
> She peddles goods, collects cinders,
> Carries water and chops wood.
> Competent in all she does, a poor man's child
> Soon learns to manage the house.

An "epic drama" brushed by tenderness, *The Red
Lantern* is charged with a high-velocity emotional appeal

inspiring a goodly number of participants-in-socialist-construction. There are close to eight hundred million people in China.

Subtleties and more profound characterization can come about in a future creative step that need not bring back into prominence the "middle characters" of dubious morality which threatened revolutionary drama before China's Cultural Revolution. A broadening of characters and story can enrich and extend the theatre of tomorrow. There are, today, safeguards and protective limits in this Oriental theatre; it is a controlled theatre, not yet ready for tolerance. Mao Tse-tung has said that absolute individualist freedom of expression will be possible only in a classless society. That may be far off, and during the time it takes, other cultural revolutions will check bourgeois growths that seem bound to crop up. In Chinese-Marxist theory there is no permissiveness in a theatre intended to educate and mold the citizens of this newly born society. Ballerina Beryl Grey was told by the head of the Chinese Theatre Agency on her visit to Peking, "This regime has succeeded in doing what nobody in history has managed before—it has united China into one country. Now, the task is to keep it that way, and to put a desperately poor land, ravaged by centuries of war and natural calamities, onto its feet. It is an immense task, and every medium that can help must do so, even—if need be—persuaded to do so."*

Persuasion comes in many forms. Learning through doing, a principle of education in the People's Republic, applies to the creators of the theatre, as well as to all artists and intellectuals, who formerly worked with their minds. Respect for manual labor and laboring people is acquired by firsthand experience. Time and again we were told, "Knowledge and understanding of the needs of the people, the majority of them peasants and workers, will come through direct participation in work and through a mutual

* *Through the Bamboo Curtain,* by Beryl Grey, Collins, London, 1965, p. 9.

learning from each other." The following example of an important Peking Film Studio director's reeducation tells its own tale:

After Liberation in 1949 he was assigned to make a documentary about peasant life. The actors, filmed outdoors in a rice paddy, realistically portrayed the peasant workers they had observed and studied. When cameramen and crew were dismissed, the fields were a trampled mess. The peasants asked the director what was to be done to restore the ruined rice. He, sympathetic but occupied by pressing duties, paid what he considered a just sum for the damage and left the wide-eyed farmers to clean up the fields and begin anew.

Change of scene: the Cultural Revolution. The same director, with the entire film studio, including carpenters and electricians, has spent several months on a May 7th Farm (a work-study brigade where cadres and intellectuals are reeducated) learning how to serve the people and what it means to plant rice and vegetables, tend pigs, and produce one's own food. Someone inadvertently stepped on a newly planted rice shoot the director had been carefully and back-breakingly tending. He cried in outrage: "What are you *doing*! You're ruining a rice plant! Do you realize the *work* involved in *one* rice shoot?"

The theatre line was stated by Mao Tse-tung in 1942 at the Yenan Forum. *The Red Lantern* is a major step in that direction. Here I will digress to mention a new opera that, to me, had not met the test as successfully.

In Shanghai a revised version of *On the Docks* (formerly *Morning on the Docks*) was about to be presented when we were there. We attended a full-dress rehearsal. I had been eager to see this performance because it meant that we would have then seen every one of the extant model productions, and because *On the Docks* is the first of these five to tackle the present day—it takes place in 1963. With the port of Shanghai as background, the story is of attempted sabotage during the loading of a ship bound for Africa with a cargo of rice. A sack mixed with glass fiber is put on board through the carelessness of Han Hsiao-chiang, a daydreaming young longshoreman tricked by a villainous warehouse keeper. A woman Communist Party branch secretary, members of the Party branch committee, and the dock workers face the immediate task of finding the ruined sack, unearthing the saboteur in their midst, and reeducating the unmilitant youth.

A valid plot. A good setting and the sets are excellent. The Shanghai wharf, full of color and poster-bright, abuzz with cranes, cargo and dockers, is great for contemporary Peking opera, offering endless opportunities for acrobatic feats and dance. And heroes and villains exist on wharves, to be sure.

The moment Chien Shou-wei enters, we see the villain; so much so that we wonder why the cast on stage doesn't. The obviousness of this slinky little man, allowed the responsible position of warehouse keeper, destroys the credibility of the otherwise alert, intelligent, and personable Party secretary acted and sung by a gifted actress and the good, honest, bright dockworkers. All of them are unaware of Chien's counterrevolutionary schemes and his influence over a gullible, irresponsible lad; it takes nearly two hours of playing before they recognize the secret enemy.

In all the other operas the villains are equally obvious— but to the heroes on stage as well as the audience. The struggle is therefore of a different nature. In *Taking Tiger Mountain*, the soldier-hero Yang, disguised as a bandit, fools the real brigands but not the theatre spectators. Never is there a doubt on either side about the villainy of the bandits and their wily chief, nor about the Japanese gendarme in *The Red Lantern* nor the Kuomintang puppet in *Shachiapang*. *On the Docks* has the problem of a hidden villain. To reveal him to the audience at the outset in his true colors (his sallow-green makeup contrasts noticeably with the healthy pink of his supposed comrades) and to keep him hidden from the vigilant characters on stage creates an uncomfortable advantage from the viewer's seat. It could be an interesting dramatic situation, but the audience would have to be in on the ruse in some other way if the dockworkers and Party people are to appear halfway intelligent. In this case, the revelation of total wickedness (counter-revolution) became unacceptable.

In *The Red Lantern* the villain, Hatoyama, represents Japanese imperialism. It isn't necessary to make him understandable, to explain his background and motives. That's not the purpose of the play. Model Chinese opera is neither pure entertainment nor an exposition of factors that explain a complicated character. "Truthful writing" or "writing honestly" and "middle characters" are scorned by those who waged and won the battle for reform of China's theatre. These terms were used before the Cultural Revolution by some writers who advocated a "modern international style," literature for "the whole people," literature which describes "universal human nature" and emphasizes characters who are neither good nor bad but whose behavior reflects personal problems and conflicts. This has been denounced by the Chinese as revisionist. They state that the purpose of revolutionary drama is to educate on class lines, with the interests of the proletariat foremost in mind; concern over "self expression," "individual happiness," "inseparable lovers, and even lovers who are class enemies," and "fallen women, rogues, nihilists and all sorts of queer characters who stand outside the mainstream of history" leads to a bourgeois—and false—concept of literature and art.

"In this 'warfare against the mind and the heart,' " explains a *Peking Review* article,* "the modern revisionists play the ignominious role of lackeys of the class enemy. While trying by every means to negate the healthy educational function of art and literature, they make a great to-do about so-called 'individual happiness' with the aim of luring young people into a blind pursuit of their individual interests and material comforts . . . What such art and literature

* *Peking Review*, No. 27, 1963.

offer to the youth is a philosophy of life characterized by extreme egoism and a nihilistic and pessimistic attitude towards the cause of the revolution and the collective."

This is not an unrealistic denial of the existence of shaded or shady characters in life—middle characters were an important cause of the Cultural Revolution; it is a theatrical emphasis on the ideal that is to fire and fix the attention of audiences on ultimate possibilities of good in their society.

"How to create a proletarian hero of brilliance and full stature, showing all facets of his character, is a political task of prime importance which we face today . . . The kind of person this is to be determines which class is to dominate the stage."* Careful, thorough preparation accompanies the creation of a Peking opera or a Chinese ballet. It is a cooperative investigation in search of proletarian truth sought through mutual work-study-criticism on the part of all involved—by no means the least of whom will eventually be members of the audience: workers, peasants and soldiers.

Chinese actors and dancers do preparatory work based on "learning from the people"; this is in many ways a deepening of the rehearsal investigations prevalent in "method" centers like New York City's Actors' Studio. But the Chinese conception of Stanislavsky is at this time entirely negative. Method students are motivated by the Stanislavsky technique, Chinese actors by political consciousness, and the ideological foundations of both are worlds apart—as distant as today's China is from societies where the emphasis from infancy up is on individualism, competiveness and motivation of material aggrandizement.

Rejecting such foreign influence—in an attempt to stand on their own revolutionary feet, and in reaction against Soviet revisionism—the Chinese, who had studied and practiced Stanislavsky's method after Liberation in 1949, inevitably condemned him as a villain—the epitome of reactionary, bourgeois behavior. Theatre people in-

* *China Reconstructs*, February 1970.

variably remind you that he not only failed to support the Russian revolution of 1905, but having gone off to Germany then, he proceeded to the United States when the October Revolution took place. Nor did he join or cooperate with the Party on his return to the Soviet Union some years later. He chose bourgeois plays and bourgeois roles—tsarist generals, aristocrats, etc.: the equivalent of the despised emperors, ghosts and monsters of discredited Peking opera. To a Westerner it may seem that he was simply apolitical and therefore uninvolved in the socialist world in which he, as a relatively old man, lived and died. But that goes against the Communists' grain. You do or you don't; you are or you aren't, and on that you are judged. If Stanislavsky only reflected the middle-class background he never repudiated, that "mistake" multiplies into mortal sin through the nature of his theatre technique—which is to identify with the character one is playing regardless of the ideological "correctness" of the motivation employed to achieve this identification. This is in direct opposition to Communist thought: the Stanislavsky system is individualism proceeding from *self* and concentrating on the personal, the ego, the I. It also counsels opposing qualities in character portrayal (look for the good in the bad, the weak in the strong); this conflicts with the Communists' image of heroes and villains.

The use of one's self, the inner I, to approach or to analyze a role contradicts unity with the proletarian masses who must be foremost in China. "To stress that we should proceed from 'self' will only distort the revolutionary struggle of the workers, peasants, and soldiers and their heroic mental outlook with the unbridled 'self expression' of the bourgeoisie."* The absoluteness of characterization in Chinese drama, inherited from the past and fostered in the present, is incompatible with the Stanislavskian principle of well-rounded, diversified interpretation: "In class society, no individual exists in the abstract or above

* *On Stanislavsky's System*, Foreign Languages Press, Peking, 1969.

classes. Nor is literature and art in the abstract or above classes . . . All the images . . . in the model revolutionary Peking opera are those of heroes and outstanding representatives of the proletariat. The excellent qualities they display are '*on a higher plane, more intense, more concentrated, more typical, nearer the ideal, and therefore more universal than actual everyday life.*' [Italics mine.] The process in which the actors study and portray these art images is one in which the actors understand, learn from and extol these heroic images and remould their own world outlook. . ."*

When I was working in the theatre, I considered the Stanislavsky system an open sesame, but I think I understand why the Chinese regard it as a Pandora's box. Theirs is an open political conception. In practice their meticulous preparation, involving actors and writers living with and learning from the actual people to be portrayed, is an aspect of the Stanislavsky method carried beyond its originator's dreams. Mao Tse-tung went far beyond Stanislavsky those years ago in his Talks at the Yenan Forum on Literature and Art; these revolutionary goals have yet to be fully attained, but the emerging theatre is on its way.

One might think that a complete fulfillment of Mao's directions on the theatre would entail utilizing the "characteristics of both aspects of a contradiction," to quote the Chairman,** Lenin's "in order to know an object we must embrace, study, all its sides" and his "the demand for all sidedness is a safeguard against mistakes and rigidity,"† all within the context of proletarian literature and art. The Chinese theatre community, aware of its particular responsibilities, is finding its own "method"; it has had, at least for now, enough of any influence that interferes with the newly born balance and unity between proletarian-based ideology and good theatre. If it is difficult to understand or accept what we might term puritanical restrictions in

* *Ibid.*
** *On Contradiction*, by Mao Tse-tung, August 1937.
† Cited in *On Contradiction*.

China's nascent revolutionary theatre, it is less so when one is on the spot seeing what is evolving and why. Foremost to keep in mind is for whom that theatre is intended.

In Yenan in 1942, Mao Tse-tung raised the questions of popularization and elevation, and the correct relationship between the two. "We must popularize only what is needed and can be readily accepted by the workers, peasants and soldiers," he said. As for raising the artistic level, he used an example of a bucket of water. "Where is it to be raised from if not from the ground? From mid-air? No . . . [the level of literature and art is to be raised] only from the basis of the masses of workers, peasants and soldiers."

Despite the length of the history of China, the cultural experience of its masses has been a limited one. Each year the scope widens. Everything is new. There is still a big gap between the tillers of the soil, the workers in the factories, and those few who have had sophisticated experiences in education or in travel. In spite of the carefully directed revolution, theatre deviated to the benefit of the intellectuals and the more "worldly wise," neglecting the needs of the masses. The Cultural Revolution has caused a full swing around to the fundamentals expressed by Mao Tse-tung two decades earlier.

Another story told to me in China underscores the point. Some years after Liberation an accomplished violinist volunteered a concert tour to reach the peasants in the far countryside. They came from long distances to hear him play Mozart and Chopin on a moonlit night in the center of the newly swept threshing ground. The Western-trained musician sat on a small stool provided for him and filled the evening air with magnificent sound. Slowly, silently, shadowy figures stole away, until at the end only one little old woman remained. The virtuoso lowered his bow, looked long and hard at the work-worn peasant, and thanked her for her appreciation. "Never mind that," she replied, "I'm just waiting for my stool."

Foreign, strange, unusual to their ears, the music had

meant nothing. A rousing song and dance of their own could have held them till the moon went down. With all the good revolutionary intentions in the world the artist had failed to learn the lesson of Yenan.

On the other hand, a full philharmonic orchestra in post-Liberation Shanghai was attended appreciatively by many working people in the city. I heard of an uneducated factory hand who saved up for a violin and practiced in his room after work. Western music opened ears receptive to a different kind of sound. During early days it influenced the newborn music of the People's Army and helped produce hundreds of songs that spread out from the liberated areas. Lacking mass appeal in pure form it nevertheless served to break down the restrictions of the traditional and create a new revolutionary "folk" music.

"From the proletarian point of view, villains . . . can only be portrayed from the class hatred of the workers, peasants and soldiers to relentlessly expose and criticize the ugly, cruel and insidious class nature of . . . reactionaries, in order to bring the brilliant images of the proletarian heroes into bold relief. If one acts from Stanislavsky's bourgeois 'self,' then monsters of all kinds, which are to be overthrown and swept away in real life, will be made into major artistic parts, and will be allowed to exercise arrogant dictatorship . . . on the stage."*

Another look has been given to *On the Docks*. One of the questions concerned the undisguised yet unnoticed villain on stage; the obviousness with which the character was played enhanced the difficulty. The actor has now approached (or has now been allowed to approach) the part in a more oblique fashion. The villain is thereby established with more subtlety and the audience gains confidence in the vigilant comrades on the docks.

According to Lee Tsung-ying, editor of *Eastern Horizon Monthly Review*, a line in a previous version, "The hearts of the awakened people (of the world) all turn to

* *On Stanislavsky's System*, Foreign Languages Press, Peking, 1969.

Peking," has been rewritten and now reads, "The hearts of the awakened people are all linked together." So, Tsung-ying says, the revision can only be construed as a sincere effort to put relations between the different nations and countries in their right perspective for the Chinese people.

The question of characters and characterization will have to be even more fully resolved in the future, for revolutionary theatre cannot stand still, nor can it ignore today's and tomorrow's problems. "Marxism embraces but cannot replace realism in literary and artistic creation . . . Dogmatic 'Marxism' is not Marxism, it is anti-Marxism. Then does Marxism destroy the creative mood?" asked Mao Tse-tung in 1942. His reply was "Yes, it does. It definitely destroys creative moods that are feudal, bourgeois, petty-bourgeois, liberalistic, individualist, nihilist, art-for-art's sake, aristocratic, decadent or pessimistic, and every other creative mood that is alien to the masses of the people and to the proletariat. So far as proletarian writers and artists are concerned, should not these kinds of creative moods be destroyed? I think they should; they should be utterly destroyed. And while they are being destroyed, something new can be constructed."

"What we demand," said Mao to the cotton-clad company at Yenan—and to the future—"is the unity of politics and art, the unity of content and form, the unity of revolutionary political content and the highest possible perfection of artistic form."

The task of constructing the "something new" has resulted in a going marriage between the valuable old and contemporary life. The offspring of this union have to solve some of the more subtle and more modern problems which the Chinese people are meeting as they forge ahead. Only twenty-odd years have passed since the new began in earnest, released from war. The source of material to meet the demand for literature and art in revolutionary China is huge. The future promises a fullfillment of Yenan.

Meanwhile, the beginning is a most welcome one.

A QUOTATION FROM CHAIRMAN MAO

> Thousands upon thousands of martyrs have heroically laid down their lives for the people; let us hold their banner high and march ahead along the path crimson with their blood!

The Red Lantern

(MAY 1970 SCRIPT)

REVISED COLLECTIVELY BY THE CHINA PEKING OPERA TROUPE

✕

CAST OF CHARACTERS

Li Yu-ho: *switchman, member of the Communist Party of China*
Tieh-mei: *Li's daughter*
Granny Li: *Li's mother*
Liaison Man: *liaison man from the Pine Peak Base Area of the Eighth Route Army*
Knife-Grinder: *platoon leader of the guerrillas of the Eighth Route Army in the Cypress Mountains*
Hui-lien: *Li's neighbour*
Aunt Tien: *Hui-lien's mother-in-law*
Guerrilla leader of the Eighth Route Army in the Cypress Mountains

Several guerrillas
Woman Gruel-Seller
Cigarette Girl
Workmen A, B, C and D: *customers at the gruel stall*
Hatoyama: *chief of the Japanese gendarmerie*
Wang Lien-chu: *puppet police inspector, an underground
        Communist who turns traitor*
Auxiliary Hou: *Auxiliary gendarme of the Japanese gen-
        darmerie*
Sergeant: *sergeant of the Japanese gendarmerie*
Bogus Liaison Man: *spy for the Japanese gendarmerie*
Cobbler: *spy for the Japanese gendarmerie*
Several Japanese gendarmes and spies

≠

SCENE ONE

CONTACTING THE LIAISON MAN

An early winter night during the War of Resistance Against
Japan. North China. Near the Lungtan railway station. The
railway embankment is visible. Undulating hills loom in the
distance.

> (*As the curtain rises, the north wind is howling. Four
> Japanese gendarmes march past on patrol. A signal
> lantern in his hand, Li Yu-ho, vigorous and calm, enters
> with firm steps.*)

Li: (*sings "hsi pi san pan"*):
    Red lantern in hand, I look round;
    The leadership is sending a man here to Lungtan;
    The time fixed is half past seven.
    The next train should bring him.

(The wind whistles. Enter Tieh-mei with a basket, heading into the wind.)

Tieh-mei: Dad!

Li: Well, Tieh-mei! (*Realizing that she must be cold, he takes off his scarf and wraps it round her neck.*) How was business today?

Tieh-mei: Humph! The gendarmes and their thugs kept searching and pestering everybody. People were too jittery to buy anything.

Li: Those bandits!

Tieh-mei: Do be careful, dad.

Li: Right. Go home and tell granny that an uncle is coming.

Tieh-mei: An uncle?

Li: Yes.

Tieh-mei: What does this uncle look like, dad?

Li: Don't ask such questions.

Tieh-mei: I'll ask granny then.

Li: What a girl!

(Exit Tieh-mei.)

Li (*gazing at her retreating figure, very pleased*): She's a good girl!
(Sings "hsi pi yuan pan")
She peddles goods, collects cinders,
Carries water and chops wood.
Competent in all she does, a poor man's child
Soon learns to manage the house.
Different trees bear different fruits,
Different seeds grow different flowers.

(Enter Wang.)

Wang: Old Li, I've been looking for you for quite a while. . . .

(Li alertly signals Wang not to speak, then looks around.)

Wang: The Japanese posted a tighter guard today, Old Li. They must be up to something.

Li: I know. We should meet as seldom as possible in the future. I'll contact you when necessary.

Wang: All right. (*Exit.*)

(*A train whistle sounds in the distance. Li goes off. Lights fade.*)

(*A train roars past. Shots are heard.*)

(*Lights brighten. Liaison Man "somersaults" down the embankment and passes out.*)

(*Li rushes in.*)

Li (*murmurs on seeing the man*): A glove on the left hand. . . .

(*Gunshots. Wang runs back.*)

Wang: Who's that?

Li: One of ours. I'll carry him away, you cover us.

Wang: Right.

(*Exit Li with Liaison Man on his back.*)

(*Shouts of the pursuing Japanese gendarmes. Sound of shooting. Wang fires two shots in the direction opposite to that taken by Li. The Japanese gendarmes can be heard approaching. In order to save his own skin, Wang shoots himself in the arm while shivering all over. He falls.*)

(*Enter Sergeant with Japanese gendarmes.*)

Sergeant (*to Wang*): Did you see the man who jumped off the train?

Wang: Eh?

Sergeant: Where's the man?

Wang: Oh! (*Points towards the opposite direction.*) Over there.

Sergeant (*in alarm*): Hit the ground!

(*All the Japanese gendarmes throw themselves down.*)

(*Lights fade.*)

(*Curtain*)

＝

SCENE TWO

ACCEPTING THE TASK

Immediately after the last scene. Li's house, interior and exterior view. The door opens onto a small lane. A table and several chairs in the middle of the room. A red paper butterfly pasted on the window pane. On the right, towards the rear, an inner room, with a curtain hanging over the doorway.

(*As the curtain rises, the north wind is roaring. It's dim in the room. Granny turns up the lamp wick and the room becomes brighter.*)

Granny (*sings "hsi pi san pan"*):
Fishermen brave the wind and waves,
Hunters (*switching to "yuan pan"*) *fear neither tigers nor wolves;*
The darkest night must end at last
In the bright blaze of revolution.

(*Enter Tieh-mei with a basket.*)

Tieh-mei: Granny.
Granny: Tieh-mei.
Tieh-mei: Dad told me an uncle is coming soon. (*Puts down the basket.*)
Granny (*to herself, expectantly*): Ah, an uncle is coming soon!
Tieh-mei: How is it I have so many uncles, granny?
Granny: Your father has many cousins, so of course you have many uncles. (*Mending clothes.*)
Tieh-mei: Which one is coming today?
Granny: Don't ask. You'll know when he comes.
Tieh-mei: Even if you won't tell me, granny, I know.

Granny: Do you? What do you know?

Tieh-mei: Granny, just listen.

(*Sings "hsi pi liu shui"*)

I've more uncles than I can count;
They only come when there's important business.
Though we call them relatives, we never met before,
Yet they are closer to us than our own relatives.
Both dad and you call them our own folk;
I can guess part of the reason why:
They're all like my dad,
Men with red, loyal hearts.

(*Li hurries in, carrying Liaison Man on his back. He pushes the door open and walks in. He signs to Tieh-mei to close the door and keep an eye on the outside, then helps Liaison Man to a chair and gives him a drink of water.*)

Liaison Man (*recovering*):   Can you tell me if there's a switchman here named Li?

Li: That's me.

(*Li and Liaison Man exchange passwords.*)

Liaison Man: I sell wooden combs.

Li: Any made of peach-wood?

Liaison Man: Yes, for cash down.

Li: Fine, wait a minute.

(*Li signs to Granny to give the lamp test.*)

Granny (*holds up a kerosene lamp and looks at Liaison Man*):   Neighbour. . . .

Liaison Man (*realizing the method of identification is wrong*):   Thank you for saving my life. I must go.

Li (*holds up the red lantern*):   Comrade!

Liaison Man (*excitedly*):   I've found you at last!

(*Tieh-mei takes the red lantern, becomes aware of its significance.*)

(*Granny signs to Tieh-mei to go out with the basket and keep watch.*)

Liaison Man: Old Li, I'm the liaison man from the Pine Peak Base Area. (*Takes a document out of the sole of his shoe*). This is a secret code.

(*Li takes it carefully.*)

Liaison Man: Get it to the guerrillas in the Cypress Mountains. Tomorrow afternoon, at the gruel stall in the junk market, a knife-grinder will contact you. Same password as before.

Li: Same password as before.

Liaison Man: Old Li, this is a difficult task!

Li: I guarantee I'll do it without fail.

Liaison Man: Fine. But time is pressing, Old Li, I must go back at once.

Li: Comrade, can you manage? . . .

Liaison Man: A moment ago I passed out simply from the fall. I'm all right now, I can manage.

Li: Wait a minute, you'd better change your clothes.

(*Helps Liaison Man change a jacket.*)

Li (*with great concern*): The enemy is searching everywhere. Things are very tight. Be careful on your way back.

Liaison Man: I will, Old Li.

Li: Comrade. . . .
(*Sings "erh huang kuai san yen"*)
Be on guard as you go—
Mountains are high, torrents swift.
Follow small lanes and short bridges,
The quiet and safe paths.
To the revolution we offer our loyal hearts.
(*Sees Liaison Man off. Tieh-mei enters.*)
(*Continues to sing*)
Shouldering the heavy task. I'll stand up to any test in the fire.

Bursting with strength, I'll be worthy of the trust of the Party.
No difficulty in the world can daunt a Communist.

(*The siren of a police car wails. With presence of mind, Li motions to Granny to blow out the lamp. With the secret code in his hand. Li strikes a dramatic pose.*)
(*Lights fade.*)

(*Curtain*)

⋈

SCENE THREE

NARROW ESCAPE AT THE GRUEL STALL

The next afternoon. The gruel stall in the junk market.

(*As the curtain rises, Workman C is sitting at the counter eating gruel. Workmen A and B walk in and sit down at the gruel counter. Cigarette Girl sits not far away from the stall. Li enters with his lantern in one hand and lunch box in the other, calm and watchful.*)

Li (*sings "hsi pi yao pan"*):
Seeking my comrade in the junk market,
I have hidden the code in my lunch box.
No obstacles whatever can stop me,
I must get it to the Cypress Mountains.
Workman C (*stands up*): Old Li!
Li (*with concern*): Ah, Old Chang, has your wound healed?
Workman C: It's much better.
Li: Watch out for yourself in the future.
Workman C: Yes. (*To himself.*) What kind of times we we live in! The Japanese devil rides in my rickshaw and won't pay, and even beats me up. What a world! (*Exit.*)

(*Li walks to the gruel stall and hangs the red lantern on a post.*)

Workmen A and B: Hello, Old Li, come here and sit with us.

Li (*warmly*):   Let's all sit down.

Gruel-Seller: A bowl of gruel, Old Li?

Li: Yes, please. How is business?

Gruel-Seller: So-so. (*She serves him.*)

(*Enter Workman D.*)

Workman D: A bowl of gruel, please. (*Takes the bowl, about to eat.*) What's this? It's mouldy!

Workman A: It's rationed mixed stuff.

Gruel-Seller: We can do nothing about it.

Workman B: *Hey!* (*Crunches bits of stone, spits them out.*) Nearly broke my teeth!

Workman A: It's full of grit.

Workman B: They just don't treat us like human beings.

Workman A: Hush! Don't ask for trouble.

Workman B: How can we eat such swill? We just can't live!

Li (*sharing their feelings, sings "hsi pi liu shui"*):
So many compatriots are suffering and fuming with discontent,
Struggling under iron heels they seethe with wrath.
Spring thunder will rumble when the time comes,
The brave Chinese people will never bow before the butcher's knife.
May our comrades come soon from the Cypress Mountains!

(*Enter Knife-Grinder.*)

Knife-Grinder (*sings "hsi pi yao pan"*):
Looking around for my comrade,
I see the red lantern hanging high to greet me.
I cry: Any knives or scissors to grind?

Li (*sings "hsi pi yao pan"*):
The knife-grinder fixes his eyes on my red lantern
And he raises his left hand to hail me.
Through a chat I'll try the password on him.

(*Before Li can speak to Knife-Grinder, a siren wails and Japanese gendarmes charge in. Knife-Grinder deliberately overturns his bench to draw the enemy's attention.*)

Li (*continues to sing: He draws the wolves to himself in order to cover me. (As he sings he coolly and resourcefully empties his gruel into the lunch box.*)
Li: Another helping, please.

(*Li lets Gruel-Seller fill his lunch box.*)
(*The gendarmes finish searching Knife-Grinder, angrily wave him away and turn towards Li.*)
(*Li deliberately holds out his lunch box for search. The Japanese push the smelly gruel away. After searching him they gesture for him to go.*) (*Li picks up his lunch box and lantern, and breaks into a serene smile. Having fooled the enemy, he walks calmly to the centre of the stage. Then he turns round and, head high, strides off victoriously.*)
(*Lights fade.*)

(*Curtain*)

SCENE FOUR

WANG TURNS TRAITOR

Afternoon. Hatoyama's office.

(*As the curtain rises, Hatoyama is talking on the telephone.*)

Hatoyama: Oh, oh! . . . What, the trail lost? . . . Eh, don't worry, I promise to get the code. . . . The case must be cleared up before the deadline! Yes, yes, sir! (*Puts down the receiver and speaks to himself.*) The Communists are really sharp! Just when the headquarters gets on their trail, they shake us off. They're hard nuts to crack, those Communists!

(*Sergeant and Hou enter.*)

Sergeant: Reporting! We searched everywhere, but found no trace of the man who jumped off the train. We've arrested a few suspects.

Hatoyama: What's the use of suspects? This fellow from the train is a liaison man of the Communists. He has a very important secret code with him. If it reaches the guerrillas in the Cypress Mountains, it will spell big trouble for our empire.

Sergeant: Yes, sir.

Hatoyama: Where is Inspector Wang?

Hou: He's here.

Hatoyama: Bring him in.

Hou: Yes, sir. (*Calling to the inside.*) Inspector Wang.

(*Enter Wang with a wounded arm in a sling.*)
(*Exit Hou*).

Wang: Captain. (*Salutes.*)

Hatoyama: Ah, brave young fellow, you've been working hard! On behalf of the headquarters, I present you this medal, third class. (*Pins the medal on Wang's chest.*)

Wang: Thank you, captain.

Hatoyama (*sings "hsi pi san pan"*):
   If you serve the empire loyally
   You have every chance to rise high;
   As the saying goes: The bitter sea has no bounds,
   Repent and the shore is at hand.
   Now everything depends on whether you are sensible
   (*Sneers.*) *or not.*

Wang: I don't follow you, Captain.

Hatoyama: You ought to. Tell me, how could it be that the man who jumped off the train fired at you from a distance of only three centimeters?

Wang: Captain. . . .

Hatoyama: Out with it, young fellow. Who was your accomplice?

Wang (*inadvertently*): Accomplice!

Hatoyama: Exactly! Without one accomplice to help him and another to cover his escape, could the man who jumped off the train have grown wings and flown away?

Wang: I was shot and fell to the ground, captain. How do I know how he escaped?

Hatoyama: You know all right. Why else should you shoot yourself?

(*Wang is taken aback.*)

Hatoyama (*presses harder*): Tell me the truth, quick, young man. Who's in the underground Communist Party? Who was your accomplice? Where's the liaison man hiding? Who's got the secret code now? Better make a clean breast of it. I have plenty of medals and rewards for you.

Wang: Your words make my brain whirl, captain.

Hatoyama: In that case we shall have to sober you up! Sergeant!

Sergeant: Yes, sir.

Hatoyama: Take this man out and sober him up.

Sergeant: Yes, sir. Guards!

(*Two gendarmes enter.*)

Sergeant: Take him away!

Wang (*begs of mercy*): Captain. . . .

Sergeant (*grimly*): Bah! (*Kicks Wang to the ground.*)

(*The gendarmes press Wang down hard.*)

Wang: I . . . I'm innocent.

Hatoyama: Beat him up!

Sergeant: Take him away! Take him away!

(*Crying repeatedly "I'm innocent," Wang is dragged out by the gendarmes. Sergeant follows.*)

Hatoyama: Let torture open his mouth and make him tell who his accomplice was.

(*Enter Sergeant.*)

Sergeant: Reporting, sir, he has confessed.

Hatoyama: Who was his accomplice?

Sergeant: Li Yu-ho, the switchman.

Hatoyama (*reflectively*): Li Yu-ho!?

(*Lights fade.*)

(*Curtain*)

✕

SCENE FIVE

RECOUNTING THE FAMILY'S REVOLUTIONARY HISTORY

Dusk. Li's house, interior and exterior view.

(*As the curtain rises, Granny is waiting anxiously for Li.*)

Granny (*sings "hsi pi yao pan"*):
It's dusk, but my son still hasn't come back.

(*Tieh-mei walks out of the inner room. A police siren wails.*)

Tieh-mei (*continues the singing*): There's such commotion in the streets, I'm worried about dad.

(*Lunch box and red lantern in hand, Li enters and knocks at the door.*)

Li: Tieh-mei.

Tieh-mei: Dad is back!

Granny: Open the door, quick.

Tieh-mei (*opens the door*):   Dad!

Granny: Yu-ho.

Li: Mother!

Granny: You're back, at last. Have you got in touch with him?

> (*Takes the red lantern and lunch box from him.*)

Li: Not yet. (*Throws off his overcoat.*)

Granny: Anything wrong?

Li: Mother!

> (*Sings "hsi pi liu shui"*)
>
> *I was trying to contact the knife-grinder at the gruel stall.*
>
> *When a police car came and the Japanese started a search.*
>
> *To protect me the knife-grinder drew away the wolves,*
> *Seizing the chance I concealed the code in the lunch box;*
>
> *They didn't find the code hidden under the gruel.*

Tieh-mei: How good Uncle Knife-Grinder is!

Granny: Where is the code, Yu-ho?

Li: Mother!

> (*Continues to sing in an affectionate and low voice*)
>
> *I've put it in a safe place to guard against any accident.*

Tieh-mei: You're resourceful, dad.

Li: You know everything now, Tieh-mei. The code is more important than our lives. We must keep it a secret even if it costs us our heads. Understand?

Tieh-mei: Yes.

Li: Hah, so you understand! What a smart daughter I've got!

Tieh-mei: Dad. . . .

Li: Ho! . . .

> (*It is getting dark. Granny brings a kerosene lamp.*)

Granny: Just look at you father and daughter. . . .

Li: I've got something to do, mother, I must go out again.

Granny: Be careful! And don't be too late.

Li: I won't.

Tieh-mei: Take this, dad. (*She wraps the scarf round his neck.*) Do come back early.

Li (*affectionately*): I will. (*Walks out of the door. Exit.*)

(*Tieh-mei closes the door.*)
(*Granny polishes the red lantern with loving care. Tieh-mei watches attentively.*)

Granny: Come here, Tieh-mei. I'll tell you the story of the red lantern.

Tieh-mei: Fine. (*Happily walks over to the table and sits down beside it.*)

Granny (*seriously*): For many years this lantern has lighted the way for us poor people, for us workers. Your grandfather used to carry this lantern, and now your dad carries it. You saw what happened last night, child. We can't do without it at crucial moments. Remember, this red lantern is our family treasure.

Tieh-mei: Our family treasure?

(*Looking at Tieh-mei confidently, Granny goes into the inner room.*)
(*Tieh-mei picks up the lantern, examines it and falls in deep thought.*)

Tieh-mei (*sings "hsi pi san pan"*):
Granny has told me the story of the red lantern,
The words are few, but meaning is deep.
Why are my father and uncle (*switches to "yuan pan"*)
not afraid of danger?
Because they want to save China,
Save the poor, defeat the Japanese invaders.
I realize I should act as they do,
And be a person like them.
I am seventeen, no longer a child,

I should share my father's worries.
If he's carrying a thousand-pound load,
I should carry eight hundred.

(*Granny comes out.*)

Granny: Tieh-mei, Tieh-mei!
Tieh-mei: Granny!
Granny: What are you thinking about?
Tieh-mei: Nothing.

(*A child cries next door.*)

Granny: Isn't that Lung-erh crying?
Tieh-mei: Yes.
Granny: Their grain has run out again! We have some
corn meal left. Give it to them.
Tieh-mei: All right. (*Gets it.*)

(*Hui-lien enters, knocks at the door.*)

Hui-lien: Granny Li!
Tieh-mei: It's Sister Hui-lien.
Granny: Open the door. Quick.
Tieh-mei: Eh. (*Opens the door. Hui-lien comes in.*)
Sister Hui-lien.
Granny (*with concern*):   Is Lung-erh any better, Hui-lien?
Hui-lien: No. How can we afford to see a doctor? Fewer
and fewer people ask me to mend and wash clothes for
them these days. We live from hand to mouth, never
knowing where our next meal is coming from. Right
now, we've nothing in the pot.
Tieh-mei: Take this home, Sister Hui-lien. (*Gives her the
corn meal.*)
Hui-lien (*greatly moved*):   . . . .
Granny: Take it. Tieh-mei was just going to send it
over to you.
Hui-lien (*takes the corn meal*):   You're so kind to us.
Granny: Don't mention it. With the wall between us
we're two families. If we pulled it down, we'd be one.

Tieh-mei: We are one family even with the wall.
Granny: That's true.

(*The child cries again, louder.*)

Aunt Tien (*offstage*):   Hui-lien, Hui-lien!

(*Aunt Tien enters.*)

Tieh-mei: Aunty!
Granny: Please take a seat.
Aunt Tien: No, thank you. The child is crying, Hui-lien. Go back and look after him. (*Sees the meal in her hand, moved.*) . . . .
Granny: Take it home and make some food for the child.
Aunt Tien: But you don't have much yourselves.
Granny (*warmly*):   Don't say yours or ours. We are one family.
Aunt Tien: We must be going now.
Granny: Don't be upset. Watch your step in the dark.

(*Aunt Tien and Hui-lien go out.*)

Tieh-mei (*closes the door*):   They are having a very hard time, granny.
Granny: Yes. Hui-lien's father-in-law was a railway transport worker and was killed by a train. The Japanese wouldn't pay any compensation. What's more, they seized her husband to work as a coolie. Tieh-mei, we two worker families endure the same suffering and feel the same hatred for the enemy. We must do our best to help them.

(*Bogus Liaison Man enters, knocks at the door.*)

Tieh-mei: Who's there?
Bogus Liaison Man: Is this Master Li's house?
Tieh-mei: Someone wants dad.
Granny: Open the door.
Tich-mei: Right. (*Opens the door.*)

(Bogus Liaison Man comes in and shuts the door be-
hind him quickly.)

Granny: You are. . . .

Bogus Liaison Man: I sell wooden combs.

Granny: Any made of peach-wood?

Bogus Liaison Man: Yes, for cash down.

Tieh-mei: Good. Just a minute.

(Bogus Liaison Man turns around and puts down his
bag.)
(Tieh-mei is going to pick up the red lantern when
Granny hurriedly stops her and takes up the kerosene
lamp to put him to the test. Tieh-mei gets the hint.)

Bogus Liaison Man *(turning round, sees the lamp)*:
Thank goodness, I've found you at last. It's been so
difficult to contact you.

(Tieh-mei's amazement turns to anger. She is burning
with indignation.)

Granny *(realizing that he is a fraud, calmly)*: Let's see
your wooden combs, master, so that we can make a
choice.

Bogus Liaison Man: I've come for the code, ma'am.

Granny: What is he saying, Tieh-mei?

Bogus Liaison Man: This is no time for jokes, ma'am.
The code is a very important Communist Party document. The revolution depends on it. Give it to me
quickly.

Tieh-mei *(angrily)*: None of your nonsense. Get out!

Bogus Liaison Man: Now, now. . . .

Tieh-mei: Get out!

(Tieh-mei pushes him out, tosses his bag after him and
bangs the door shut.)

Tieh-mei: Granny!

(Granny quickly stops Tieh-mei from speaking.)
(Bogus Liaison Man signals to two plain-clothes men,

indicating that they should watch the house. Then they go off in different directions.)

Tieh-mei: He nearly fooled me, granny.

Granny: Child, someone must have turned traitor and let out the secret.

Tieh-mei: What's to be done, granny?

Granny (*whispers*):   Tear off the sign at once.

Tieh-mei: What sign?

Granny: The red paper butterfly on the window pane.

Tieh-mei (*suddenly understands*):   Ah! (*About to tear it off.*)

Granny: Tieh-mei, open the door to screen the window. You tear off the sign while I sweep the floor to distract attention. Quick.

(*Tieh-mei opens the door. Li strides in and closes the door behind him. Tieh-mei is startled. The broom drops from Granny's hand.*)

Li (*senses something wrong*):   What's happened, mother?

Granny: There are dogs outside!

(*Showing no fear, Li makes a quick appraisal of the situation.*)

Granny: Son, son!

Li: Mother, it looks like I'll be arrested. (*Seriously.*) I've put the code under the stone-tablet beside an old locust tree on the west bank of the river. You must do everything to deliver it to the knife-grinder. The password is the same.

Granny: The password's the same!

Li: Yes, but you must be careful.

Granny: I know. Don't worry.

Tieh-mei: Dad. . . .

(*Hou enters, knocks at the door.*)

Hou: Is Master Li in?

Li: They've come, mother.

Tieh-mei: Dad, you. . . .

Li: Open the door, Tieh-mei.

Tieh-mei: Yes.

Hou: Open the door!

(Tieh-mei tears off the red paper butterfly while she opens the door.)

Hou *(entering the house)*: Are you Master Li?

Li: Yes.

Hou: Captain Hatoyama invites you to have a drink. *(Presents an invitation card.)*

Li: So Captain Hatoyama invites me to a feast?

Hou: Yes.

Li: Ha! What an honour! *(Throws the invitation card on the table scornfully.)*

Hou: He just wants to make friends with you. Come along please, Master Li.

Li: After you. *(To Granny, firmly and gravely.)* Mother, take good care of yourself. I'm going.

Granny: Wait a minute! Tieh-mei, bring some wine.

Tieh-mei: Yes. *(Fetches some wine.)*

Hou: Don't bother, ma'am. There's plenty at the feast for him to drink.

Granny: Bah! . . . The poor prefer their own wine. Each drop of it warms the heart. *(Takes the bowl of wine from Tieh-mei and, gravely and with deep feeling, she bids Li a hero's farewell.)* Son, take this bowl and drink it!

Li *(taking the bowl solemnly)*: With this wine to put heart into me, mother, I can cope with whatever wine they give me. *(Drains the bowl at one gulp.)* Thank you, mother.

(Heroically, sings "hsi pi erh liu")

I drink the wine mother gives me at parting,

I'm filled with courage and strength.

Hatoyama is giving a feast to make "friends" with me,

Even a thousand cups I can handle.

The weather is treacherous, with sudden wind and snow,
Be prepared always for unexpected changes.

Tieh-mei: Dad. (*Rushes over to Li, sobbing.*)

Li (*kindly and meaningfully, continues singing*):
Dear Tieh-mei,
When you are out selling wares, keep an eye on the
weather
And remember well all the "accounts."
Beware of curs lurking outside
When you feel drowsy;
Listen for the magpie's lucky song
When you feel low.
You must run errands for the family
And share your granny's burdens and cares.

Tieh-mei: Dad! (*Clasps him and sobs.*)

Hou: Let's go, Master Li.

Li: Don't cry, child. Always do as granny says.

Tieh-mei: I will.

Granny: Open the door, Tieh-mei, so your father can go
to the "feast."

Li: I'm going now, mother.

(*Li and Granny clasp each other's hands firmly, encour-
aging each other to be staunch in the fight.*)
(*Tieh-mei opens the door. A gust of wind. Li strides out
into the wind, head high. Hou follows.*)
(*Tieh-mei runs after Li with the scarf, crying: "Dad!"
Spies A, B, and C rush in and bar her way.*)

Spy A: Stop! Go back.

(*He forces Tieh-mei back. The spies come into the
room.*)

Tieh-mei: Granny! . . .

Spy A: Make a search! Stay where you are!

(*They rummage the house. One of them comes out of
the inner room with an almanac, leafs through it, then
tosses it away.*)

Spy A: Let's go.

(They go off.)

Tieh-mei *(closes the door, draws the curtain and looks around the room)*:   Granny! *(Falls into Granny's arms and sobs. A pause.)* Will dad ever come back, granny?

Granny: Your dad. . . .

Tieh-mei: Dad. . . .

Granny: Tieh-mei, tears cannot save your dad. Don't cry now. It's time to tell you everything about our family.

Tieh-mei: What, granny?

Granny: Sit down. I'll tell you.

(Granny looks at the scarf. Revolutionary memories float before her eyes; hatred, old and new, for the enemy comes to her mind.)
(Tieh-mei gets a stool and sits down beside her.)

Granny: Tell me, child, is your dad a good man?

Tieh-mei: Of course.

Granny: But . . . he's not your own father.

Tieh-mei *(startled)*:   Ah! What are you saying, granny?

Granny: Neither am I your granny.

Tieh-mei: Granny, granny! Are you out of your mind?

Granny: No, child. We three generations are not from the same family. *(Stands up.)* Your surname is Chen, mine is Li and your dad's is Chang.
(Sings "erh huang san pan")
For seventeen storm-tossed years I've kept quiet,
Several times I wanted to speak,
But I was afraid you were too young for the truth.

Tieh-mei: Tell me, granny. I won't cry.

Granny *(sings "erh huang man san yen")*:
It's most likely your father will not return,
And granny may be jailed too.
Then the heavy burden of revolution will fall on you.
When I tell you the truth, Tieh-mei,
Don't cry, don't break down, be brave and staunch,

Learn from your father his loyalty, courage, and iron will.

Tieh-mei: Granny, sit down and tell me everything. (*Helps Granny to a seat.*)

Granny: It's a long story. Your grandfather was a maintenance man in the Kiangan Locomotive Depot near Hankow. He had two apprentices. One was your own father, Chen Chih-hsing.

Tieh-mei: My father, Chen Chih-hsing?

Granny: The other was your present dad, Chang Yu-ho.

Tieh-mei: Oh, Chang Yu-ho?

Granny: At that time, the country was torn by strife among warlords. Then, Chairman Mao and the Communist Party led the Chinese people in waging revolution. In February 1923, workers of the Peking-Hankow Railway set up a federation of trade unions in Chengchow. One of the warlords, Wu Pei-fu, a stooge of the foreign invaders, tried to ban it. At the call of the federation, all the workers on the line went on strike. More than ten thousand in Kiangan took to the street and demonstrated. That was another cold, dark night. I was so worried about your grandfather I couldn't sit still or go to sleep. I was mending clothes by the lamp when I heard someone knocking at the door, calling, "Aunty, aunty, quick, open the door." I did, and in rushed a man.

Tieh-mei: Who was it?

Granny: Your dad.

Tieh-mei: My dad?

Granny: Yes, your present dad. He was covered with wounds, and in his left hand he held this very signal lantern. . . .

Tieh-mei: The signal lantern?

Granny: In his right arm he held a baby.

Tieh-mei: A baby. . . .

Granny: A baby less than one year old.

Tieh-mei: That baby. . . .

Granny: That baby was none other than. . . .

Tieh-mei: Than who?

Granny: Than you.

Tieh-mei: Me?

Granny: Hugging you tightly to his chest, with tears in his eyes your dad stood before me and shouted, "Aunty, aunty. . . ." For several minutes he just stared at me and couldn't go on. Terribly worried, I urged him to speak. He . . . he said, "My master and Brother Chen . . . have been murdered. This is Chen's child, a future successor to the revolution. I must bring her up to carry on the revolution." He added, "Aunty, from now on I am your own son and this child is your own granddaughter." Then I took you and held you tight in my arms.

Tieh-mei: Granny! (*Buries her head in Granny's arms.*)

Granny: Be brave and listen.
(*Sings "erh huang yuan pan"*)
In the strike those devils murdered your father and mother,
Li Yu-ho worked untiringly for the revolution;
He swore to follow in the martyrs' steps, to keep the red lantern burning;
He stanched his wounds, buried the dead and went on with the fight.
Now the Japanese brigands are burning, killing and looting,
Before our eyes your dad was taken away to prison;
Remember this debt of blood and tears,
Be brave and determined to settle accounts with the enemy,
A debt of blood must be paid with blood.

Tieh-mei (*sings "erh huang yuan pan"*):
Granny tells a heroic and stirring episode of the revolution,
Now I know I was raised in wind and rain.
Dear granny, for all those seventeen years,

Your kindness to me has been vast as the sea.
Now with high aims I see my way clear.
Blood must pay for our blood,
Successors must carry forward the cause of our martyrs.
Here I raise the red lantern, let its light shine far.
Dad! (*Changes to "erh huang kuai pan"*)
My father is as steadfast as the pine,
A Communist who fears nothing under the sun.
Following in your footsteps I shall never waver.
The red lantern we hold high, and it shines
On my father fighting those wild beasts.
Generation after generation we shall fight on,
Never leaving the field until all the wolves are killed.

(*Tieh-mei and Granny hold high the red lantern in a dramatic pose. It casts a radiant red light.*)
(*Lights fade.*)

(*Curtain*)

≍

SCENE SIX

STRUGGLING AGAINST HATOYAMA AT THE FEAST

Immediately after the previous scene. Hatoyama's reception room. A feast is laid.

(*As the curtain rises, Hou enters.*)

Hou: Please come in, Master Li.

(*Li enters calmly and with firm steps. Exit Hou.*)

Li: (*sings "erh huang yuan pan"*):
A poisoned arrow is hidden in the invitation card,
Sudden burst of a storm means traitors lurking,
I laugh at his feast spread amid swords and axes,
With revolutionary righteousness in my heart,

I will face the enemy with composure, firm as a mountain.

(Enter Hatoyama.)

Hatoyama: Ah, my old friend. I trust you've been well?

Li: Ah, Mr. Hatoyama. How are you?
(Li ignores Hatoyama's extended hand. Hatoyama withdraws it in embarrassment.)

Hatoyama: So we meet again after all this time, eh? Do you remember I once treated you in the railway hospital?

Li: In those days you were a rich Japanese doctor and I was a poor Chinese worker. We were like two trains running on different tracks, travelling in different directions.

Hatoyama: No matter how you put it, we're not strangers, right?

Li *(pretending a civility)*:   Then I'll expect you to be "helpful."

Hatoyama: That's why I've invited you for a good chat. Please sit down. This is a private feast, old friend. We'll talk of friendship and nothing else, all right?

Li *(sounding the enemy out coolly)*:   I am a poor worker and like to be straightforward. Anything you have in mind, just speak out.

Hatoyama: Quite frank! Come on, old friend, drink up.

Li: It's very kind of you, Mr. Hatoyama. Sorry, I don't drink. *(Pushes the cup away, takes out his pipe and lights it.)*

Hatoyama: You don't drink? There's an old Chinese saying, "Life is but a dream." It passes in a flash. Therefore, as is well said, "Enjoy wine and song while we can, for tomorrow we die."

Li *(blowing out his match contemptuously)*:   Yes, listening to songs and drinking the best wine is the life of an immortal. I hope you always lead such a life and I

282

wish you "long life," Mr. Hatoyama. (*Throws away the match sarcastically.*)

Hatoyama: Hah. . . . (*Forcing a smile.*) Old friend, I am a believer in Buddhism. A Buddhist sutra tells us, "The bitter sea has no bounds, repent and the shore is at hand."

Li (*counter-attacking*):   I don't believe in Buddhism. But I've heard the saying, "The law is strong, but the out-laws are ten times stronger!"*

Hatoyama: Well said, my friend. But this is only one kind of creed. As a matter of fact the highest human creed can be condensed into two words.

Li: Two words?

Hatoyama: Right.

Li: What are they?

Hatoyama: "For myself."

Li: For yourself, eh?

Hatoyama: No, every man for himself.

Li (*pretending not to understand*):   "Every man for him-self?"

Hatoyama: Right. Old friend, you know the saying, "Heaven destroys those who don't look out for them-selves."

Li: Oh? Heaven destroys those who don't look out for themselves?

Hatoyama: That's the secret of success in life.

Li: So there's such a thing as a secret of success in life?

Hatoyama: There's a secret for doing everything.

Li: Mr. Hatoyama, for me your secret is like trying to blow up a fire through a rolling-pin. It just doesn't work.

(*Hatoyama is taken aback.*)

* Here "law" means the reactionary ruling class while "outlaws" means the revolutionary spirit of rebellion of the proletariat and revolutionary people in their struggle against the reactionaries. In striking back against Hatoyama, Li Yu-ho uses this saying to imply that the Japanese bandits may ride roughshod for a time, but it is the revolutionary people who are really strong. The Japanese bandits are doomed. The Chinese people are sure to win.

Hatoyama: No more joking, old friend. Now I'd like to have your help.

Li: How can a poor worker help you?

Hatoyama: Let's stop this shadow-boxing now. Hand it over!

Li: What?

Hatoyama: The secret code.

Li: Ha. . . . A code? I don't have anything to do with such things. All I know is to work switches.

Hatoyama (*threateningly*): If you want to do it the hard way, friend, don't blame me if we get rough.

Li (*unruffled*): As you like.

(*At a sign from Hatoyama, Wang Lien-chu enters.*)

Hatoyama: Look, my old friend, who is this?

(*Wang cringes and trembles beneath Li's piercing gaze.*)
(*Hatoyama indicates for Wang to persuade Li.*)

Wang: Old Li, you mustn't be too. . . .

Li: Shut up!

Wang: Old Li, you mustn't be too pig-headed. . . .

Li (*pounds the table and jumps to his feet. Pointing at Wang, he denounces*): Shameless traitor!
(*Sings "hsi pi kuai pan"*)
Only a coward would bend his knees,
Afraid of death and clinging to life.
How often did I warn you
Against enemy threats and bribes?
You swore you would gladly die for the revolution;
How could you sell out and be their pawn?
They are treating you like a cur,
Yet you count disgrace an honour.
The day will come when the people bring you to trial,
Your betrayal is an unpardonable crime.

(*Terrified by Li's revolutionary integrity, the traitor hides behind Hatoyama.*)

Hatoyama (*quite pleased with himself*): Keep cool, my friend. Ah. . . . (*Waves Wang away.*) I didn't want to play my trump card but you forced me to. I had no alternative.

Li (*in sharp retort*): I expected as much. Your trump card is nothing but a mangy dog with a broken back. You'll get no satisfaction out of me, Hatoyama.

Hatoyama (*frustrated, reveals his true colours*): You know very well what my job is, Li Yu-ho. I'm the one who issues passes to Hell.

Li (*giving tit for tat*): And you know very well what my job is. I'm the one who will demolish your Hell.

Hatoyama: You ought to know my torture instruments are hungry for human flesh.

Li (*contemptuously*): I am no stranger to those gadgets of yours.

Hatoyama (*menacing*): Take my advice and recant before your bones are broken.

Li (*overwhelming the enemy*): I'd sooner have my bones broken than recant.

Hatoyama: Our gendarmes are pitiless. Once in the torture chamber you won't come out alive.

Li (*categorically*): We Communists have a will of steel. We look on death as nothing! Hatoyama!
(*Denouncing the Japanese bandits, sings "hsi pi yuan pan"*)
The Japanese militarists are wolves
Hiding their savagery behind a smile.
You kill our people and invade our land
(*Switches to "kuai pan"*)
In the name of "Co-prosperity in East Asia."
The Communist Party and Chairman Mao are leading the people's revolution;
We have hundreds of millions of heroes
Fighting against Japan to save our country.
Your reliance on traitors is of no more use
Than fishing for the moon in the lake.

Hatoyama: Sergeant!

(Sergeant and two gendarmes enter.)

Hatoyama *(sings "hsi pi san pan")*:
I'll let you taste all of my torture instruments.

(Militantly, Li throws open his coat in a dramatic pose.)

Li *(smiles sardonically)*:   Huh! . . .
Sergeant: Get moving.
Li *(sings "hsi pi san pan")*:   You can only limber up my joints.
Sergeant: Take him away.

(The gendarmes seize Li.)

Li: I don't need your help.

(Li flings out his arms and they stagger backwards.)
(Calmly, Li buttons his coat, picks up his cap, flicks the dust off it and holds it behind his back. Turning round, he strides off in a manner that overwhelms the enemy.)
(Sergeant and gendarmes follow.)

Hatoyama *(crestfallen and helpless)*:   He's a hard one!
(Recites "pu teng ngo"*)
What makes a Communist tougher than steel?
My persuasion and threats are of no avail,
I hope torture will make him speak.

(Enter Sergeant.)

Sergeant: Reporting! Li Yu-ho would rather die than speak.
Hatoyama: Rather die than speak?
Sergeant: Let me take some men to search his house again, captain.
Hatoyama: Forget it. Communists are very vigilant. He must have put the code somewhere else.
Sergeant: Yes, sir.

---

* A recitative accompanied rhythmically by percussion instruments.

Hatoyama: Bring him in.
Sergeant: Bring Li Yu-ho here!

(Two Japanese gendarmes drag Li in. Blood-stained and covered with wounds, Li advances militantly on Hato-yama. Then, turning round in a dance movement, he stands erect, supporting himself on a chair.)

Li *(sings "hsi pi tao pan")*:   You beast with the heart of a wolf!
Hatoyama: The code. Give me the code.
Li: Hatoyama!
(Continues to sing, switching to "hsi pi kuai pan")
No matter how cruel your tortures,
Pure gold fears not tempering in fierce fire.
No matter what, I'll never bow my head!
Ha. . . .

(The enemies are terrified by his heroic spirit.)
(Li strikes a dramatic pose.)
(Lights fade.)

(Curtain)

⇌

SCENE SEVEN

HELP FROM THE MASSES

One morning several days later. Li's house, interior and exterior view.

(As the curtain rises, Cobbler, a spy in disguise, is sitting not far from the door watching the house.)
(Knife-Grinder cries offstage: "Any knives or scissors to grind?" He enters repeating his cry while warily looking around. He sees that the red paper butterfly on the win-

dow pane is gone and notices the spy. He decides to make contact some other time.)

(Granny and Tieh-mei come out of the inner room and look out of the window.)
(Knife-Grinder leaves, calmly uttering his cry. The spy looks at him but sees nothing unusual.)

Granny: That knife-grinder probably came to contact us, Tieh-mei.

Tieh-mei: I'll run after him with the lantern and see whether he's our man or not.

Granny: It won't do, child, not with that dog outside. You can't go.

Tieh-mei: Then, what shall we do? *(Meditating.)* Granny, I have an idea. I'll go out through Hui-lien's house!

Granny: How can you do that, my child?

Tieh-mei: The other day, in the inner room where our bed stands the stone at the foot of the wall came loose. When I was helping dad repair the wall I pulled it out and crawled through for a visit.

Granny: What, you crawled through?

Tieh-mei: Yes, Hui-lien's room is right on the other side.

Granny: Let's ask their help, then. You can go out through their house. Do you remember the password your dad told you, Tieh-mei?

Tieh-mei: Yes, I do.

Granny: If you catch up with the knife-grinder, and he gives the right password in reply, go to the west bank of the river and get the code from under the stone-tablet beside an old locust tree.

Tieh-mei: Under the stone-tablet by an old locust tree?

Granny: Didn't you hear your dad mention it? You must be very careful, child.

Tieh-mei: Don't worry, granny.

Granny: Look out!

Tieh-mei: I will.

(Taking the red lantern, Tieh-mei goes into the inner room. Exit.)
(Cobbler throws away an empty match-box, walks over and knocks at the door to ask for a match.)

Cobbler: Open the door.
Granny: Who's there?
Cobbler: Me. The cobbler.
Granny: Wait a moment. (*Opens the door.*)
Cobbler (*enters*):   Ma'am.
Granny: What do you want?
Cobbler: I want a match.
Granny: There are some on top of the cupboard.
Cobbler: Thank you. Where's the girl? (*Lights his cigarette.*)
Granny: She's not well.
Cobbler: Not well? Where is she?
Granny: In bed in the inner room.
Cobbler: Oh! Thank you. (*Exit.*)
Granny: Filthy dog.

(Two spies enter at Cobbler's signal. They whisper together. As Granny closes the door they push into the house.)

Granny: Who are you?
Spy B: We are checking up.
Spy A: Where's your granddaughter?
Granny: She's ill.
Spy B: Ill? Where is she?
Granny: In bed in the other room.
Spy B: Tell her to get up!
Granny: She's ill. Let her rest.
Spy B: Get out of the way! (*Pushes Granny aside and reaches to lift the door curtain.*)

(Voice from behind the curtain: "Granny, who's there?")

Granny: Police checking up.

(Looking at each other helplessly, the spies go out. Granny closes the door behind them. She turns round and stares in surprise.)

(Hui-lien comes out of the inner room.)

Granny: Ah! What brings you here, Hui-lien?

Hui-lien: Granny Li!

(Sings "hsi pi liu shui")

Tieh-mei has slipped away through our house,
My mother-in-law sent me to let you know.
When I heard those spies questioning you
I pretended to be Tieh-mei lying ill in bed.
When Tieh-mei returns, she can come through our house,
With me helping, you don't have to worry.

Granny (*gratefully*):   You've been a tremendous help.

(Tieh-mei comes out of the inner room.)

Tieh-mei: Granny! Sister Hui-lien!

Hui-lien: So you're back, Tieh-mei.

Granny: If it weren't for Hui-lien we'd have been in serious trouble.

Hui-lien: It's good you're back. I must be going now.

Tieh-mei: Thank you.

(Hui-lien enters the inner room. Exit.)

Granny: Go and put the stone in place, Tieh-mei.

(Tieh-mei goes into the inner room. Granny hangs up the lantern. Tieh-mei enters again.)

Granny: Did you find the knife-grinder?

Tieh-mei: I searched several streets but couldn't find him. I hurried back for fear those spies might discover that I was out.

Granny: You did right!

(Enter Hou. He sends Cobbler away and knocks at the door.)

Tieh-mei: Who's there?

Hou: Captain Hatoyama is coming to pay you a visit.

Tieh-mei: Granny!

Granny: If I am arrested, Tieh-mei, you must try your best to deliver the code to the Cypress Mountains.

Tieh-mei: Don't worry!

Hou: Open the door!

Granny: Go and open the door.

Tieh-mei: Yes. *(Opens the door.)*

(Hatoyama enters and comes into the house. Hou follows and stands by.)

Hatoyama: How are you, madam?

Granny: So you are Mr. Hatoyama?

Hatoyama: Yes, I'm Hatoyama.

Granny: Just a minute, please. I'll tidy up and go with you.

Hatoyama: Oh, that's not what I came for. Li Yu-ho said that he left something with you, madam.

Granny: Left what?

Hatoyama: The code.

Granny: What does he mean, child?

Hatoyama: It's a book.

Granny: A book?

Hatoyama: That's right.

Granny: Mr. Hatoyama.
(Sings "hsi pi yuan pan")
My family has always suffered from hunger and cold,
None of us three knows how to read.
What would we want with a book in our home?

Hatoyama *(continues the singing)*:
Since Li Yu-ho has told me about that book,
Why try to hide it and fool me?

Tieh-mei *(continues the singing)*: *Let my dad come and find it. Why trouble yourself?*

Hatoyama: Now, now. If you give me that book I'll send Li Yu-ho straight home and make him a vice-section chief. I promise all of you wealth and fame.

Granny: Hum!
(Continues to sing)
I look upon wealth and fame as dust,
We poor people find coarse food very tasty.
Since you have taken such trouble to come for it—
(To Tieh-mei.) Go and find it for him.

(Tieh-mei goes into the inner room and brings out the almanac which she hands to Granny.)

Granny *(to Hatoyama, continues to sing)*:
So that you will not have come for nothing.
(Hands the "book" to Hatoyama.)

Hatoyama: That's it. That must be it. An almanac? *(Leafing through it.)* I'll take it with me and study it. What about going to see your son, madam?

Granny: Very well! Look after the house, Tieh-mei.

Hatoyama: No! The girl must come too!

Tieh-mei: Let's go, granny!
(Sings "hsi pi san pan")
Filled with courage and strength like dad,
I have nothing to fear—

(Granny and Tieh-mei leave the house.)
(Hatoyama follows. Hou orders the spies to seal the door.)

Granny *(continues the singing)*:
Revolutionaries can stand the collapse of heaven and earth!

(Granny and grand-daughter walk straight forward, then strike a dramatic pose.)
(Lights fade.)

(Curtain)

≍

SCENE EIGHT

STRUGGLE ON THE EXECUTION GROUND

Night. A corner of the prison in the headquarters of the Japanese gendarmerie.

(As the curtain rises, Sergeant and Hou stand waiting. Enter Hatoyama.)

Hatoyama: It seems direct questioning won't get us the secret code. The hidden microphone?

Hou: Already installed.

Hatoyama: Good. We'll hear what they say when the old woman meets her son. Perhaps we'll find out something this way. Bring the old woman in.

Hou: Yes, sir. (To offstage.) Come along!

(Enter Granny.)

Hatoyama: Do you know this place, madam?

Granny: It's the gendarme headquarters.

Hatoyama: This is where your son will ascend to heaven! When a man has committed a crime and his mother refuses to save his life when she has it in her power, don't you think she is cruel?

Granny (sternly, putting the vile enemy on trial): What kind of talk is that! You've arrested my son for no reason. Now you want to kill him. You are the criminals, it's you who are cruel. You kill the Chinese, and you want to shift the blame on to the Chinese people, on to me, an old woman?

Hatoyama: All right! Go and see your son!

(Granny walks off resolutely. Hatoyama signs to Hou to follow her.)

Hatoyama: Take Li Yu-ho there.

Sergeant: Bring Li . . . Yu-ho! . . .

(*Dark change.*)
(*A corner of the execution ground: A high wall, a steep slope, a sturdy pine reaching to the sky. In the distance a high mountain pierces into the clouds.*)

Li (*offstage, sings "erh huang tao pan"*):
    At the gaoler's bloodthirsty cry . . .
    (*Enters and strikes a dramatic pose.*)
    I stride forth from my cell.

(*Two Japanese gendarmes push him. With a strong sense of righteousness, Li stands chest out, undaunted. Then he performs a series of characteristic Peking opera dance movements: moving briskly sideways on both legs, backing a few steps on one leg, a pause; turning round on one leg and then swinging the other and striking a dramatic pose. He advances boldly, forcing the two Japanese gendarmes to retreat.*)
(*Li rubs his wounded chest, then places one foot on a rock and nurses his knee. He casts a contemptuous glance at his chains and fully displays his noble spirit.*)

Li (*sings "hui lung"*):
    Though heavy chains shackle me hand and foot,
    They cannot fetter my spirit that storms the heavens.
    (*Feeling a sharp pain in his wounded legs, he backs a few steps on one leg, nurses his knees and finally stands on one leg in a dramatic pose.*)
Li (*sings "yuan pan"*):
    That villain Hatoyama used every torture to get the
        code,
    My bones are broken, my flesh is torn,
    But my will is firmer than ever.
    Walking boldly to the execution ground, I look afar:
    The red flag of revolution is raised on high,
    The flames of resistance spread far and wide.
    Japanese bandits, let's see how much longer you can
        age!

Once the storm is past (*changes to "man san yen"*)
    flowers will bloom,
New China will shine like the morning sun,
Red flags will fly all over the country.
This thought heightens my confidence
And my resolve strengthened.
(*Changes to "yuan pan"*)
I have done very little for the Party,
I'm worried that the code hasn't got to the mountains.
Wang's only contact was with me,
The wretch can betray no one else;
My mother and daughter are as firm as steel.
Hatoyama, try and get the secret code!
You may ransack heaven and earth
But you will never find it.
Revolutionaries, fear nothing on earth,
They will forever march forward.

(*Enter Granny.*)

Granny: Yu-ho!
Li (*looks back*):   Mother!
Granny (*runs over to support Li, sings "erh huang san pan"*):
    Again I live through that day seventeen years ago,
    And burn with hate for the foe of my class and country.
    These . . . Japanese devils, cruel and treacherous,
    Have beaten you black and blue,
    My son, my son!
Li: Don't grieve for me, mother!
Granny (*continues to sing*):
    With such a fine son . . . I shouldn't grieve.
Li: My good mother!
    (*Sings "erh huang erh liu"*)
    Brought up by the Party to be a man of steel,
    I fight the foe and never give ground.
    I'm not afraid
    To have every bone in my body broken,

I'm not afraid
To be locked up until I wear through the floor of my
*   cell.*
It makes my heart bleed to see our country ravaged,
I burn with anger for my people's suffering.
However hard the road of revolution,
We must press on in the steps of the glorious dead.
My only regret if I die today
Is the "account" I have not settled.
(Gestures to indicate the secret code.)
I long to soar like an eagle to the sky,
Borne on the wind above the mountain passes
To rescue our millions of suffering countrymen—
Then how gladly would I die for the revolution!

(Enter Hou followed by two Japanese gendarmes.)

Hou: Old woman, Captain Hatoyama wants to have a talk with you.

Granny (*to Li*):   Son, I know what he is going to say.

Hou: Come on.

(Granny goes out fearlessly, followed by the two Japanese gendarmes.)

Hou: Bring Li Tieh-mei here!

(Tieh-mei runs in.)

Tieh-mei: Dad!

(Exit Hou.)

Tieh-mei (*sings "erh huang san pan"*):
Day and night I've been longing to see you again,
And now you . . . so battered and covered with blood. . . .
Dear father!

Li: You mustn't cry, child! (*Strokes Tieh-mei's hair lovingly, with determination.*) Be brave, daughter! (*Helps Tieh-mei to her feet, with feeling.*) My child!
(*Continues the singing*)

One thing I have wanted to tell you many times,
It's been hidden in my heart for seventeen years.
I. . . .

Tieh-mei (*quickly stopping him*):   Don't say it, dad, you
are my own father. (*Kneels.*)
(*Sings "erh huang kuai pan"*)
Don't say it, father,
I know the bitter tale of these seventeen years.

(*Li helps Tieh-mei to her feet, his feelings like turbulent*
waves.)

Li (*sings "erh huang yuan pan"*):
People say that family love outweighs all else,
But class love is greater yet, I know.
A proletarian fights all his life for the people's liberation.
Making a home wherever I am,
I have lived in poverty all these years.
The red lantern is my only possession,
I entrust it to your safe keeping.

Tieh-mei (*sings "erh huang kuai san yen"*):
Dad has given me a priceless treasure
To light my path forward forever.
You have given me your integrity
To help me stand firm as a rock;
You have given me your wisdom
To help me see through the enemy's wiles;
You have given me your courage
To help me fight those brutes.
This red lantern is our heirloom.
Oh dad, the treasure you leave me is so vast,
That a thousand carts and ten thousand boats
Cannot hold it all.
I give you my word I will keep the lantern always safe.

Li (*sings "erh huang san pan"*):
As wave follows wave in the great Yangtze River,
Our red lantern will be passed on from hand to hand.
(*To Tieh-mei.*)

If some day to home you return,
Find our relatives, make a living, clear that "account,"
(Gestures to indicate the code.)
I'll have no worries.

(Japanese gendarmes enter pushing Granny. Enter
Sergeant.)

Sergeant: Captain Hatoyama gives you five more minutes
to think it over. If you still refuse to give up the
secret code, you will all be shot. (*Drags Tieh-mei away.*)
Our five minutes left, girl. Give up the code and save
the whole family. Understand? Speak up!

(Firmly, Tieh-mei walks back to her dear ones.)

Sergeant: Where is the code?
Tieh-mei: I—don't—know!
Sergeant: Shoot them all.
Gendarmes: Yes.
Li: No use baring your fangs! Tieh-mei, let's take granny's
arms and go together.

("The Internationale" is played, Bravely and firmly, the
three walk arm in arm up a slope with their heads high.)
(Enter Hatoyama.)

Hatoyama: Wait! I give you one more minute to think
it over.
Li (*with a spirit that shakes the universe*):   Hatoyama, you
can never kill all Chinese people, all the Chinese Communists. You must think of the end in store for you
scoundrels!
Hatoyama: Terrible! (*To Sergeant.*) Act according to
plan! (*Exit.*)
Sergeant: Shoot them!

(To the militant strains of "The Internationale," the
three revolutionaries of three generations, heads high,
walk up the slope, defying death. They go out.)
(Japanese gendarmes follow.)

(*Silence. Offstage, Li shouts: "Down with Japanese imperialism!" "Long live the Chinese Communist Party!" The three of them shout with their arms raised: "Long live Chairman Mao!"*)

(*A volley of shots. Two Japanese gendarmes drag Tieh-mei in and throw her down.*)

Tieh-mei (*standing up, turns to call*):   Dad! Granny!

(*Enter Hatoyama with Hou and Sergeant.*)

Hatoyama: Give me the code, Li Tieh-mei.
Hou and Sergeant: Speak up!

(*Tieh-mei glares at Hatoyama.*)

Hatoyama: Let her go!
Sergeant: Yes, sir. Get out!

(*Sergeant pushes Tieh-mei away. They go out, followed by the gendarmes.*)

Hou: Why did you let her go, sir?
Hatoyama: It's called using a long line to catch a big fish.
Hou: Right!

(*Lights fade.*)

(*Curtain*)

SCENE NINE

ADVANCING WAVE UPON WAVE

Immediately after the last scene. Dawn. Li's house, interior and exterior view.

(*As the curtain rises, Tieh-mei enters the room, leans back against the door. Looking around, full of sorrow and hatred, she thinks of her martyred father and grand-mother.*)

Tieh-mei: Dad! Granny! (*Rests her head on the table and sobs. A pause. Slowly rising, she sees the red lantern, hurries over and takes it.*) Granny, dad, I know what you died for. I shall carry on the task you left unfinished and be the successor to the red lantern. I'm determined to deliver the code to the Cypress Mountains and avenge your bloody murder. Hatoyama, you may arrest me or release me at will, but you'll never get the secret code!
(*Sings "hsi pi tao pan"*)
I burst with anger when I think of the foe!
(*Changes to "kuai san yen"*)
Repressing my rage I grind my teeth.
Using every trick to get the code,
Hatoyama has killed my granny and dad!
(*Changes to "erh liu"*)
Biting my hate, chewing my rage,
I force them down my throat,
Let them sprout in my heart.
I'll never yield, I'll never retreat,
(*Changes to "kuai pan"*)
No tears shall wet my cheeks,
Let them flow into my heart
To nourish the bursting seeds of hatred.
Flames of rage, ten leagues high,
Will burn away this reign of the forces of darkness.
I'm prepared: arrest me, release me,
Use your whips and lash, your locks and chains.
Break my bones, you will never get the code.
Just wait, you villain Hatoyama,
This is Tieh-mei's answer!
I'll go now! (*Picks up the red lantern, ready to leave.*)

(*Hui-lien comes out of the inner room.*)

Hui-lien: Tieh-mei!

Tieh-mei: Sister Hui-lien! (*Puts down the lantern and bolts the door.*)

Hui-lien: My mother has come to see you.

(*Aunt Tien emerges from the inner room.*)

Aunt Tien: Tieh-mei!

Tieh-mei: Aunty. . . . (*Runs into her arms.*)

Aunt Tien: Child, we have heard what happened to your dad and grandma. We'll see how much longer those beasts can ravage our land! There are spies outside, Tieh-mei, you mustn't leave by this door. Slip out through our house. Hurry, change jackets with Hui-lien.

Tieh-mei: No, aunty, I mustn't get you into trouble.

Aunt Tien: My child! (*While helping Tieh-mei to change jackets with Hui-lien she sings "hsi pi san pan"*)
None but the poor help the poor,
We are two bitter gourds on the same vine;
We must save you from the tiger's jaws,
So that you can go forward on your course.

Tieh-mei: But what if something happens to you?

Aunt Tien: We are both working-class families. We have shared bitterness and hatred for many years. No matter how risky it is, I must see you safely away.

Tieh-mei (*with gratitude*):   Aunty. . . .

Aunt Tien: Hurry up, child!

Hui-lien: Be quick, Tieh-mei!

Tieh-mei: I shall never forget you, sister and aunty.

Aunt Tien: Go quickly.

(*Picking up the red lantern, Tieh-mei goes into the inner room. Exit.*)

Aunt Tien: Be very careful, Hui-lien.

(*Aunt Tien goes into the inner room. Exit.*)
(*Hui-lien wraps Tieh-mei's scarf round her head, covering the lower part of her face. She steps out of the*

*house with the basket and closes the door behind her.
Exit.)*
*(Spies B and C emerge from behind an electric pole and
trail her.)*
(Lights fade.)

(Curtain)

═

SCENE TEN

AMBUSHING AND ANNIHILATING THE ENEMY

Immediately after the last scene. On the road leading to the
Cypress Mountains.

> *(As the curtain rises, enter Knife-Grinder with two
> guerrillas dressed as peasants. Enter Tieh-mei. They
> meet.)*

Tieh-mei: Uncle Knife-Grinder! *(Takes out the red lantern from the basket and holds it aloft.)*

Knife-Grinder: Tieh-mei! *(Turns to the guerrillas.)* Keep
guard!

Tieh-mei: I've found you at last, Uncle! My dad and
Granny. . . .

Knife-Grinder: We know everything. Don't grieve, Tieh-
mei. Turn your sorrow into strength. We'll be avenged!
Have you got the code with you?

Tieh-mei: Yes.

Knife-Grinder: That's fine.

Tieh-mei: Uncle, my neighbour Hui-lien helped me. She
disguised herself as me and led the spies off after her.
That's how I was able to get the code and bring it here.

Knife-Grinder: The enemy must be suspecting Hui-lien's
family.
(To Guerrilla A.) Old Feng, help the Tiens move as
quickly as possible.

Guerrilla A: Right! (*Exit.*)

(*A police car siren is heard.*)

Guerrilla B: The enemy's coming, Old Chao.
Knife-Grinder: You take Tieh-mei up the mountain.
We'll deal with them.

(*Guerrilla B leads Tieh-mei off*).
(*Wang shouts offstage: "Halt!" Japanese gendarmes en-
ter, with Hatoyama and Wang in the lead. Knife-
Grinder blocks their way. Hatoyama shouts: "Take
him!" Knife-Grinder snatches Wang's pistol and kills a
Japanese gendarme. Then he strikes Wang with his
bench.*)
(*The guerrillas jump out of a grove. Dramatic pose.*)
(*On the crag a guerrilla kills a Japanese gendarme.*)
(*Hatoyama and Wang run off, Knife-Grinder and the
guerrillas pursue them.*)
(*The guerrillas dash down from the crag and chase the
enemy.*)
(*A guerrilla with a red-tasselled spear fights two Japanese
gendarmes. They flee, followed by the guerrilla.*)
(*Knife-Grinder chases Wang. They lock in struggle.*)
(*Enter Hatoyama with Japanese gendarmes. Fighting
at close quarters. The guerrillas wipe out all the enemies,
shooting down the traitor Wang, and running Hatoyama through with a sword.*)
(*The ambush has been a great success. The guerrillas
form a tableau of heroes, in a valiant dramatic pose.*)
(*Lights fade.*)

(*Curtain*)

≍

SCENE ELEVEN

FORWARD IN VICTORY

Immediately after the last scene. The Cypress Mountains.

(*As the curtain rises, red flags flutter against a clear blue sky. The guerrilla leader walks down the hill slope. Knife-Grinder enters with Tieh-mei. All the guerrillas enter. Solemnly, Tieh-mei hands the code to the guerrilla leader. Brandishing their rifles and swords, all rejoice in their victory. Tieh-mei holds aloft the red lantern while crimson light radiates. The curtain slowly falls.*)

(*The end*)

Do-It-Yourself Theatre

≋ "IN PEKING, THE EFFECT OF BRINGING THE people, old and young, literate and illiterate, into the theatre, has been a very marked one," wrote Rewi Alley from the capital of the People's Republic the year after Liberation. "The Chinese language is not easy to learn, and many people still find reading a formidable task. But the theatre does not allow thinking to lag behind. And as I sit and write this, from a compound nearby, I hear the orchestra of the railwaymen's theatrical group practicing. The People's Liberation Army has its trained theatre group, for the Army today is very much a part of the life of the people. Schools and other organizations all have theirs. The theatre both educates and finds expression for all sections everywhere in China today, and belongs, in the truest sense, to the people themselves. Only a revolution could have produced the contrast between the theatre of today and the theatre of the past."*

Among the very poor in the uncountable back-country villages of old China, theatre was rarely, if ever, seen. The substitute was the strolling players and storytellers who wandered from place to place earning their scrubby keep by means of song and fiddle. Releasing the miserable peasants from their sordid existence for an hour or so meant dinner bowls filled with a meal. Often the players performed at the village water wheel, where newly ground flour served as payment for the entertainment. People would listen interminably, warmed with the glimmer of self-respect engendered by the tales of old heroes fighting against injustice.

Rewi Alley recalls the performance of a favorite storyteller in the area of Sandan in northwest China. A huge man with bulging eyes and nimble tongue, the actor regaled the local residents with his personification of a giant warrior who stripped down before plunging into battle with swords flashing in the teeth of the enemy. The storyteller would prance around with great gusto and heighten the climax by removing his own pants—to the delight of the audience, who let the coppers fly after his bare bottom.

Another favorite of this region was the ancient *kun chu* opera *Hsiao Fang Niu* (Little Buffalo Boy), whose plaintive song "All the World Is Poor but None So Poor As I" was the most popular of all.

Twenty years later, theatre, music, song and dance remained an important part of people's lives. From schoolchildren to factory hands, from university students to farmer-peasants, everywhere we went some manifestation of this love of expression was obvious. Often time was diverted for us by the songs and dances of small troupes of strolling PLA players as we waited to be called to a plane or train. Coming back late in the evening to our hotel we sometimes encountered a busload of *tung chih* ("comrade"

* *Yo Banfa!* by Rewi Alley, New World Press, Peking, 1952.

waiters and maids) returning in bright make-up after entertaining in a suburban commune. High-pitched, childish
notes floated from crocodile lines of youngsters walking
home from school. Tots in primary grades, and practically
"dots" in kindergarten, backed up by a teacher at a piano
or organ, welcomed us with songs and poems. Middle-school
kids put on full-fledged shows of Peking opera tunes, costumed folk dances, and original musical sketches boasting
such titles as "Celebrate the Communiqué of the Second
Plenary Session" and "People of the World Unite to Defeat
U.S. Aggression"—hardly candidates for "Top of the Pops,"
but we were duly impressed.

It's almost all do-it-yourself, which in Chinese could
be translated into *tze li keng shen* or "self-reliance." A
remarkable number of talented people are around, ready to
perform at the drop of a hint.

On the grounds of the Capital Iron and Steel Company outside Peking we sat on tiny stools to watch a performance put on by five- and six-year-olds of the company's
kindergarten. The children, dressed in tiny replicas of PLA
uniforms and caps, sang and danced a program which included "Rely on the Masses," "Tibetan Dance," and "We
Must Liberate Taiwan." One little girl with finely shaped
eyes and tassle-silk hair was already a striking performer. She
was so pretty and unusually graceful that I wonder if she's
not headed for a Peking opera or ballet training school in
a year or so. We were told scouts are constantly on the
lookout for talent. I watched the child later in the morning
playing tag outside with her friends. In the school's tree-
sprinkled courtyard there is a protruding cement structure
—the entrance to the ubiquitous air-raid shelter that silently
reminds one of China's concern.

This huge steel plant, a town in itself, has amateur
theatrical productions of model operas as well as propaganda
teams who put on skits and plays based on factory and local
problems. Often the worker-actors go out to entertain the
members of nearby farm communes. Our September visit

found them engaged in rehearsals for *The Red Lantern*, to be performed in Peking's Tien An Men in front of Mao Tse-tung, they proudly told us, for the forthcoming October first celebration.

This month preceding National Day was a busy one. Peking's Temple of Heaven buzzed with young adults practicing marches and songs on the once-upon-a-time preserves of sacred emperors. A group of pilots twirled and whirled huge crimson flags in complicated patterns on the field beside Peking's airport. Primary school pupils and militia troops rehearsed on city side-streets; Pei Hai Park swarmed with students practicing marches and songs. In every provincial capital and in thousands of towns and villages China reverberated with preparation. Floats went up in the back lanes near our hotel, their wooden frames like enormous fish skeletons. One morning they suddenly had become painted and decorated beauties, ready for the parade. Every sector of society seemed represented, from professional and amateur theatre and ballet troupes to minority groups dressed in unusual native costumes. The model revolutionary productions each rated a special float, the actors frozen in representative scenes held for ten minutes at a time without an apparent blink, as music rolled over them and pompons held by thousands of people in the background varied patterns of brilliance and shapes. It was a time of color, gaiety, pageant and pride, with holiday excitement tangible in the air.

But this is special, as are the May Day song and dance festivities given each spring in the profuse parks of China. During workaday most-of-the-year the population expresses its ancient love of song, dance, storytelling, and such simpler forms of entertainment (and instruction) in performances that vary in time, talent and location. One sunny day I walked through lake-divided T'ao Ran Ting (Joyous Pavilion Park) with an old resident of Peking. Families were boating, children splashing and diving. (In winter the lakes become ice-skating rinks.) Under the roof of a tiled pavilion, teen-aged Red Guards were telling stories and playing instruments as they acted before a knot of kindergarten babies grouped at their feet. I commented on the scene, warmed by the beauty found in the quiet center of a teeming commercial district. My friend nodded in agreement, then remarked that the lakes had been mosquito-infested swamps used for garbage dumping and that the area had served as execution grounds, first by the emperors and war-lord governors, and last by Chiang Kai-shek. How many people had been beheaded or shot in this now-peaceful park? We left the storytellers in silence and went off to have tea.

In Sian we spent a day at the No. 1 Textile Mill, with its 3400 workers and staff. At the end of hours of questions asked, and mostly answered, we were ushered into a hall where the factory's theatrical team put on an entertainment for us and their fellow workers—the same show they bring to outlying areas around this northern capital. There was no proscenium, no curtain; doors on either side of the back wall served as entrance and exit. The men wore white shirts and dark blue overalls; the girls were in blue pants, pink blouses and white aprons. A sixteen-piece orchestra—Western and Chinese violins, Chinese mandolins, the wonderfully clear and wild horn called *sona*, a *pi-pa*, an accordion, drums, cymbals, and "pan-style" pipes—was led by a virtuoso musician who himself played practically every instrument. They played orchestral music from *The White Haired Girl* and the theme song from the film *Tunnel Warfare*. Verve, good will, hard work and talent blended in an almost two-hour performance. Shy and grave, a girl of some sixteen years sang "If I Live I Must Follow His Example"—Tieh Mei's solo from *The Red Lantern*. We had seen her during the day working in the factory shop putting thread on spools—a middle-school graduate doing her *lao tung* (manual labor).

A very fast "patter number" between a young man and woman discussing the new Party Constitution, combined chant, mime and dance in what is called *yao yen-chao*. A chorus of men wearing the white head towels of Shensi peasants and girls in the local large straw hats danced *yang ko* steps to native Yenan music. The subject was the opening up of land at Naniwan, a nearby farm area that has endured since early revolutionary days. The Mao Tse-tung poem "Snow" was sung while two young girls performed an acrobatic dance. Korean and other minority dances changed the pace, the long silk skirts and bodices softening the bodies of the factory girls.

The show was straight and simple, but the words sung by a boy accompanying himself on an accordion were "People are not afraid of U.S. imperialism; U.S. imperialism is afraid of the people all over the world." And there we were. They ended the show waving magically appearing "Little Red Books" and singing "Socialism Is Good." We walked up to them as they stood in line and shook hands with every one. They beamed with friendliness and the exuberance of having given a first-rate performance. When we left the factory the cast, still in make-up and costume, came out onto the covered portico to say goodbye. A long triple-deep row of children and adults was waiting in the rain to clap and wave us away.

We passed another rainy evening, this time outdoors, in entertainment, provided within the shadow of the Great Wall near its seacoast terminal. Our hosts were members of a commune made up of people once so poor that they owned together only three legs of a donkey—the fourth leg belonged to a family that did not want to join the cooperative. Here in Shi Pu, a hundred miles from Peking, we sat on special seats in the midst of an audience which included nursing mothers and venerable oldsters, watching a spirited, spritely show put on by young actors costumed in scarlet cotton jackets and blue pants. The songs and dances were from the new Peking operas, regional folk music and original compositions that ranged from the three-legged donkey tale to a song-and-mime whose humor contrasted with its title, "I Just Heard on the Loudspeaker that the Soviet Revisionists Want Two Chinas!"

The stage is a permanent roofless stone structure in the center of the village square. When rain began toward the middle of the performance, enormous straw hats were immediately placed on our heads as the show went on. I was reminded of Jack Belden's account of wartime theatre; the intermittent drizzle caused the lights to go out several times. Out came the handy ladder, up went the ready actor, on came the lights. It bothered nobody (as in any good amateur company in the world). What impressed me was the spontaneity and fervor that permeated the performance. Directed by two Peking students doing their manual labor in the countryside, the performers were unsophisticated farmers whose knowledge of Peking opera and dance came mainly from radio and television. They had "dared to do," and they did well.

The most professional of the amateur groups we saw was a children's unit in Nanking. We had been told they were "worth the trip," and they were. These "Little Red Soldiers" are students of seven to fourteen who belong to a special school where, along with regular studies, they are trained to entertain. They are all kids of theatrical promise and eventually some of them will become professionals, though that word can be applied to them today, judging from the show they put on—full of smiles, spirit and sparkle. They "sell" themselves, if one can use such a nonproletarian term.

A large orchestra made up of Western and Chinese violins, flutes, a cello, an accordion, the low, soft-toned *erh hu*, the moon-shaped guitar called *yueh ch'in*, and a myriad of string instruments, was composed of boys and girls obviously trained by somebody who cares. Eleven dancers, in green army uniforms with bright red arm-bands, entered in an explosion of march and song. Every girl had a long black pigtail and all were made up to equal the casts we had seen in Peking. Energy socked out to the audience and held straight through the show. A party of PLA soldiers near us sat on the edge of their chairs in obvious enjoyment.

The hit of the evening was an eleven-year-old boy who, with marvelous twisting and lifting of eyebrows, sang two of Yang Tzu-jung's solos from *Taking Tiger Mountain*; a born comedian, he didn't know it, which made it all the more delightful. He was joined in an aria from *Shachiapang* by a doll of an eight-year-old girl in the part of Aunt Sha. They brought the house down. Another hit was a condensed version of *Little Sisters on the Grassland*, about two Tibetan girls who risk their lives in a snowstorm to save the sheep entrusted to their care. A lively African dance by eight boys and girls dressed in the blackest of leotards, which left their feet startlingly bare and white, was supplemented by choral singing of "Asian, African and Latin American People Want to Make Revolution."

Individual fledgling musicians were extraordinary, handling Western violins as skillfully as Chinese *pi-pas*, and producing odd but charming music from the bamboo-piped mouth organ *sheng* and a wooden ball instrument that sounded like horses' hooves, throughout a Mongolian folk song.

So it continued wherever we went; the successors to the revolution are full of song. From such youngsters, far-flung over the country, China will draw its new citizens and its newly emerging theatre. What will it be—and for whom? I trust it will fulfill what I saw at the time, not only for the People's Republic, but for the rest of the world as well.

The following Glossary is an attempt to clarify some of the terms used in Peking opera by literally translating into English the Chinese words that make up each term. The same has been done for the ballet language where the classical French terms, familiar to the West, have been taken into the Chinese language through descriptive definitions that in most cases result not only in an understanding of the action but also in a word picture of the physical image to be achieved. The list is not complete, and in some instances the author has employed a bit of guess-work or intuition. The blend of Peking opera and ballet steps sometimes makes it difficult to be precise.

Glossary of Chinese Theatre and Dance Terms

FORM	TERM					EXPLANATION
Ballet	*Chiao*	*Chu*				"Twisting the enemy's arm while fighting"
	Cross	Stop				
Ballet	*Chien*	*Shih*	*Pien*	*Shen*	*Tiao*	*Jeté entrelacé* "Scissors stance leap"
	Points	Style	Side	Body	Leap	
Peking Opera	*Chuan*	*Fan*	*Shen*			"Successive body turns in a circle while holding on to a stick"
	Twirl	Turn	Over			*Fan Shen* in Peking opera 1) Somersault 2) Cartwheel

Form	Term				Explanation
Peking Opera	*Chi*	*Pu*	*Yuan*	*Chang*	"Quick step around"
		Step			
Ballet	*Chien*	*Yueh*			*Sissonne ouverte* "Forward leap"
	Points	Leap			
Ballet	*Chan*	*Chih*	*Tun*	*Chuan*	"Squatting and turning with wings outspread"
	Spread	Wings	Squat	Spin	
Peking Opera	*Chien*	*Chiao*			"Forward bridge"
	Points	Bridge			
	Fei	*Chiao*			"Flying feet"
	Flying	Feet	(Kick	Legs)	
Ballet	*Hsuan*	*Feng*	*Kung*	*Chuan*	*Grand assemblé en tournant* "Whirlwind mid-air spins"
	Swirl	Wind	Air	Turn-spin	
Peking Opera	*Hsuan*	*Tzu*			"Amid-air whirl" Jump into the air and make a complete turn in a horizontal position.
	Swirl				
Ballet	*Hsien*	*Shen*	*Tan*	*Hai*	*Attitude basse*
		Body	Plunge	Sea	
Ballet	*Hsi*	*Tui*	*La*	*Chuan*	*Tour lent à deux* "Spinning with one knee folded"
	Fold	Leg	Move	Twirl-spin	
Ballet	*Hsi*	*Tui*	*Tiao*		*Temps levé, jambe repliée* "Leaps with knee (leg) folded"
	Fold	Leg	Leap		
Ballet	*Hsi*	*Tui*	*Ta*	*Tiao*	"Great leap with knee folded"
	Fold	Leg	Great	Leap	

Form	Term				Explanation
Ballet	*Ho*	*Li*		*Hsuan Chuan*	*Grande pirouette attitude*
	Crane	Stand		Spinning	"Stork or heron spin" (Spinning in place)
Ballet	*Hsiao*	*Peng Tzu*			*Serie de renversés* "Little spirals"
	Little	Spin			
Peking Opera	*Hu*	*Tiao*			Cartwheel
		Jump			
Peking Opera	*Hsiao*	*Mao*			Light forward tumbling
	Little				
Ballet	*Ho*	*Li*	*Shih*		*Attitude* "Stork or heron pose"
	Crane	Stance	Style		
Ballet	*Hua*	*Cha*			"Splits on the flat ground"
	To Slide	Splits			
Ballet	*Kung*	*Chien*	*Pu*		"Bow arrow stance step"
	Bow	Arrow	Step		
Peking Opera	*Ko*	*Tzu*			(Landing on his bottom)
Peking Opera	*Kao*	*Pu*	*Hu*		"Pouncing on the lion" (Jump up and land on hands ... used for fighting)
	High Pounce on Tiger				
Peking Opera	*Kuei*	*Chuan*			"Spin on knees" (Used for anguish, desperation, anger)
	Kneel	Spin			

Form	Term					Explanation
Ballet	*Kung*	*Chuan*				*Tour en l'air* "Spin in midair"
	In the Air	Spin				
Peking Opera	*Kua*	*Tui*				Pose on one leg, then stride forward
		Leg				
Ballet	*Kua*	*Yeh*	*Tui*	*Kung*	*Chuan*	Folded legs high spin in the air (Men only)
		Fold	Leg	Air	Spin	
Ballet	*Kuo*	*Men*	*Kan*			"Crossing the door sill"
	Crossing	Door	Sill			
Peking Opera	*Liang*	*Hsiang*				A convention of Peking opera. It is a still, statuesque pose assumed for a brief moment by the principals and others while entering or leaving the stage, sometimes after a dance or an acrobatic feat, in order to bring out sharply and concentratedly the spiritual outlook of the characters.
	Bright	Appearance				
Ballet	*La*	*Tui*	*Peng Tzu*			*Grand jeté en tournant* "Spirals with legs outspread"
	Spread	Leg	Leap			
Ballet	*Ling*	*Kung*	*Yueh*			*Grand jeté*
	Mid Air Off Ground		Leap			"Leaps in midair"

Form	Term				Explanation
Ballet	*Ling*	*Kung*	*Yueh*	*Chuan*	*Jeté par terre en tournant*
	Mid	Air	Leap	Spin	"Leaps and springs in midair"
Ballet	*Pan*	*Feng*	*Shih*		*Écarté* "Stance for climbing heights
	Climb	Peak	Style		
Ballet	*Pi*	*Cha*	*Tiao*		*Pas de chat* "Sharp thrusting jumps" *Pi Cha* is the Peking opera term for a widespread split
	Spread	Legs	Lead		
Ballet	*Pi*	*Cha*	*Ta*	*Tiao*	*Grand pas de chat* "Doing the splits while running"
	Spread	Legs	Great	Lead	
Ballet	*Pu*	*Pu*			Pouncing or bouncing step
Ballet	*Ping*	*Chuan*			Chaîne "Spinning on the level"
	Level	Spin			
Ballet and Peking Opera	*Pi*	*Cha*			Probably sharp thrusts to frighten enemy
	Spread-legs (deep split)				
Peking Opera	*Pei*	*Tao*	*Fei*	*Chiao*	"With sword on back and flying feet" (Warrior scenes)
	Back	Sword	Flying	Feet	
Peking Opera	*Pei*	*Shen*	*Kuei*	*Pu*	"With back to audience while taking steps on knees"
	Back	Body	Kneel	Step	
Ballet	*Pang*	*Yueh*	*Pu*		*Jeté fermé* *Pang* is ninety degrees of side
	Side	Leap	Step		

FORM	TERM				EXPLANATION
Ballet	*Pien*	*Tui*	*Chuan*		"Kick spin" *Pien* means forty-five degrees of side
	Side	Leg	Spin		
Ballet	*Pien*	*Tui*			*Grand rond de jambe en dehors*
	Side	Leg			
Ballet	*Pang*	*Tui*	*Kung*	*Chuan*	*Grand temps levé en tournant à la seconde* "Side leg midair turns"
	Side	Leg	Air	Spin	
Ballet	*Pien*	*Shen*	*Tiao*		*Grand fouetté* Change of body leap
	Side	Body	Leap		
Peking Opera	*Shang*	*Pu*	*Fan*	*Shen*	"High step body turn"
	High	Step	Turn	Over	
Ballet and Peking Opera	*Shen*	*Yen*	*Ta*	*Tiao*	"Goose shooting grand leap" (Two arms in shooting position)
	Shoot	Goose	Great	Leap	
Peking Opera	*Shen*	*Yen*			"Goose shooting squat"
	Shoot	Goose			
Peking Opera	*Sao*	*Tang*	*Tui*		Squat on one leg and make a complete circle with other leg extended
Ballet	*Shuang*	*Peng Tzu*			Double spiral
	Double	Spin			

FORM	TERM					EXPLANATION
Ballet and Peking Opera	*Tsu*	*Chien*	*Kung*	*Chien*	*Pu*	One leg straight like an arrow; other leg bent like a bow. In Peking opera, flat feet. Ballet adds on points.
	Foot	Point	Bow	Arrow	Step	
Ballet	*Tsu*	*Chien*	*Sui*	*Pu*		*Pas couru* "Mincing steps on toes"
	Foot	Point	Mince	Step		
Peking Opera	*Tao*	*Ti*	*Tzu*	*Chin*	*Kuan*	"Purple crown back kick" (Back kick so as to knock off something on your head; flat feet)
	Back	Kick	Purple	Gold	Crown	
Peking Opera	*Tan*	*Hai*	*Fan*	*Shen*		"Turning one's body in search of the sea"
	Plunge	Sea	Turn	Over		
Ballet	*Tso*	*Pu*				*Chassé*
	Gliding	Step				
Peking Opera	*Tsao*	*Hsing*				A sculptural dancing pose struck by the artists in the course of a dance or during a pause, in order to present a harmonious unity of physical appearance and the mental world of the characters
	Build	Image				
Peking Opera	*Tan*	*Man*	*Tze*			Somersault sideways
Peking Opera	*Ti*	*Tui*				Kick one leg up and turn
	Kick	Leg				

Form	Term						Explanation
Peking Opera	*Tao*	*Hua*					"Sword flower" (Brandishing a sword)
	Sword	Flower					
Ballet and Peking Opera	*Tse*	*Shen*	*Hsi*	*Tui*			"Toe pointing with one knee folded"
	Turned	Body	Fold	Leg			
Ballet	*Tsu*	*Chien*	*Ping*	*Li*			*Soutenu en tournant* "Standing on toes"
	Foot	Point	Together	Standing			
Ballet	*To*	*Ni*					"Mud" (Pounding the earth)
	Pound	Earth					
Ballet	*Ta*	*Chuan*					"Big turn"
	Big	Spin					
Ballet	*Yeh*	*Tui*	*Chuan*				*Tour en dedans*
		Leg	Turn-spin				
Ballet	*Yen*	*Shih*	*Tiao*				"Swallow leap"
	Swallow	Style	Leap				
Ballet	*Ying*	*Feng*	*Chan*	*Chih*			*Arabesque* "Spreading one's wings in the welcoming breeze"
	Welcome	Wind	Spread	Wing			
Ballet	*Yi*	*Ti*	*Hsi*	*Tui*	*Kung*	*Chuan*	*Saut de basque*
	Move	Place (or Position)	Fold	Leg	Air	Spin	

Index

About the Author

Lois Wheeler Snow was born in Stockton, California. She was educated there and received her B.A. degree from the University of Pacific. She received a scholarship to the Neighborhood Playhouse in New York City and worked there for two years with Sanford Meisner, Herbert Berghof, Martha Graham and David Pressman. She has appeared in many Broadway plays, including the Theatre Guild production of *The Innocent Voyage*, with Herbert Berghof and Oscar Homolka; Michael Todd's production of Elsa Shelley's *Pickup Girl*; Dorothy Baker's *Trio*, with Richard Widmark and Kirk Douglas; *Dear Ruth*; *The Young and Fair*, with Julie Harris; *Dinosaur Wharf*; Arthur Miller's *All My Sons*, produced by Harold Clurman and directed by Elia Kazan; Norman Rose's version of *The Brothers Karamazov* and *The Troublemakers*. She was a founding member of The Actors Studio. Lots of television and lots of soap—best known is probably *The Guiding Light* in which she played a nasty nurse for years.

Lois Wheeler married Edgar Snow in 1949. Their children are a son, Christopher, age twenty-two, and a daughter, Sian (Western Peace), age twenty-one. The family moved to Switzerland in 1959. Lois Wheeler Snow went to China for the first time in 1970, with her husband. She spent five months there. Her articles subsequently were published in *Vogue, The Nation, Saturday Review, National Elementary Principal, Le Monde, World Health Organization* magazine, and various other publications in Italy, Finland and France.

Frederick H. Little
Theatre Collection

In memory of Frederick H. Little,

for thirty years Director of the

Theatre Program at the Horace Mann

School in New York City

Donated by
Phyllis Little of Wells, Vermont
August 1994